THE BATTLE FO

Copyright © 2020 A V J Brassell

All rights reserved. This book or any portion thereof may not be reproduced or used in any manner whatsoever without the express written permission of the author except for the use of brief quotations in a book review.

First Printing, June 2020

DEDICATION

This book is dedicated to the memory of all the Guernsey people who died under German Occupation during the Second World War. They never had the chance to enjoy Liberation and the return of freedom.

With special thanks to my beautiful wife for her patience and support as I have worked on this novel.

Front Cover is based on an image called: 'Into the Jaws of Death, which shows US Troops wading ashore through water and heavy enemy gunfire on the 6th June 1944. Image from the Franklin D Roosevelt Library, public domain photographs, World War II. Photo ID 7298

For the purpose of this story let's imagine they are the support platoons provided by the US Army wading ashore on L'Ancresse Beach during the Battle for Guernsey.

ISBN: 9798654472144

FORWARD

I have just spent a wonderful few hours lying in the sun and enjoying the beauty of our favourite beach, Pembroke Bay, in Guernsey.

This beautiful beach was bathed in the summer sun and rang to the sound of children playing and adults laughing, enjoying the company of family and friends.

Various beach toys were in play, including blow up toys of various kinds, paddle boards and kayaks as well as the inevitable beach cricket and football.

Ice creams were melting too fast and picnics and even beer were being consumed as the care free beach goers, local and visitor alike, enjoyed the sun and the warm sea. Surrounding the beach is an anti-tank wall and numerous bunkers, legacies of the German Occupation of the Channel Islands which began in June 1940.

It is hard to believe that in 1943 as the English and Americans started to plan the invasion of Europe, to support the Russian counter offensive in the East, this same stretch of beach was being considered as the starting point for that offensive. With the Channel Islands occupied, serious thought was given to taking the Islands back from the German occupiers. They could then have been used as steppingstones for the invasion of France.

As with the beautiful beaches of Normandy, this would have given a whole different meaning to the name Pembroke Bay and the area of L'Ancresse where the beach is situated.

Let us roll the dice of fate again and see how history might have looked if different decisions had been made and the fate of Europe had centered around this beautiful stretch of beach on the sunny Island of Guernsey.

THE PLAN

Lizzie Jones poured hot water into the silver tea pot. As the tea brewed, she made sure the three cups were perfectly clean and matched the saucers they stood on. She opened an old tin and found a handful of biscuits which she put on a small plate.

She counted the Digestives and realised she had put seven on the plate by mistake.

'That won't do,' she muttered to herself.

She looked around the empty room like a naughty schoolgirl, checking no-one could see her, then snatched a biscuit off the plate and quickly devoured it. Lizzie dabbed around her mouth with a napkin to remove any crumbs that might point to her guilt. She was careful not to disturb her ruby red lipstick.

The tea pot, plate, cups and saucers were placed on a silver tray along with a small bowl of sugar lumps.

She checked herself in a large mirror by the door, smoothing down her dark grey skirt. She tugged at her slightly tight white blouse to try and ensure the buttons were not noticeably pulling in all the wrong places.

I wish they had given me a larger size, she thought to herself but she was secretly pleased at the way the blouse emphasized her figure. She smiled at her reflection and checked her lipstick had not found its way on to her teeth.

Satisfied she would pass muster, she placed the tray on a wooden trolley and wheeled it to the heavy wooden door at the end of the room. She paused for a moment to compose herself and tapped on the door with her knuckles three times.

'Come,' came the reply from the room.

She opened the door and entered the room. It was almost dark, with just the light from two desk lamps illuminating the table and the faces of the three men pouring over a pile of maps and photos. She wheeled the squeaky trolley to the desk, as she had done many times before.

The room was thick with cigar smoke which made everything seem darker yet.

The men had gone quiet as she came in and she was conscious that three pairs of eyes followed her every move as she handed out the cups and placed the biscuits on the table.

'Shall I be mother?' she offered in a very precise English accent.

Without waiting for an answer she began pouring the tea and handing out the sugar. She knew exactly how each man liked their tea.

Once that was done, she turned and wheeled the trolley back out of the room. Still nothing was said.

As she closed the door one of the men spoke.

'By God she's a looker, what do you reckon Freddy.'

'Can't say I noticed Louis,' Major General Frederick Morgan replied with a wicked smile.

Lord Louis Mountbatten turned to the third man.

'What do you reckon Winnie, don't tell me you haven't noticed her?'

Winston Churchill looked up from the maps and smiled.

'I'm too old for all that Louis, besides which Clem would give me a clout if I even looked at another woman.'

They all laughed.

Churchill brought them back to the job in hand.

'Gentlemen, back to business. We must decide tonight what we recommend to our American cousins as regards the invasion of Europe. As much as I hate the idea of losing more young lives, we must give the Germans another front to worry about. We promised Stalin at the Trident Conference we would act soon and if we don't the Russians may lose their battle against the Nazis.'

He cleared the aerial reconnaissance photos away and looked at the map of the English Channel set out before him.

'What do we think of the Pas de Calais?'

'Too obvious,' Morgan replied. 'That's the closest point to England and the Germans will be expecting us to cross there. It would be good as a diversion but not for the real show.'

'I totally agree,' Louis Mountbatten replied, not mincing his words.

Winston put a black cross against the Pas de Calais but wrote Diversion on the map as a reminder.

Next, they looked at the Normandy beaches.

'What do you think of this option?' he asked, looking at the two senior officers over the top of his glasses.

'Could work but I am really worried about how well defended and exposed these beaches are,' Freddy replied without hesitation. They had been pouring over these plans for weeks now and they all knew the options.

Winston wrote a large question mark on the map over the beaches, glancing once again at an aerial photograph which showed a mass of sea defences and gun emplacements all around the beaches.

'Remember we can take them out from behind if we plan the attack properly, using paratroopers.'

'Yes,' agreed Morgan, 'but they would have to go in at night and the chances of the plan going to shit are high, excuse my language.'

Winston Churchill grunted in agreement.

'What about Normandy's western coastline? If we could cut off the Cotentin peninsula from Dielette and take Cherbourg we would have a great harbour to work with, and its within easy reach of the south coast ports.'

Louis Mountbatten coughed, a little irritated by all the cigar smoke.

'Just one problem, the Channel Islands are in the way and Hitler has fortified them heavily. I have no doubt some of the guns on Alderney and Guernsey could damage our invasion fleet. We would need to take them at the same time.'

Morgan nodded in agreement. After a little thought he reached for his cup and had a sip of tea, then seemed to make a decision.

'The real opportunity here is twofold. First, as Winston said we would get a great harbour in Cherbourg and have the small port of Dielette to act as a staging point for the invasion. Guernsey would give us a fallback position and a base for command and control until we are firmly established in France. At the same time, we would get the Islands back from Hitler and free our people.'

'That will really make him mad!' Mountbatten added.

Both Winston and Louis Mountbatten picked up their cups and leaned back in their chairs. Winston took a biscuit and for a long minute silence enveloped the room as each man considered the options.

'The Islands would also give us air bases and as such, close air support, to help further the attack.' Louis added thoughtfully.

Churchill and Morgan both nodded.

'What about the local population on Alderney and Guernsey, they would be in mortal danger?' Churchill said, breaking the silence.

'According to sources, Alderney is a concentration camp with no British citizens left and Guernsey evacuated a huge proportion of its population. If we go in hard and fast before the German garrison knows what has hit them and use overwhelming force, there should be minimum casualties on the Island.'

Morgan had suddenly become deadly serious.

'Louis, can the navy take out the big guns on Alderney and Guernsey?' Churchill asked.

'I don't see why not. Alderney should be easy as there is no civilian population to worry about but from the aerial photos we see of Guernsey, some of their big guns are among civilian dwellings so I can't promise there wouldn't be casualties. We might need to consider using commandos to go in and take out some of the big emplacements.'

All three fell silent again and finished their tea and biscuits.

After a couple of minutes, Winston Churchill leaned forward and picked up his pen. He underlined the word Diversion next to the Pas de Calais and put a cross against the Normandy Beaches. He then drew lines from Weymouth, Exmouth, Torquay and Plymouth to a point between Alderney and Guernsey and then across to Dielette on the French coast. After a pause he added another line straight to Guernsey.

'What about Jersey?' Morgan asked.

Mountbatten thought for a moment and looked back at the chart. 'It may be that once Guernsey is taken, and we are established on France, the garrison on Jersey will see they are in a hopeless situation and surrender.'

'Would the guns in Jersey put the invasion in danger?' Churchill asked.

'I don't think so.' Morgan replied.

'Well let's check and be sure.'

The three men looked at each other through the cloud of smoke emanating from Winston Churchill's cigar.

'I take it from the smoke signals Winnie that this is our chosen plan.' Mountbatten remarked with a gentle cough.

Lord Louis Mountbatten and Frederick Morgan both smiled.

Winston looked over his glasses and pointed at the lines which converged on Dielette.

'Gentleman, here is our plan. Mark this date, 14th July 1943, for this is the day the planning for the invasion of Europe begins and the day we decided to take back our Channel Islands. Freddy take this chart back to the Americans at COSSAC and let us see if they agree to this plan of action. Tell them I have a good feeling about this.'

'Yes sir!' Freddy stood, rolling up the plan as he turned to leave. 'I'll report back tomorrow.'

The door shut and the two men looked at each other.

'This is a big moment Winnie if we get this wrong...'

'I know,' Winston Churchill replied. 'We could face another Dardanelles and lose a lot of British civilians in the process. I don't think history will think much of me if that happens.'

After a brief pause Lord Louis Mountbatten stood.

'In that case Mr. Prime Minister, we'll make sure that doesn't happen. I will not let you down and I am sure the British armed forces won't either. The world is depending on us to succeed and by God we will.'

Mountbatten put on his cap, gave Winston an unusually impressive salute and announced. 'I'm off to bed!'

With that he turned and walked out of the room.

Winston sat back in his chair and enjoyed a few more puffs on his cigar then stubbed it out in a brass ashtray on his desk.

'By God we had better succeed,' he muttered to the room. He looked up at the portrait of the King which hung opposite his desk. 'Or God have mercy on my soul.'

He picked up a file marked Italy and went back to work.

*****

The following day the telephone rang on Winston Churchill's desk just as Lizzie had brought in a mid-morning cup of tea.

She paused as he spoke.

'Thank you,' he said and put the phone down.

He turned to Lizzie and smiled. She could not recall him smiling quite like that before.

'Take away that damned tea and bring me a whisky,' he said. 'I have something to celebrate.'

'Yes sir,' she replied pouring him a stiff tot from the decanter which sat on a large bureau opposite his desk.

'To victory and the King,' he said, raising his glass towards the King's portrait.

'Now fetch my car. I want to have a drive around London.'

Lizzie rushed out and got on the phone to Winston's driver and within minutes the Prime Minister of Great Britain was heading out into the battered city wearing his trademark, dark coat, bowler hat, cane and cigar. He was all smiles, waving his trademark V for Victory to anyone who looked his way.

Lizzie sipped at the tea and nibbled on a biscuit. She was not one to see good food going to waste.

'I wonder what all that was about?' She asked herself and with a shrug went back to her desk.

*****

In November, Winston Churchill travelled to Cairo to meet President Roosevelt and there the final elements of the plan were thrashed out. The numbers of men and machines that would take part in the invasion were agreed. The command structure for the campaign was also agreed and General Eisenhower was nominated as Supreme Allied Commander. General Omar Bradley for the Americans and General Montgomery for the British would head up the two army groups.

Montgomery would be in overall charge of the landings. Admiral Ramsay was put in charge of the naval forces that would be brought to bear and Air Chief Marshall Leigh-Mallory would command the allied air forces. It was a strong team, full of experience and confidence.

It was agreed that the invasion would take place in May of 1944.

With that the buildup for the campaign began.

It was given the designation –

OVERLORD.

INTO ACTION

The four Lancasters of 617 squadron skimmed the waves as they headed South across the channel. They skirted to the west of Alderney and lifted slightly as they approached Guernsey to clear the invasion fleet which sat waiting to follow them in.

As they had done in the industrial heart of Germany, they dropped their bouncing bombs into the relatively calm waters of Pembroke Bay just as dawn broke on that Saturday morning in June 1944. Sporadic gunfire headed their way, but they were already climbing away from the Island, their job was done.

Three bouncing bombs slammed into the huge anti-tank wall, ripping great holes in the German defences. The 4th bomb cleared the wall and bounced inland coming to rest just in front of a cottage on the L'ancresse Road. There it exploded destroying the building completely. 92-year-old widow, Edith Le Page was the first civilian casualty that day. She had lost her husband a few years earlier and her only son had died in the first world war. The neat cottage had been her home for over 50 years. The only saving grace was that she was sound asleep when she died.

The guns of the support fleet, which included two cruisers and a dozen destroyers, opened fire, trying to increase the damage to the wall and targeting the bunkers and forts that protected the bay.

They also bracketed the gun emplacements on the low hill overlooking the beach. That hill provided a commanding view of the bays and common land that bordered the beaches and had exceptional views inland towards higher ground and the airport a few miles away.

Further north more ships, including a battleship were pounding the defences on Alderney, pummeling the huge bunkers that had been built on that Island.

The Battle for Guernsey had begun.

NINE MONTHS EARLIER

September 1943.

Lieutenant General Frederic Morgan and Vice Admiral Louis Mountbatten sat in folding chairs in a field overlooking Chesil Beach. Alongside them was US Army Brigadier General, Ray Barker. All three were members of the joint Chiefs of Staff Committee.

In front of them a Brigade of troops were carrying out a test landing on the beach using American landing craft. It was not going well.

Offshore a destroyer sat in the mist as if minding her flock. Her presence quite intimidating.

One landing craft let down its ramp early and the troops inside got a soaking and had to wade a long way to shore under the orders of a very angry platoon sergeant. The expletives aimed at the pilot of the landing craft and at his troops for their tardiness out of the ramp could be heard on top of the cliff.

Freddy stood up and waved his swagger stick at the troops as if pointing a gun.

'If I had a hundred men and a couple of machine guns no-one would be getting off that beach. What a debacle.'

Louis Mountbatten was more focused on the Destroyer, no doubt imagining being her skipper. 'Give them a chance, this is their first exercise. There will be many more.'

Ray Barker looked at them. 'Do you want to use our boys for this General?'

Frederick 'Freddy' Morgan paused for a moment.

'No, this part of Operation Overlord has to be a British mission, Guernsey is our territory and we should be the ones to take it back from Hitler. Your troops need to focus on capturing Cherbourg. Once that is done we need Monty and Patton to be our swords, to thrust deep into the heart of Hitler's troops in France and then on to Germany.'

Ray Barker nodded. 'Have it your way gentlemen, but if you need anything just let me know.'

'Well, we need more landing craft, that's for sure. We've barely enough for Guernsey let alone the invasion of France.' Morgan stated.

The three men sat back down again and watched as more landing craft came into the beach and discharged their troops. Sergeants and Corporals bellowed orders as men scrambled up the gravel and then lay down at the top as if ready to fire their guns at the imaginary defenders.

Louis Mountbatten looked across to Freddy Morgan and asked if this was a good replica of the proposed landing point in Guernsey.

'Not really,' Freddy replied, 'come into the tent and I'll show you what we're faced with.'

With that the three officers on whom the order of battle depended walked into the tent where a map and several aerial reconnaissance photographs were spread out on a number of trestle tables.

Freddy pointed his swagger stick at the photographs first and indicated the beach defences at Pembroke Bay. These included a full-length anti-tank wall, what looked like sea defences on the beaches, bunkers at each end of the bay as well as gun emplacements at the entrance to the bay and more on a low hill overlooking the beaches.

A large tower which was marked as an observation point was off to the west of the bay and numerous smaller towers were dotted around behind the anti-tank wall. Freddy explained that these were Napoleonic, and it was unlikely that they were being used by the Germans as defences.

'Looks a bit of a big ask to land here,' Barker suggested.

Louis Mountbatten looked concerned. 'We're not going to be able to get our big guns close to shore either are we?'

'That's the trouble with these islands, they have extremely rocky coastlines, but I think you'll be able to get near enough to the north of Guernsey to provide accurate fire.' Morgan replied.

He pointed at the common land behind the anti-tank wall. 'This land provides us with a good marshalling area after the landing and has potential for a parachute assault.'

'There are other things we need to be aware of,' Morgan added with an air of concern. 'The main German garrison we believe is here in what is called Fort George. There are other pockets all over the Island, the most notable being here in Castle Cornet and here, in these barracks, next to this large battery near the islands west coast.'

'Have you an idea of what the total garrison on the Island is?' Ray Barker asked.

'Our estimates are that there could be around 20,000 troops on the Island but in the main they are thinly spread, divided amongst the myriad of coastal defences. We also have little evidence of any heavy armour on the Island. The important target for us is that heavy battery I pointed out before. Those guns look like battleship guns and could be used against the main invasion fleet. They have to be neutralised separate to the main attack.'

'With due respect Freddy, I think you need to focus on the main invasion rather than worrying about the Guernsey element. I think it's time we appointed someone to manage the Channel Islands invasion and that the three of us worry about the French beaches and how we push out from those into France and Germany.' Ray Barker looked adamant.

Lieutenant General Frederic Morgan thought for a moment and with some reluctance nodded in agreement. 'Anyone come to mind?'

'We need a Major-General.' Louis suggested. 'British with a Channel Island connection, if possible,' he added.

Freddy rubbed his chin. 'Let me talk to a few of my colleagues. I'll come back to you with some suitable candidates, and we can take it from there. Good call Ray.'

With that the three men went back to their folding chairs and watched the rest of the exercise.

*****

Lieutenant General Frederic Morgan returned to Norfolk House in London later that evening. The building was buzzing with noise and people, even at this late hour, but was completely blacked out from the outside. As he walked through the corridors, he made a mental note to talk to Winston Churchill with a view to finding a larger space for his team. He called in an aide and ordered tea. 'Who's in?'

'Captain Best is here sir,' the aide replied.

'Good, send him in.'

The aide bustled out and around five minutes later there was a knock on Morgan's door.

'Come!'

With that Captain Ian Best walked through the door, his cap almost concealing his curly red hair.

'Ian, thanks for coming so quickly, take a seat. Working late?'

'Lot's to do sir.' Ian replied, taking off his cap as he sat down.

'There certainly is Ian, I need your help. You know our the invasion plans for France include neutralising the defences on Alderney and taking back Guernsey to prepare the way for our landings on the French beaches?'

Ian nodded not wanting to spoil the Lieutenant General's thread.

'Well the Joint Chiefs of staff and our American allies need to focus on the invasion of Europe and how we proceed beyond the French beaches. I need someone to head up the invasion of Guernsey. We need to find a Major-General within the army to plan and lead the invasion. Can you look through the personnel records and find a few potential candidates? If any have active experience or local knowledge of Guernsey, then flag those for me. I do not want any desk types Ian. The chosen candidate needs to have dirt on their boots and be ready to get blood on their hands. Is that OK?'

'Clear as a bell Sir, I'll get right on it.'

At that moment there was another knock on the door.

'Thanks Ian, I know I can depend on you. Get the door on your way out.'

Captain Ian Best got up from his seat, placed his cap back on his head and offered a crisp salute to the Lieutenant General before turning to leave. When he opened the door the General's aide was waiting with a tray of tea and biscuits. 'After you Jimmy,' Ian offered, holding the door for the Aide. Once the General's Aide was on his way Ian closed the door behind him and headed back to his desk on a lower floor.

I wonder if I can get in on the action, he thought with a smile. He was desperate to get away from his desk and get stuck into the fight.

Once back at his desk he went over to a large wooden filing cabinet and hooked out the current troop placements focusing on the Hampshires, Devonshires and Dorsetshires. As they were south coast regiments he surmised that any Channel Islanders in the services were likely to be embedded there rather than with regiments based further north.

He brought out the files for the 50th Division which included those regiments and started to work through them, looking for any mention of Guernsey amongst the senior ranks. The 50th were currently in action in Italy and recently there had been some issues with a few members of the Division which was being loosely described as a mutiny. Officers on the ground were dealing with it but it had put a cloud over the 50th and there were a lot of unhappy senior officers and NCOs out there, keen to repair their personal reputations.

After working through the files Ian hoped that the 50th would be chosen for the invasion of Guernsey. He had found that there were enough Channel Island officers and men in the regiments to ensure that there would be a lot of local knowledge on the ground when they hit the beaches.

As he went through the files, he lost track of time and it was the early hours of the morning before he finally put his pen down and looked at his list. It was not a long list by any means, but he felt he had some good candidates. He had focused on people with the rank of Colonel and Brigadier knowing that if the right man were found he could easily be promoted to the rank of Major General and thus be able to command the Division.

The short list was as follows:

Colonel Ronald 'Ronnie' Krimp
Brigadier Harold 'Harry' Vaudin
Colonel Bruce Mahy
Colonel John 'Jonno' Hood
Brigadier Mark Heaume

All were either Guernsey born or had lived in Guernsey for many years, He was in fact surprised at just how many Guernsey men were in the regiments. Most were in the Hampshires though a few were in the Devonshires.

Ian had stumbled across Colonel Krimp by accident. He had been noted in a file as a friend of Brigadier Heaume. Krimp was currently in the 6th Airborne Division, which had not long been created and was in a period of intensive training. He had been with the Green Howards in Sicily and Italy before their conversation to a paratrooper regiment and had won a Distinguished Service Order (DSO) while out there.

Best pulled out a fresh piece of paper and re-wrote the list in a neat and tidy fashion. He had put together five files, one for each of the candidates and after he had signed the list he placed the accumulated information in a large brown envelope, marked it for Lieutenant General Morgan's attention and stamped it URGENT and TOP SECRET. He then walked it back up to Morgan's office, leaving it in the in-tray on a desk outside his office door.

Ian was confident the General had long gone to bed so did not try knocking on his door. Anyway, they all needed some sleep. He looked at his watch. It was 2.30am and he was very tired. He walked back down to his desk and picked up his coat and walked out into the cool night air. He took a few deep breaths, looked up at the stars, noting there had been no raids that night on London, and then headed for his digs a short walk away. He wanted to be back at his desk by 8am so he did not have much time for sleep.

Next morning Freddy was back at his desk at 8.30. He had stopped to talk to Ian on the way in to see if he had been able to find any suitable candidates. The General had noted how tired Ian looked and when he had heard that he had been up most of the night had told him to get back to his digs and get some more sleep. A meeting was arranged for 3pm to go through the five candidates.

When Morgan had settled down, he picked up the envelope and emptied the contents on his desk. His Aide had already brought tea and while he drank, he made his way through the files, taking stock of each man by their service record. He was impressed enough to mentally earmark the 50th for the Guernsey invasion and realised that his chosen candidate would have to replace Major General Sidney Kirkman who was currently in charge of the Division. As his team was expanding, he had already considered Kirkman as a potential HQ officer and thought that bringing him into HQ would be a viable course of action. Morgan needed good men around him.

Now all he needed to do was to make the final choice so he could recommend his chosen candidate to the Joint Chiefs of Staff. This was not a decision that could be taken lightly.

By 3pm he had a good picture in his mind of the strengths of each candidate. As the clock on the mantel piece behind him chimed the hour there was a knock on his door.

'Come!' He called out in his normal brusque manner. The door opened and his Aide announced that Ian was waiting to see him.

'Send him in Jimmy.'

Captain Best strode in and saluted, waiting to be offered a seat.

The General waved at him to sit down and Ian took off his cap and sat in the single chair in front of Morgan's desk.

'Jimmy, bring us some tea will you, and if you can rustle up a biscuit or two that would be perfect.'

'I'll see what I can do Sir,' Jimmy replied with a smile, closing the door quietly as he left Morgan's office.

The five files Ian had prepared the night before were laid out on the leather top of Morgan's desk. As he sat, Ian looked around the office. He had rarely seen it in daylight.

The sun shone in through the heavily taped windows and cast a pattern across the floor between the desk and the window. Tables around the room were covered in maps as were the walls. An in-tray on Morgan's desk was full to the brim with reports and files.

There were two telephones on his desk. A standard black one and a red one. Ian knew that the red one was a direct line to the Prime Minister, Winston Churchill. He also knew the black phone would not ring while there was anyone in the office with the General. Meetings were always short but if something important did crop up, Jimmy would interrupt the meeting so Morgan could clear the room before the call was put through.

'I like your choices Ian,' the General began. 'We have some good men here.'

'Thank you, sir,' Ian acknowledged.

'Do you have a ranking for me?'

'I wasn't sure if that was my place sir,' Ian responded.

Morgan paused for a moment. 'Imagine you were this side of the desk Ian. You have read all these files and analysed each man. Who, if you were sitting in this chair, would you put your faith in to carry out the invasion of Guernsey?'

Ian shifted uncomfortably in his chair. He cleared his throat.

"Well sir, if I was in that chair, I'd have ordered cake with the tea.'

Morgan paused for a moment then burst out laughing. 'Thanks Ian, that's the first good laugh I've had in a long time. I'll make a note for next time.'

Ian smiled.

'Thank you, sir. Well as regards the officers on the table, I would have faith in all of them. They have all had dirt on their boots and have all led and inspired their men. I wish we had more Guernsey men in the army sir.' Morgan nodded in agreement.

'But if I were going to follow one of these men into battle, and I'll come back to that later if I may, I would suggest Colonel Hood is your man sir.'

Morgan picked up Colonel Hood's file which was the middle one of the five and flicked through it. He had read them all that morning, so the action was in truth unnecessary, but he made a show of reading it again. The file had a black and white head and shoulders image of the Colonel.

Hood looked a kind man, the type of officer who would care for the soldiers under his command. Full head of hair and glasses, Morgan thought he had the look of Jimmy Stewart about him. A career soldier he had attended Elizabeth College in Guernsey as a border where he had his first taste of the army in their CCF (Combined Cadet Force). He entered the army in 1930 and steadily progressed through the ranks. Hood had been with the British Expeditionary Force that went to France in 1939 and had helped defend Dunkirk before making a break for Cherbourg and getting back to England on one of the last boats out of that port. Once back in England he had immediately been involved in organising the defence of the country against the anticipated invasion.

In 1941 he had shipped out with the division to Africa and had distinguished himself at Tobruk and El Alamein. He was wounded in the leg at Wadi Akarit and shipped home to recover. He rejoined the 50th Division in Sicily and was currently with the 1st Battalion of the Royal Hampshire Regiment in Italy somewhere near Pizzo.

There were several mentions in dispatches all through his career, even in the last few weeks, as he had led his men ashore in Italy. Promotion seemed long overdue.

Morgan nodded his head. He closed the folder and put it back in the centre of the row of five files.

'He was my choice too,' he stated quietly.

'Thanks Ian, I think I know what's coming next.' Morgan leaned back in his chair.

'That's why you're on that side of the desk, sir.' Ian replied with a smile. 'I want in on the action.'

'Why?' Morgan replied crossing his arms.

'I was at Dunkirk sir; Jerry nearly took my leg but I've worked hard to get fit again and I want to go back to the front lines. I want revenge.'

'I am not sure revenge is the best attitude to have when you hit the beaches Ian. That sort of thinking can get a man killed.'

'Sorry Sir, I just want to get out there again and play a part.'

'You play a hugely important role here. Your decisions can save countless lives and above all you're important to me.' Morgan still had his arms crossed defensively.

Ian looked disappointed. 'Would it help if I told you I know Guernsey. I was there for a summer 5 years ago, fishing and sailing. I know the Island quite well.'

Morgan uncrossed his arms and leaned forward.

'If you want to do this Ian, I won't stop you but if I am going to put you into the 50th I will need you to find me a replacement for you.' Morgan smiled. 'Now get these files put away and draft me a report proposing a promotion for Colonel Hood to Major General and get him back here as soon as possible. I want him to start planning the assault as soon as he can. If your name as a staff officer on his team is in that report don't be surprised if I sign it.'

Captain Ian Best smiled and stood up from his chair. He replaced his cap and gave General Morgan his sharpest salute. 'Thank you, sir.'

Morgan gathered up the files and handed them to Ian. 'I wonder if you will still be thanking me when you are in a landing craft approaching the beach in Guernsey?'

Ian took the files and smiled. 'Thank you again sir, I'll try and make you proud.'

'Just get that damned Island for us Ian. If we fail in Guernsey, our war efforts could be put back years. In the worst-case scenario, we will hand Europe to the Russians.'

'We'll not let you down sir.' Ian saluted again and this time Morgan stood and saluted back.

Ian walked down to his desk and put the files back in the filing cabinet. He looked around his small, relatively safe space and sat down in his chair. He leaned back and put his hands on his head.

What have I let myself in for? He thought.

He shook his head and went back to work. The first thing he did was write that report. Once that was done, he started to look for his replacement.

TIME TO PREPARE

After pushing into Italy in September 1943 the 50th returned to Sicily in October and were shipped home in November, arriving in Liverpool.

They were met by their new commanding officer, Major General John "Jonno" Hood.

Newly promoted General Hood watched proudly as the troops disembarked, happy to be home again. There were smiles all around and more than one bent down and kissed the ground as they stepped off the gangplanks. He had arranged for them to enjoy a couple of weeks leave and then they were all due to assemble again near Salisbury before training began for the invasion of Guernsey.

He had flown back to England from Sicily and met General Morgan to discuss the plans. Morgan wanted Hood to prepare his troops for an invasion of British soil and pull together as much local knowledge of the Island from the 50th and anywhere else he cared to look for the invasion.

Morgan had recommended the four other officers Captain Best had found and suggested they would make good brigade leaders or at least provide him with a core staff to discuss what tactics to employ on the ground in Guernsey.

He emphasised it would be Hood's call.

Morgan suggested Hood should get as much intelligence about the Island as possible. Information about German troop placements, which units were on the Island, how battle sharp they were and what the mood was amongst the locals. He also advised Hood that he should get to know what weaponry they had. If there were armoured units on the Island that could prove a serious threat to the breakout from the beach head.

With those ideas in mind he brought Hood up to speed concerning the plans for the invasion of France. Morgan explained that intense efforts would be put in place to fool Hitler into believing the attack would come in the Pas De Calais region. General Patton was 'assigned' to that mission and the buildup in that area was established overtly using such deceptions as blow up tanks, trucks and planes. Special missions to convince German intelligence operatives were to be undertaken to back up the visible troop buildup on the ground and two Canadian Divisions were stationed in the Dover area to support the false intelligence.

Morgan explained that the real troop buildup had begun with American Units being stationed around the ports of Southampton, Poole and Weymouth with British troops located around the West Country ports of Torquay, Dartmouth and Plymouth. The town of Slapton Sands was to be evacuated and taken over by the Army to provide a training ground for the invasion and different divisions took turns in using the few available landing craft to carry out mock attacks on the beaches and town.

Up to date with the current situation Hood headed down to Exeter, where he had established his base to begin assembling his team. He had the senior officers of the various battalions assigned to the 50th to draw on for the overall planning and he called them his HQ team.

While Hood was happy to let his HQ team focus on the physical aspects of the invasion like the accumulation of landing craft, logistics, support, etc., he brought together his senior Guernsey team as he called them to try and establish some intelligence to help with the planning.

The clock was ticking, and he had to ensure the men and equipment he needed for 'his' invasion were not lost amongst the huge amount of resources that were being absorbed by Operation Overlord. The Guernsey invasion was given its own Codename, Coverlet, and the full Guernsey team met for the first time in December of 1943 to start working on the plans Hood had begun to formulate.

They met in the White Hart Hotel in Exeter which Hood had commandeered as his Headquarters for the duration of the planning and training phase of the operation.

He had converted one of the lounges as a command centre and Captain Ian Best, who had been assigned to him by General Morgan, was busy setting up the room with any maps and photographs he could find of the Island.

Ian had scoured local libraries and obtained as many documents as possible to provide reference material for the Guernsey team. Hood used one of the larger bedrooms on the first floor of the hotel as a meeting room and had a large table put in the room to replace the bed. At a push he could sit up to a dozen people around the table for briefings and meetings. The kitchens had been taken over by his personal staff and they prepared food and drinks as required for the officers and men dotted around the hotel.

As well as the Guernsey Team, Hood had to coordinate and assemble the various Battalions and Regiments which formed the 50th. As the plan developed, he also had overall control of additional units including mechanical units, logistics corps, medical corps and the 7th Light Infantry Parachute Battalion which he had assigned to Colonel Ronald 'Ronnie' Krimp.

Hood stood up from the table and got the meeting started.

'Merry Christmas Gentlemen, I am sorry you are having to spend it away from your families, especially those with families and friends in Guernsey. With luck and good planning by this time next year, I hope we'll all be enjoying roast Turkey at home followed by a walk to Pleinmont to work off our meals.'

'Here, here,' Brigadier Vaudin replied, 'but for me it would be a walk around L'Ancresse common.'

Brigadier Heaume and Colonel Mahy both nodded in agreement as that was where they had both been brought up. They had also enjoyed the occasional round of golf before the war on the L'Ancresse links so knew each other from there.

'That may be a big ask gentlemen as we are going to mess the common up good and proper by the time we are finished with it! I have asked Captain Best to join us today as he will be the main liaison between us and the logistics corps to ensure we have enough materials and men for the invasion. Gentlemen I want us to come up with a workable plan for the invasion of Guernsey by the end of January so we can get it approved by Lieutenant General Morgan.'

He looked across at Captain Best. 'Ian bring everyone up to speed as to where we are currently.'

'Yes sir,' Ian replied.

Hood sat down and everyone turned to Ian as he got up and walked over to where an Ordnance Survey map of Guernsey was pinned to the wall.

'Gentlemen you all know Guernsey well and know that the Island is well protected by fortifications which date back to Napoleonic times.' He pointed to a composite aerial reconnaissance image of the Island which hung next to the Ordnance survey map, it was pretty much the same scale.

'This is the latest image we have of the Island and as you can see it isn't the same place, we all remember. There are several bays where anti-tank walls have been built, some of the old Napoleonic fortresses have been strengthened and enhanced and new gun emplacements and bunkers cover the Island. We can see several barracks units and a slave labour camp. The Germans have even installed a railway which is used to supply the numerous bunkers and defences around the Island. The beaches are heavily mined and the cliffs on the south coast are protected by numerous bunkers and gun emplacements. We have observation towers here at Pleinmont, L'Eree, Chouet and one inland here at Bordeaux.'

He paused for a second as the impact of the news sank in. All the men realised for the first time, just how much their home had been changed forever.

'What we do lack is up to date intelligence on troop compositions on the Island and the equipment they have. We can see what look like 88mm guns here at L'Ancresse supported by anti-aircraft batteries and there are a mix of different types of guns in some of the open emplacements. The best guess is that they have brought in some captured French ordinance and installed them around the Island, but we can't be sure. We got lucky and have a rather good view of these large gun emplacements inland from L'Eree. You can also see that the airport is well defended. They have converted Castle Cornet into a fortress and have even put an anti-aircraft battery on Brehon Tower in the Little Russell. The Island is a very impressive fortress, a pretty big nut to crack so to speak.'

Colonel Krimp cleared his throat. 'How are we going to crack this nut General, without killing thousands of our friends and family on the Island?'

'Good question,' Hood replied. 'Ian, continue.'

'Thank you, sir.' Ian turned back to the Ordnance survey map.

'The current plan is to attack from the north concentrating our main forces on L'Ancresse. We will land on these beaches, breach the walls, then take out the high ground and form a bridgehead here on L'Ancresse common. Colonel Krimp's paras will drop on to the common half an hour before the main attack and secure this area around the Vale Church to stop the anticipated reinforcements that will be sent to L'Ancresse from St Peter Port. He will also put pressure on the rear of the defenders. As that is happening, we propose that we attack these big guns using commando forces who will land under cover of darkness here on the L'Eree headland.'

Ian took a sip of water before continuing.

'We have the support of the Navy and they will bombard the beach head area to try and take out as many of the mines and defences as possible. They will also bombard the headlands and surrounding gun emplacements. We can also count on the RAF, weather permitting, to make precise bombing raids on Fort George, at the barracks behind the battery near L'Eree and on some of the West Coast strongholds using Typhoons and Mosquitos. This should cause complete confusion and blur the picture so to speak as to where the ground attacks are coming from.' He paused for a moment. 'Any questions so far?'

'Thank you Ian, can I just add before you all chip in, our plans include the need for some intelligence gathering and any ideas you may have to help with that would be appreciated. In short, we need boots on the ground before the invasion.'

General Hood sat back while the Guernsey team took stock.

Colonel Krimp started the conversation. 'There isn't much room for my boys to drop into General, I could lose men into the sea or into the marshy ground beyond Vale Church. The gorse on the common may not provide a comfortable landing zone either. If the weather is bad, we won't be able to drop from any great height and have a reasonable chance of success.'

General Hood looked at the map. 'Understood Ronnie, maybe your boys will need some specialist training. If we set out a similar drop zone somewhere and practice low level drops would that help?'

Krimp nodded. 'That would help sir.'

'How are we going to get off the beaches? That wall looks pretty impenetrable.' Colonel Mahy asked.

'We have some ideas Bruce, we hope to breach the walls before the boys hit the beaches. Put that down as a work in progress. The important area for this team to focus on now, is how we break out of L'Ancresse and take the rest of the Island. In an ideal situation we will find the defenders in total confusion, and most will surrender at the earliest opportunity. The last thing we need is a large land battle with so many of the population still in situ. I cannot imagine the consequences for the Guernsey people if we end up engaged in house to house fighting in St Peter Port. Remember we also need the harbour and the airport intact.'

Brigadier Heaume was the next to speak. 'Sir, I have a brother in Guernsey, he made the choice to stay there and was quite high in local government when the Germans invaded. People used to think we were twins. If I were to get on the Island, I might be able to get some intel from him or even take his place for a while using his ID?'

'Nice thought Mark but I need my senior officers here. I can't risk you getting captured and interrogated.'

'They wouldn't get anything from me sir.'

'You say that now Mark but you don't know what the SS are capable of; but that's an example of the issues we face. Are the SS even on the Island. They are fanatics and if we attack, they could do anything to hold on to the Island, including using the civilian population as hostages.'

'Sir, with respect, this could be the best way we have to infiltrate the German command systems and see what we are up against.' Brigadier Heaume was intent. 'It would also put me in a great position to advise the troops on the ground when we go in.'

'Assuming you get back Mark. Look, I know you mean well but crawling around in hostile territory is not what I expect my Brigadiers to be doing. Let me think about it. Anyone else have any ideas?'

'We could send a commando team in sir. We must have someone with local knowledge who would volunteer?' Krimp suggested.

'My worry is that if they get caught or the Germans become aware of them, it will tip off Jerry that we are considering an invasion. If you all can give it some thought and get back to me, Ian and I will assess the best way forward. For now, we are making regular reconnaissance flights across the Islands as well as the Pas de Calais and the Cotentin so will update the aerial picture each time we get new information. We are also trying to monitor radio traffic but it's not proving easy.'

Hood turned to Ian. 'Ian can you get some tea set up, my throat feels like a badger's arse.'

'Yes sir.' Ian replied with a smile. He made his way out of the room and down to the kitchen.

While he was away the General turned to Colonel Mahy. 'Bruce, I want your boys to lead the assault and I want you to take Ian with you. He is desperate for action, and I can't think of a better way to blood him but to include him in the first wave.'

Colonel Bruce Mahy was a senior officer in the 1st Battalion of the Royal Hampshire regiment. He had been in Malta, Egypt, Sicily, and Italy, serving with distinction in all campaigns. He was proud of his regiment and knew it was an honour to be chosen to lead the attack. 'No worries General, I'll incorporate him into my team. His local knowledge will be useful on the ground. I can't promise to keep him safe mind.'

'I'm not asking you to do that Bruce, I am sure he can look after himself, just get him ready and keep an eye on him.'

Just then Ian came back in with a tray of tea and some local scones. 'This should keep the wolf from the door sir. I'll be mother.' With that he started to pour the tea.

Once the tea was poured and everyone was enjoying their scones, General Hood brought the discussion back on topic.

'Right gentlemen, the best way to tackle this is one step at a time. We will let the navy focus on the targets we give them and work out how to get us on the beach. We have some ideas on how to breach the wall and we have the paras going in first. If we assume the commandos do their job and take out those big guns and we are on L'Ancresse Common in force. Where do we go from there?'

They looked at the plans and Brigadier Vaudin spoke up.

'Well sir, the obvious route is along the Route Militaire, over St Clair Hill and down as far as the seafront. Then it is a short run along the coast into town. I would lay good money that they have their HQ in either the Royal Hotel or Elizabeth College. If we can cut the head off the snake, they may just surrender that little bit quicker.'

'That's the way they'll expect us to go and I would also lay good money that every junction along that road will be defended and reinforced from the moment we hit the ground.' Colonel Bruce Mahy replied. General Hood nodded in agreement.

'If I may sir?' Ian asked.

'Go on son, all ideas are welcome here.'

Ian got up again and walked over to the map.

'I think we need to push down the route Brigadier Vaudin mentioned to focus their attention. But that should be a feint. We should push our main forces along here towards L'islet and down Route Carre and then push across towards the coast behind the Halfway. There is a lot of open ground that way which would reduce the possibility of causing too many civilian casualties. Another brigade could push across towards the coast at Bordeaux and take St Sampson's harbour.'

Ian paused to gather his thoughts. 'St Sampsons Harbour would give us a supply point, well at least either side of high tide, and secure the northern part of the Island. I also think we should ask the commandos to push on to the airport once they have destroyed those batteries. That way we can focus on St Peter Port and cut the head off the snake as you put it Brigadier. With luck the other defences will start to fall if they lose contact with their leaders. We can then mop up with the use of overwhelming force; if they don't surrender first.'

The room went silent.

General Hood stood and walked across to the map as Ian sat down. He took a good look at the map. Then he went across to the aerial photographs and studied them for a few minutes.

He walked back to his seat but did not sit down.

'Gentlemen, I think we have heard enough for one day. We have a lot to think about. Ian, you go with Colonel Mahy, he has something to talk to you about and I want you and him to work on those ideas of yours. Ronnie get your paratroopers as sharp as you can. I want them able to land on a sixpence. Mark, you're with me. Harry, put yourself in the head of the defenders and tell me how you would stop us getting into St Peter Port. I want you all back here in a week and we can decide how best to proceed.'

With that they all got up except for Brigadier Heaume. Each saluted in turn as they left the room.

'Well Mark, got any photos of this brother of yours?'

'Yes sir.'

'You can call me Jonno when we are on our own Mark.'

The Brigadier smiled. 'Just like when we were back at home eh!'

The General nodded.

'I hate the idea of you going ashore in Guernsey ahead of the invasion but we need that intelligence. If you can convince me that you and your brother would pass for each other and you can come up with a plan to get ashore, and back again, safely, then I will consider it. I'm not saying yes, just a maybe, Is that clear?'

'Yes Jonno. I'll come back to you in the next couple of days.'

He stood up and saluted the General. 'And thank you sir.'

General Hood got up and saluted back with a smile. 'I haven't said yes yet.'

Brigadier Mark Heaume smiled as he turned and left the room. As he shut the door behind him, he muttered to himself. 'I'm going home.'

He bounced down the stairs and out into the fresh air with a spring in his step. The sun was shining despite it being the middle of winter and he took in a deep breath. *Not quite the salty air of Guernsey*, he thought and then headed for his billet to find a few photos of his brother.

CHRISTMAS 1943 - GUERNSEY

The table at the Heaume's house was a bit sparse to say the least. They had boiled potatoes, some cabbage, and a chicken. The family around the table had not eaten much meat for a few weeks so this was a real treat. Laura Heaume had even managed to make some passable stuffing to complete the treat as the five of them sat down to try and celebrate their fourth Christmas under German occupation.

'Remind me where you got the chicken from Rob?' Laura asked smiling.

'Best not ask dear but let us just say the Germans have more than enough to go around. They won't miss one.' He leaned across and gave his wife a kiss much to the amusement of the children who started giggling.

'You just be careful Robert Heaume, we all depend on you for our livelihood. I am not sure what we would do without you. Now let us say a prayer for absent friends and then we can tuck in.'

The family held hands and the adult's heads were filled with images of family and friends who had left the Island when the evacuation took place. As always Rob thought of his brother, wondering if he was still alive and where in the world he might be.

In German HQ in the Royal Hotel the Guernsey Kommandant was enjoying a turkey dinner with all the trimmings.

GeneralMajor Rudolf Von Graf was surrounded by his key staff in the hotel's main restaurant. A German chef oversaw the catering but many of the staff were locals employed by their German masters. The Kommandant was annoyed that the civilian leader of the Guernsey government had turned down his invitation to join him for the meal, citing a preference to be with his family. Personally, he could understand his decision but turning down a request from the German Kommandant was, he considered, just plain rude.

Von Graf could have ordered Ambrose Sherwill to join him, but he had considered the mood around the table may have been soured so decided against it. As it was there was a jovial mood in the room, after all life could not be much better than it was for the Germans here in Guernsey. They could have been on the eastern front fighting the red army. *There will be no turkey dinners out there*, he thought.

He too called for silence and then asked the assembled officers to give thanks to god and the Fuhrer for their meal. He then asked them all to stand.

'Fill your glasses gentlemen and join me in a toast,' he turned to the painting of Adolf Hitler above the fireplace in the lounge, 'to Adolf Hitler.'

'Adolf Hitler,' they all repeated in unison. One of them called out Seig Heil, and they all chanted 'Seig Heil.' They drained their glasses and sat back down and began to eat.

As always, the conversation was about the war and the Eastern front. They discussed reports they had received and articles they had read in Signal Magazine. The assembled officers felt secure in the knowledge that they were now the protectors of a combined Europe. It was their sacred duty to ensure no-one invaded the territories they had conquered. Here in Guernsey, they were part of Hitlers Atlantic wall, the blade on which any invaders would be impaled.

The news in Signal Magazine was all good. There were no troops that could match their prowess and this occupation showed just how beneficial the German way of life could be for the conquered.

They had built new sea defences, installed a railway, built a large underground hospital and re-numbered the roads. The cinemas and theatres were open, and no-one was starving as there was plenty of work for those happy enough to work with the occupying forces.

The Germans had even worked with the local government to give them some self-control, allowing them to keep their own police force and ambulance service. Above all they had installed sufficient defences to protect the inhabitants against any invasion.

Von Graf was unusually quiet. He had just been notified that there were indications of a military buildup in the Kent countryside opposite the Pas de Calais region and it was expected that the British and Americans might make an attempt to open up a Western front in that area. He had decided not to share that news with the officers around the table as he did not want to spoil the mood. The Kommandant was secretly pleased that the rumoured invasion was many miles away. They would all be safe here in Guernsey.

He looked around the table at the officers joking and laughing as they drank too much wine and ate too much food. He held a glass in his hand, but he wasn't drinking.

We are growing soft, he thought. *I need to put a stop to this, or we will not be an effective unit. The Fuhrer may need us if the allies invade and we need to be ready to move at a moment's notice.* He resolved that in the New Year he would arrange a series of exercises to make sure his troops were fighting fit.

He smiled and called the table to order.

'Gentlemen, another toast. To 1944, let us make it a year we will never forget.' They all raised their glasses and in unison called out. '1944!'

Somehow, they managed to put aside the reverses they were suffering in Italy and the losses they were incurring in the East, not to mention the increasingly frequent bombing raids on Berlin and enjoyed the rest of the day. News like that was not included in Signal Magazine.

Most of the officers were roaring drunk by the time the festivities broke up. They had agreed they were confident the allied advances in Italy could be stopped and the Russians would run out of steam. New night fighters were being developed to combat the RAF's Lancaster bombers so even the raids on Berlin would be stopped soon. They were all extremely happy.

The GeneralMajor went back to his office and looked at the latest reports. Even though it was Christmas the reports still came in from Germany via Manche HQ.

The first report was news that Berlin had been bombed again. He wondered how his friends that lived in the city had faired. His aides had been given the evening off, so he sat reading the reports on his own. He looked at the plans of the Island on the wall and the new defences that were being built.

A new observation tower was being built on the south coast and one of the reports detailed progress, and included a photograph of the part-built tower. He noted that some local men were involved with the building of the tower as well as the Russian and French prisoners of war that had been sent to the Island. The rumour was that some of the bunker designs came from the Fuhrer himself but all he could see was the potential for being trapped in a concrete coffin, as some of the builders called them. He was glad he was not stationed in one of those.

Tunnels were being dug everywhere to store equipment away from prying eyes and to add to the Island defences.

Organisation Todt were doing an amazing job, he had to admit the pace of development was impressive even for his beloved Germany.

He was almost at the bottom of the reports when he spotted a memorandum from Berlin. Generalfeldmarschall Erwin Rommel was due to visit the Islands in early January to inspect the defences. He sat back in his chair. *What fool left this in the middle of the pile*, he thought to himself. *This should have been given the highest priority.*

There was nothing he could do about this now, so he placed the report to one side and made a mental note to have a word with his aides in the morning.

He stood up from his desk and moved into the adjoining room which he used as his quarters. He got undressed and settled into bed even though it was quite early and picked up a book from the bedside table. The rooms in the hotel were heavily blacked out, so he could use the electric lamp by the bed without any fear of light leaking through into the dark night outside. He had brought a glass of whiskey with him and settled down to get through another chapter of Volk ohne Raum by Hans Grimm. Smiling at how it supported the expansionist view of Hitler and showed the need to provide space for the German people to truly flourish.

Von Graf had a dream that once the war was over, Hitler himself would visit these Islands, maybe create a playground here for the German elite classes.

He read a chapter before putting the book down and thought again about Rommel's visit.

We need to make a good impression, he thought to himself. *Starting on the 1st January we will hold regular exercises and sharpen the troops so we can show the Generalfeldmarschall how ready they are, maybe I can get myself a promotion out of this.*

With that thought in mind he finished his whiskey and turned off his bedside lamp, promising himself an early start the next day to get his aides working on plans for the different types of exercises he had in mind.

He also needed to plan how to meet the Generalfeldmarschall and deal with him while he was here. He fell asleep dreaming of grand parades and motorcades around the Island.

The following morning, he was up bright and early and even over breakfast he was issuing orders. His plan was to carry out his own tour of the defences and make sure all was well. His inspection would be a surprise and he was looking forward to seeing how each defensive position was being run and if the troops were well prepared.

He decided there was no time like the present, so he called his driver and together with two of his aides and a couple of motorcycle outriders he set out up St Julians Avenue towards the West Coast. The miniature cavalcade swept down to Vazon Bay and headed up to the bunker complex known locally as Fort Hommet. The GeneralMajor knew the strongpoint as Stutzpunkt Rotenstein.

The network of defences and searchlights protected the beaches and surrounding coastline and included a bunker with a multi loopholed Cupola, two casemates with 10.5cm guns covering Vazon Bay, an anti-tank gun and an M19 automatic mortar. There were also flame throwers, and machine gun pits.

The whole headland was surrounded by barbed wire and minefields ensuring the area was protected from attack from the rear as well as from the sea.

As the cavalcade drove up the access road the guards at the barrier snapped to attention and one ran across to a hut to no doubt notify the unit commander that they had visitors.

The motorcycle outrider waved to the guards and the barrier was hastily moved to one side to allow the Kommandant's car and entourage to pass. The guards snapped to attention as he drove past and he waved at them with a the shortened form of the Nazi salute showing them the palm of his hand.

As soon as the Kommandant had passed, the barrier was put back in place. His car drove up the low hill, pulling up in front of the concrete barracks room. Troops were spilling out, some still in the act of pulling on their jackets and began forming up under the instruction of a couple of NCOs.

An Oberwachtmeister was in overall charge of the troops at this point and had soon formed up a reasonable guard as the Kommandant's aide opened the car door for him.

GeneralMajor Rudolf Von Graf smiled at the Oberwachtmeister and acknowledged his salute as he brought the troops to attention.

'Good morning Oberwachtmeister, where is Hauptmann Fischer?'

The Oberwachtmeister hesitated. 'I am not sure Herr Kommandant.'

'Well I suggest you find him, and while you do that, I want your Unteroffizier to give me a guided tour of the defences.'

'Yes Herr Kommandant, Unteroffizier Becker will be honoured.' He turned to the troops lined up behind him. 'Becker!'

Unteroffizier Becker marched over to his Oberwachtmeister and saluted.

'Becker, can you take the Kommandant on a tour of the defences. I suggest you start at the casemate below us.'

The Kommandant coughed to gain the Oberwachtmeister's attention. 'If you don't mind, I'll decide where to start and we'll begin with the searchlight block and accommodation.'

A look of barely disguised panic came across the Oberwachtmeister's face as he nodded, and he turned back to the Unteroffizier who also looked shocked. 'You heard the Kommandant Becker, lead the way.'

As the party moved off the Oberwachtmeister doubled down to the Guard House. 'Where the hell is Hauptmann Fischer?'

'I think he is visiting someone in one of those cottages Oberwachtmeister,' the guard said pointing towards a row of cottage across the minefield and barbed wire.

'Bloody hell. I will stay here, you two get down there as fast as you can and get him back here. Tell him the Kommandant is holding a snap inspection.' The guards looked at each other. 'Schnell, schnell!' he shouted. The guards ran off down the access road and were soon knocking on the cottage doors.

Hauptmann Fischer was having a lovely start to the day. He had spent the night with a local girl and was enjoying her company over a relaxed breakfast. His reverie was disturbed by a banging on the door. The girl answered and the guard pushed past her into the kitchen where he was sitting eating breakfast. Fischer was not properly dressed yet so reacted by shouting at the guard. 'What is the meaning of this - get out, imbecile.'

The guard stood his ground. 'Herr Hauptmann, the Kommandant is here making a snap inspection. He wants to see you now! The Oberwachtmeister sent us and told us to tell you that he was starting at the searchlights.'

'Bloody Hell,' the Hauptmann muttered as he rushed back to the bedroom and got himself dressed as quickly as he could. He checked himself in the mirror before donning his cap. He had no time to shave but right now that was the least of his worries. Without saying a word to the girl, he pushed past the guards and ran across the road up towards the guard house where the Oberwachtmeister was waiting.

'Bloody hell Oberwachtmeister, why didn't you send the Kommandant to one of the bunkers.'

'I tried Herr Hauptmann, but he insisted he wanted to go to the searchlights.'

'Shit, come on we'd better get up there and try and sort this out.'

With that they double timed it up the hill and across the complex to the large searchlight complex built on top of an old Napoleonic fort.

When they got there, not a soul was to be seen. They rushed into the staff quarters and there stood the Kommandant. He was surrounded by Christmas decorations in various states of disarray plus the remains of the party the men had enjoyed the night before. Bottles were scattered all over the floor as were piles of dirty plates.

'Ah, Hauptmann Fischer, kind of you to join us.' He was absentmindedly slapping the swagger stick he always carried against his leg.

Hauptmann Fischer snapped to attention. 'Herr Kommandant, apologies for this, the men had a bit of a party last night and we haven't had a chance to clean up yet. You should have let me know you were coming.'

The Kommandant walked towards Hauptmann Fischer. 'Do you think the British army would let you know they were coming? Do you think being away from your post with some whore would have proved a threat to a sea borne invasion? Your job is to keep this stronghold in fighting order, whether it is Christmas or not.' His voice was getting louder and louder as he spoke.

Hauptmann Fischer's mind was working overtime. He had two options, apologise or try and face it out. He chose wrong.

'Sir, the men are far from home and lonely, they needed to let their hair down and have a party. I am sure the British would not invade on Christmas Day.'

The Kommandant raised his swagger stick and struck Fischer across the face. Blood seeped from the wound and Fischer staggered back. Von Graf was virtually screaming when he replied. 'And that is precisely the reason they would invade, because you don't think it would happen. When I am in my HQ, I must trust that my officers are keeping this Island, my troops and me safe.'

Fischer tried to compose himself and stood back up to attention trying to ignore the pain and the blood dripping down his face.

The Kommandant walked right up to the young officer and ran the handle of the swagger stick across the wound. 'Do you know there are Prussians who would give anything for a scar like you are going to have?'

He turned away and walked back towards the door. 'I know your record is exemplary Fischer and I am going to give you a chance. I am going to come back tomorrow, and I want every weapon, every room, every bed and every damned rifle shining. If I see so much as a speck of mud on a soldier's boots I will make sure you spend the rest of the war on the Eastern front. DO YOU HEAR ME?'

'Yes, Herr Kommandant, what time will you be visiting us?'

'Wouldn't you like to know. I'll be here as soon as I am ready.' As he was about to walk out the door, he turned back one last time. 'I assume you will be warning your fellow officers at other strong points around the Island about this as soon as I leave. Tell them that I will be visiting them all over the next week and in a couple of weeks Generalfeldmarschall Erwin Rommel will be here. If you think I am a bastard, wait until you meet the Desert Fox in person.'

With that he stormed out and together with his aides was soon back in the car and on his way past the guard house.

I will give them a day, he thought.

'Driver, take me around the Island, let's scare the shit out of the lazy bastards. Then we will inspect them all over the next few days.'

With that, the car with the motor bike escorts proceeded to drive past all the west coast and north coast gun emplacements and strongholds, he had the driver slow down at each one. He could see troops scattering at each position in preparation for the visit that didn't come. He smiled at their panic. T*hat is one job done*, he thought to himself. *Tomorrow, it gets serious.*

INTELLIGENCE

Brigadier Mark Heaume knocked on the door and entered as soon as he heard General Hood's call. He was carrying a file under his left arm.

He walked in and offered a brisk salute and took the seat offered to him by the General. He placed the file in front of General Hood and took off his cap.

'Good to see you Mark, I take it you managed to get the information I asked for?' Mark just nodded. 'Before I open this file have you given the idea any more thought, or should I say have you changed your mind?'

'I haven't changed my mind Jonno, in fact I am more convinced than ever that this is the best way for us to get the information we need. Look at the pictures and you'll see what I mean.'

General Hood opened the file and on the top of the small stack of papers was a photo of two young men. He could see straight away that they were brothers, in fact they could have been twins. He looked up at Mark and studied his face and those of the men in the picture. 'OK, I give up, which one is you?'

'That's me on the right Jonno, as you can see, I am slightly taller than Rob but apart from that we are like two peas in a pod.'

'When was this taken Mark?'

'It was taken about 5 years ago. I was on leave in Guernsey. That is Bordeaux Harbour in the background, it's about half a mile from Robs house.'

'You know he could have changed a lot over the years, especially while they have been occupied. He could be thinner, he could have a beard.'

'I know Jonno, but I won't know how much he has changed until I get there.'

'How do you plan to get ashore?'

'I have sketched it out in the file sir, but in short, I think we should ask the Navy to drop me off by submarine on a moon less night, offshore from Bordeaux harbour. It would have to be at high tide so we wouldn't need to worry about being swept off course. From there I could paddle ashore, or better still be paddled ashore because then I would not have to worry about hiding the dinghy. I would then make my way under cover of darkness to my brother's house and hide out there. I could then take his place, taking walks with his wife or even go to his work to get a good idea of what is going on in the Island. I will not really know just how much I can achieve until I talk to him.'

General Hood thought for a moment. 'You know if you get caught you will probably be shot as a spy. And goodness knows what they will do to your brother and his family if they catch you there.'

'I am not worried about me Jonno, but I do worry about my brother and his family. But I have reflected long and hard and I think it is worth the risk. I know the area well and am confident Rob would want me to do this.'

'You knew the area Jonno,' he corrected as he looked across at the aerial photographs, 'hell, there's a damned railway between Bordeaux Harbour and your brother's house. That was not there when you were having fun 5 years ago. Who knows what else lies in wait and how many patrols there may be in the area?'

'I know sir, but I'll be careful.'

'I am bloody sure that every married man who volunteered for the first world war told their wives that they would be careful, but it didn't stop them getting slaughtered in huge numbers!'

General Hood paused for a moment, tapping a pencil on the desk. He looked again at the photo.

'How long are you planning to be there?'

'Give me a week sir.'

'That means on your way back you won't have a moon less sky and you may face a different tide? And let us not even mention the probability of bad weather at this time of year.'

The General thought for a moment.

'When?'

'No time like the present, we just need to organise the sub sir.'

'Damn it Mark, I am not happy about this but have a word with the weather guys and get yourself a window for the mission. Once you have that come back here and I'll decide whether it is a go or not. In the meantime, I will read your proposal and discuss it with upstairs. We can't let you jeopardise the whole invasion.'

'Yes sir, I'll get right on it.'

'Look, I am not being obstinate for no reason, I don't want to risk losing one of my best men but on the other hand we need intelligence. I want to make sure this is achievable before you set off in that submarine. There is more than just your life at risk here.'

'I understand Jonno, but if I didn't think I could do this I wouldn't be volunteering.'

'And I don't think I would trust anyone else to get what we need. Now get me that window and I'll run it up the chain of command.'

Mark stood, placed his cap back on his and saluted.

General Hood didn't look up but opened the file and started reading. The Brigadier took that as a signal to leave and turned smartly and left the room.

Once he was on his own, Hood sat back in his chair and thumped the table with his fist. 'Damn,' he muttered to himself. 'I wish there was another way.'

A worried aide popped his head around the door. 'Everything all right sir?'

'Tickety-boo, bloody tickety-boo.' He muttered gruffly. 'Get us a cup of tea while you are here Jock. Make it a thick one with two sugars if you can find any of the stuff in the kitchen.'

The aide backed out and shut the door, deciding it wasn't time for a conversation with the old man, as his aides had started calling him, which was a bit harsh as he wasn't much past 30 years old.

Brigadier Heaume talked with the Meteorological officers, and it was confirmed that early morning on January 22nd would be the best day for the mission, and recovery would take place exactly a week later, on the morning of the 29th.

2pm in the morning was the agreed time with a half hour window either side for pick up. A special unit of the commandos would provide the paddle power.

Once the plan was passed upstairs and approved the navy was asked if they could provide a submarine and the S-Class HMS Sealion was taken off its exercise schedule and sent south for the top-secret mission.

General Eisenhower, now Supreme Allied Commander and Major General Frederick Morgan had both signed off the mission but it was made clear that Brigadier Heaume was not to take any identification with him, nor anything which linked him to the British Army. The fallback position was that the mission was far enough in advance of the proposed attack not to jeopardise Overlord itself, the final date for which was the best of best kept secrets, and well beyond the pay grade of the Guernsey team.

That meant that the clothes he was due to wear for the incursion had to be authentic. Given that the Island had been occupied for nearly three years, they also had to be well worn. The team looked to their own wardrobes and amongst the clothes that were chosen was a traditional Guernsey jumper, which was well worn and slightly too big for him. Nothing that was army issue was allowed, down to his socks and underwear.

During the early weeks of January 1944, Brigadier Mark Heaume was given a crash course in German, it was reasonable to assume his brother had picked up at least the basics during the occupation. He was also trained in basic unarmed combat by the team of commandos who would be rowing him ashore. His orders were not to engage with the enemy under any circumstances, but he needed to be able to defend himself just in case. The worry was that if the Germans lost a man then they would be highly likely to put two and two together and realise that the allies had made an incursion into the Island.

After all the work and two weeks of reduced rations, Brigadier Heaume stood on the docks in Weymouth Harbour getting soaked by a heavy downpour of rain. It was late in the morning on the 21st January.

Dressed in a dirty, sad looking Guernsey, with a woollen hat on his head, worn dark grey corduroy trousers and a pair of battered black shoes he felt he looked the part and that he was ready. To counter the cold and wet he wore an oiled fisherman's coat, dirty and frayed around the edges. He looked gaunt and filthy.

His very loose cover story was that he was a merchant sailor who had been lost at sea and drifted ashore in Guernsey. He hoped he never had to use the story as he knew precious little about life in the merchant navy.

General Hood and Mark's good friend Colonel Ronnie Krimp were there to see him off.

'Godspeed Mark, we'll see you in just over a week,' the General said offering him his hand. Mark shook his hand firmly and then also shook Ronnie's hand. 'Give my best to Rob,' Ronnie added with a smile.

'Will do Ronnie,' Mark replied smiling back.

'And kiss the granite for me too, I miss the place so much,' Ronnie added as a parting shot.

Mark laughed and turned to walk over the short gangplank on to HMS Sealion. The captain was there to welcome him aboard as were a dozen of the crew. The coxswain of the boat piped him on board and the deck crew lined up as the captain led him up to the conning tower and then down into the depths of the boat. Lines were cast off and the crew saluted the General and Colonel on the dock. Hood and Krimp saluted back as the ship pulled away from the land.

The crew then scampered down various hatches until all Hood and Krimp could see were the boats number one and a duty watch keeper at the top of the conning tower as they took the ship out to sea.

While General Hood and Colonel Krimp made their way back to their HQ, Mark was being squared away in his temporary quarters. He met his four-man commando team again in the crowded wardroom and it was agreed he should enjoy a last good meal with them before he was put ashore.

Mark hoped he would get a little sleep prior to them dropping him off. The submarine made its way into deeper water and headed East towards the Isle of Wight just in case they were being watched. As soon as they were happy that everything was working well, the skipper called for the boat to dive and as soon as they were submerged, they changed course to the south.

The Commandos seemed able to sleep anywhere and were soon snoring away while Mark could only try and imagine what he was going to find when he got to Guernsey. Eventually he did manage to close his eyes but it seemed no time at all before he was woken by the call of 'Grubs up.'

The ships cook brought them plates of fried bully beef, mash and carrots in a thin gravy. The skipper popped in to see if they were being looked after properly and to let them know they would soon be passing to the west of Alderney.

Once the food was finished, the commandos settled down for more sleep. Mark made his way to the main control room and took a look at the chart the skipper and his navigator were pouring over. He could see that they were now just passing Alderney and heading towards the Little Russell which was the strip of water between Guernsey and Herm. The skipper explained that the tide was coming up which they needed because the waters were quite shallow where they were going. There was a cross on the chart which marked the spot off Bordeaux Harbour they were aiming for.

'How will it work on the way back skipper?' Mark asked knowing that normally the week after a high tide it would be roughly a low tide.

'It will be tight, but we think there will be enough water, the tide will be neaping so it won't go as far out as it normally does. This definitely is our best option sir.'

Mark thanked the skipper and went back to the mess and tried to rest. His eyes were heavy and he was half asleep when he noticed a change in the sound of the engines as the submarine began its approach to Guernsey.

One of the ratings popped his head around the curtain. 'Wakey, wakey boys. Show time! Brigadier, the Skipper wants to see you in the conning tower.'

When Mark got to the conning tower the room was lit by a dull red light. The skipper was looking through the telescope, cap turned round on his head. 'Brigadier, do you want to have a look?'

Mark had a look through the periscope but was not sure what he was looking at. All he could see where some vague changes in the dull light. 'What am I looking at?' he asked.

'Guernsey, Brigadier. Guernsey.'

Mark smiled at the captain. 'Thank you, Captain, you don't know how much this means to me.'

'Rather you than me,' the captain replied. 'Good luck and I'll see you in a week. We will be here from 1.30 to 2.30 am, don't be late.'

They shook hands and Mark went to join the commandos who were preparing the rubber dinghy. The ship was running silent, and no lights were allowed. At a signal from the captain, a rating carefully undid a hatch and two commandos climbed on to the deck. They dragged the deflated dinghy out on to the deck and using a hose from the inside of the submarine carefully and quietly inflated the rubber boat. The other two commandos followed and then reached down and offered Mark a hand. He was unceremoniously pulled out into the cold night. There was quite a chop going on but that was good as it helped disguise the waves made by the submarine when it surfaced and submerged.

The dinghy was finally ready and one by one the commandos took their places. There was a moment of panic as one of the oars was dropped into the sea but a commando managed to grab it before it drifted off. Next it was Marks turn to climb in.

They had practiced this on land but now they were doing it for real. He felt his legs shaking as a deck hand helped him take the big step down into the bottom of the dinghy. Before he could settle himself on the floor of the small boat paddles were in the water and they were making their way towards the shore. They were about half a mile out and it was proving hard work for the commandos as they fought the waves, trying to make sure they made as little noise as possible.

Each was dressed in black and carried holstered pistols, the metal dulled and black to avoid any glint of light. They also carried knives for silent killing. Even the rubber of the dinghy had been roughened to avoid any potential reflections. They all wore balaclavas, except for Mark who had his face blackened with charcoal. He would wash that off when he got to Rob's house. If he got to Rob's house.

His night vision was really good now and he was starting to make out details on the shore, familiar lumps of land were appearing out of the dark and he could also see the outline of the Vale Castle off to his left. The leader of the team held up a clenched fist and they all stopped rowing. An ominous black shape started to drift past them on their right.

It was a German sea mine and must have been there to prevent any boats entering or leaving the small Bordeaux harbour. As the mine drifted past the two commandos in the front of the boat started paddling gently again looking out for more mines as they went.

The two in the back steered using their paddles, while watching out for mines or sentries.

Bordeaux Harbour has a small slipway which leads into the sea on the outside of the small pier that protects the harbour. It was this slipway that had been chosen as potential landing point. During the planning concern had been expressed that the slipway may have been mined or patrolled so they eased towards the rocks to the left of the slipway and gently bumped against the seaweed and barnacle covered granite.

Mark felt a tap on the shoulder which almost made him jump out of his skin. The commando leaned forward and whispered into his ear. 'See you here in a week sir. Good Luck.'

Next, he felt another hand grab his arm and soon he was half lifted off the dinghy on to the rocks. Without another word the dinghy pushed away and rapidly disappeared out into the dark.

Mark never felt so alone. He sat there for about half an hour until he was sure the commandos were back on board before he took stock. The smell of the seaweed reminded him of fun days spent on these very rocks when he has a young boy. Fishing for crabs and small fish from these rocks had been part of every summer and he knew them like the back of his hand. He turned towards the shore and kissed the rock in front of him.

That's for Ronnie, he thought to himself.

He looked over the top of the rocks at the slipway and noticed a barbed wire barrier. He knew some barriers like this were mined so he had to be careful. The barbed wire rolled across the top of the rocks over towards the Vale Castle to the south of Bordeaux Harbour. On the other side of the slipway there was just water. He had to find a way off the rocks.

He crept as far as the barbed wire and froze. A German sentry was walking in his direction, patrolling the barbed wire defences. Mark hugged the rocks and prayed the sentry did not look too closely over the fence. The guard reached the top of the slipway and then turned and started to make his way back. Once he was over 50 yards away, Mark went back to looking at the barbed wire. He spotted a small gap underneath where it spanned a fissure in the rocks. *If I could squeeze through there*, he thought.

The guard turned at the far end of the small bay to the south of Bordeaux Harbour and made his way back. Mark mentally timed how long he took and waited until he had passed where he was, had turned and was walking back again. He was worried he would dislodge some pebbles and listened to the noises of the night.

The waves breaking on the small pebbly beach to his left made quite a bit of noise so he guessed that once the guard was around 50 yards away, he would not notice any small noises he might make.

Mark reached in the crack and pulled out as many loose pebbles as he could and once the guard had done another rotation took his chance.

Slipping under the wire, he eased himself up on to the rough land above the rocks. Carefully he hurried across to the road before the guard turned to make his way back. He slipped down into the road and paused to take stock of his situation.

He looked north towards the cottages by the beach that formed the western end of Bordeaux Harbour. There in the road by the wall another guard stood looking out to sea. He had his rifle slung over his shoulder and seemed to be focused on something he could see in the harbour.

The guard behind him was getting closer, his steady footsteps making a crunching noise, as he paced across the rough ground. Mark was sure the guard could hear his heart beating out of his chest as he got nearer and nearer. Then the pacing stopped, not ten yards from where he was crouched.

The guard behind him whistled and the other sentry looked across. 'All OK,' he called out in German.

'I think I can see some geese,' the other guard called back.

'They'll be seagulls you idiot,' the guard behind him yelled. 'Get back on your patrol.'

The guard over by the beach made some sort of gesture and started to walk towards the northern side of the bay while he heard the guard behind him turn on his heels and start to walk away. Away in the distance he could hear what sounded like a motor bike and he knew he had to get out of the road.

He glanced across to Bordeaux Bay. That guard still had his back to him and a quick look over the wall told him that the closest guard also had his back to him. Seizing the moment, he quickly scurried across the road and vaulted over the wall landing in a patch of stinging nettles. He cursed silently but did not stop, he scurried along, bent almost double until he reached a copse of trees and carefully eased himself amongst them.

A few minutes later a motorcycle and sidecar drove past and stopped at the top of the beach. The passenger got out and the driver stepped off the bike. The two sentries came over and swapped places, changing the guard. The new guards took their places and the other two got on to the bike and swinging around drove back towards the south.

The new guards had a quick chat before they resumed their patrols. All was quiet again.

Mark watched for a while before edging out of the copse of trees and looked across the field. What used to be a flat field when he was last in Guernsey now had a large embankment across it which held the railway line the Germans were using to supply gun emplacements around the coast with munitions and materials.

Over to his left the railway line bridged a small lane. That was the way he wanted to go but he could see a guard on top of the embankment patrolling up and down the railway line. He knew he would be exposed if he crossed over the top of the line but equally, he could be seen from above if he followed the lane. *These boys are on the ball*, he thought.

Once again, he watched the guard patrolling the track, timing how long he took to walk up and down his route. He also tried to work out if there might be others who could see the area where he was planning to cross the track. He knew the guard patrolling where he had come ashore could possibly see him against the skyline, if he looked Mark's way but he couldn't think of any other option to get to the other side of the tracks.

Slowly, while the guard was at the far end of his patrol, he crawled up the bank until he was near the summit. He waited for the guard to come back towards him and then turn away before edging himself up on top of the embankment, lying as flat as he could.

He eased himself on his belly across the tracks and then slid himself over the other side, pausing near the top of the slope to check what was below him and to see if there was any reaction from the guards. All was quiet apart from the distant pacing of the guard on the railway track. With nothing dangerous in sight on this side of the railway he slipped down the embankment and waited once more until the guard followed his patrol.

Once he was again walking away, Mark scurried across the rest of the field and crouched down on the far edge, next to some bushes. His heart was still beating fifty to the dozen, but he hoped the worst was over.

He waited there for another few minutes before making his way along the field edge to a gate which led out on to the lane he had originally wanted to follow. He did not want to risk opening the gate in case it creaked, so he climbed over the wall and dropped quietly into the lane. Looking back, he couldn't see the guard on the bridge or any other sign of life in the lane.

Mark knew there would be some sort of curfew so did not expect to see any locals on the roads at night. Quietly he crept along the lane, hugging the hedges and walls on the way, occasionally stepping into a gateway to pause and check if he could hear anything. The Island was silent apart from the wind in the trees.

Eventually he reached the gate of his brother's cottage and crept in. The gravel drive was a problem as it crunched under his feet, but he carefully made his way along a strip of gravel that had been worn flat and slipped around the back of the cottage out of sight of the road. He breathed a huge sigh of relief.

From here he could not be seen by anyone. His only problem now was not knowing if his brother still lived here. The cottage could have been commandeered by the Germans for all he knew so he chose to wait until dawn. There was a shed in the back garden, so he crept into that and curled up in a corner and went to sleep. He was exhausted.

He was awoken by the sound of rain on the shed roof as a sudden downpour of rain and hail passed over the Island. It made what little light there was at that time-of-day dimmer than usual and he estimated it might be around 7 am. The shed had a window which looked out towards the cottage, and he watched for any sign of activity. He did not have to wait long.

The first thing he noticed was the room gently illuminated by the light of a candle. Through the window in the dim light, he could see his brother filling an old kettle at the kitchen tap and placing it on the aga. A plume of grey smoke was coming from the small chimney on the back roof of the cottage, and he thanked goodness that they still had some heat in their house. He was freezing.

He watched a bit longer and soon Rob's wife joined his brother in the kitchen as she started to prepare breakfast for the family.

Convinced there was no-one else in the small cottage he waited until his brother and his wife had settled down for their breakfast and crept across to the back door and gave it a knock.

He could hear a flurry of voices in the house as they no doubt puzzled as to who would be knocking on their back door at that time of the morning. The door opened and there stood his brother. They looked at each other for what seemed like ages before Rob spoke.

'What the hell,' were his first words then, 'what are you doing here?' He looked around behind Mark to see if there was anyone else in his back garden then grabbed Mark's arm and dragged him into the house.

Rob's wife had to stifle a scream at the sight of her brother-in-law. She had not seen him for nearly 5 years, and he was the last person she expected to see in the current circumstances.

'Morning Rob, Laura,' Mark managed, tears of joy filling his eyes. 'Long time no see.'

Rob, still in a state of shock hugged his brother and was hugged back.

'Sorry to impose but I am so pleased to see you,' Mark managed. There had been times when he wondered if he would ever see his brother and his family again.

'Good to see you too Mark, take a seat, you look frozen and you look a mess.'

Mark smiled. 'That's intentional, behind this half-drowned sailor is a Brigadier in the Hampshire Regiment, but we'll keep that to ourselves.'

Laura managed to get three cups of the weakest tea Mark had seen in a long time out of the pot and suddenly he regretted he hadn't brought any supplies with him.

Rob asked again what he was doing there. Mark explained that he was trying to get some intelligence about German strength on the Island and what sort of equipment they had but did not mention the possible invasion.

Mark also put forward the idea that he and Laura could perhaps have a walk out later using Rob's ID, if he could dress himself and do his hair in a way that made him look as much like his brother as possible.

After he was finished the room went quiet. He broke the silence.

'I am here for a week and hopefully I can scout around while I am here. Is there any chance we can do this and that I can stay with you while I am here?'

'Bloody hell Mark, do you realise how dangerous this is. We have the kids to think of and we barely have enough food for ourselves let alone for someone else.'

'I know, I know,' Mark replied guiltily. 'This is a big ask but I hoped you would be able to help me as much as possible, for the sake of the Island. It could make a big difference to us all.'

Laura put her hand on her husband's arm. 'I know you are worried Rob but if Mark thinks this is the best thing we can do to help everyone in the long term then we need to trust him and help as much as we can.'

Rob turned to his wife putting his hand over hers. 'I am scared for the kids love. If the Germans find out, Mark will be shot, and we could end up being sent off the Island to some god forsaken concentration camp and we might never see the kids again. I'm not as brave as Rob and we have responsibilities, three of them.'

'Then we had better make sure the Germans don't find out eh love.' She turned to Mark. 'Mark, you are always welcome in our house, war or no war, just be bloody careful eh!'

The men both smiled as they could not recall Laura swearing before.

'I'll be careful, I promise, and in a week, I'll be gone and out of your hair.'

'That's settled then,' Laura stated getting up from the table, 'let's see if I can find another slice of bread.'

The kids came down an hour later and were introduced to their Uncle Mark. None of them remembered him as they had been too young last time they had seen him. The youngest had not even been born when Mark left for the army. They didn't tell them why he was here or that he was in the army. They just said he was from the other side of the Island, and he was a fisherman.

The weather was still pretty atrocious and there seemed little point in venturing out while the rain persisted so while Laura busied herself getting the kids washed and fed, Rob and Mark sat in the small lounge and Rob brought Mark up to speed with how things had been over the last three and half years.

Mark also updated Rob on the war and how things were going from the British perspective. All Rob had heard was the news in the local paper as portrayed by the Germans and a few whispers from those brave enough to keep crystal radios.

Over the course of the morning Rob told Mark that he was still working for the Government and was involved with the Essential Commodities Committee which sourced products from France to keep the islanders fed. He had been to France with the Germans many times over the years and had got to know several of them very well. As had been suspected he now knew quite a bit of German, but he was also quite fluent in French.

After the Germans had landed life had become quite tough, he had been forced to give up his precious car and now relied on a very old bike to get to work but in the summer, he tended to walk. Rations were just enough to keep them healthy though other non-essential things like furniture, tools, etc., were hard to come by.

Many of the houses had been left unoccupied by the people who had been evacuated so their contents had become fair game for people needing things like furniture and carpets. The house next to his cottage was empty and he knew people had raided it from time to time. He admitted he had raided their garden for fruit and vegetables, and he used their small Greenhouse all year round to grow vegetables to supplement their meager diet.

Rob explained that the Island was incredibly well defended, and he had seen all type of guns and vehicles over the years including a few small tanks which someone had told him were French. He had never heard of the bigger tanks Mark mentioned. They did have a lot of trucks, mostly commandeered from the locals and a few halftracks, and loads of motorcycles with sidecars.

Rob also explained how the police were still operating as were doctors and the ambulance service, but no fishing boats were allowed out of the harbour without German troops on board. This meant a limited supply of fresh fish was available.

During the discussion, Rob mentioned that he had seen hundreds of slave workers. They were being used to build many of the large defences and create tunnels and other military buildings. The investment in terms of time and materials was huge and he described how he saw examples of bunkers and defences every day, just on his way to work.

He had kept all the newspapers from the occupation so if Mark wanted he could read through those to get a feel for what was happening.

Finally, Rob mentioned that he had noticed that the troops seemed to be more drilled and sharper than normal over the last week or so. He was regularly stopped to show his ID and patrols were more frequent than ever. There had been speculation that something was happening and that maybe an invasion was about to take place.

With the rain showing no sign of abating and it being a Saturday the family decided to hunker down for the day. Laura kept the kids busy in the kitchen while Mark and Rob spent the afternoon reading the papers to see what intelligence they could glean from the news, as edited by the Germans. Later in the afternoon Rob asked if he thought there was any chance that Hitler could be beaten.

'Oh yes,' Mark replied, 'we have pushed them back in North Africa, driven them out of Sicily and are now pushing north towards Rome. Italy will be free soon. The Russians are also pushing them hard so yes, they can be beaten and we will beat them. It is just a matter of time.'

Rob smiled and got back to scouring the papers and secretly wished he had joined up when he had the chance.

*****

The same day that Mark landed on Guernsey the Kommandant of Guernsey, GeneralMajor Rudolf Von Graf, was in the middle of a frenzy of activity. He had driven his aides mad with constant orders and demands. The troops had been drilled and drilled again. Inspections seemed to be almost daily since the start of the year and every weapon and boot had been polished to perfection.

Dress uniforms were prepared and ready because tomorrow Generalfeldmarschall Erwin Rommel, the Desert Fox himself and hero to almost every German, was to arrive on the Island at 9 am. A special suite had been prepared at the Royal Hotel with a picture of Hitler above the bed. Flags were ready to be hung from the balcony of the Hotel when he arrived and would stay there for as long as Rommel was on the Island. The only thing that the Kommandant wasn't sure of was the length of his visit.

He took a moment to get up from his desk and looked out of the window across the rough beach next to the harbour. The weather was foul, and he just hoped it would improve in the morning. He doubted if the Generalfeldmarschall's plane would even fly in this weather. On days like this he wished he were back in Germany, playing in the snow with his wife and children. 'Bloody rain,' he muttered to himself.

All he could do was make sure that everything was ready for the morning. He had organised a cavalcade for the visit which consisted of his own personal car which he would share with Rommel, four outriders, a second car which would be in front of his car and would carry a couple of his senior officers and a half track which would follow his car and provide troop cover in case they ran into any trouble. Not that he anticipated that happening.

The local population were unaware of the visit and only the senior ranks around the local strongholds knew who was coming, the other ranks just knew they were being inspected by a senior officer.

Every button, medal and piece of metal on his uniform was cleaned and polished, as was his ceremonial dagger.

He was sure everything was ready, but he decided to check again and went back to his desk but this time he decided to consider what could go wrong and started to think.

Von Graf called in one of his aides. 'What happens if we get a puncture in the Generalfeldmarschall's car?' he asked. The aide shrugged his shoulders.

'Bloody hell must I think of everything. Make sure the half-track has at least one spare wheel. If that happens, we transfer cars and let the driver repair the wheel on the other car. Now what else could go wrong?'

And so, the planning went on until by early evening he was confident that he had thought of every eventuality.

That evening he played the role of the Generalfeldmarschall at a lavish meal which would be replicated exactly the following evening for Rommel in the Hotel's main lounge. All the senior officers including Oberleutnant's and above, who could be spared, were due to attend but that night just the officers based in the Royal Hotel occupied the top table for the practice meal.

The food was excellent as always, roast pork and venison with the finest available vegetables and fruit were the order of the day. After the meal he walked into the kitchen and complimented the chef and checked if he was confident that he could feed the hundred or so officers that would be attending the following day. He was assured that would not be a problem as he had more catering staff coming in the following evening.

He shook the chef's hand and after a quick look around the kitchen made his way back up to his office. He looked through the window again, it was still raining. He could do no more, so he retired to his bedroom, got himself into bed and set his small alarm for 6.30 the following morning. He picked up his book and started to read.

Eventually Von Graf fell asleep after going through the visit in his head numerous times. Next morning, he was awake before the alarm.

The first thing he did was poke his head through the blackout curtains. It was still pitch dark outside but from what he could make out it was not raining.

'Thank you, god,' he said to himself and with renewed enthusiasm he got himself ready. By 7 am he was enjoying a breakfast of bread, cold meats and cheese washed down with a black coffee. As dawn started to break, he was pleased to note the skies were relatively clear. After ensuring all the main rooms in the hotel were spick and span he called for his car and escort vehicles.

At 8 am he stepped out of the hotel and into the road and checked the flags were hanging correctly from the balcony. The long red banners with the swastika emblazoned in the middle fluttered in the gentle breeze and made him smile.

'Good, good,' he muttered as he got into his car and together, the small group of vehicles drove from St Peter Port to the Airport. The guards on duty were sharp and in good form, checking each vehicle through the gates and barbed wire barricade which surrounded the airport approaches.

A second set of gates were opened to let the vehicles on to the tarmacked area in front of the small airport building and there they waited. It was 8.30.

At 8.45 am a guard of honour together with the army band arrived from Fort George in several trucks. They all dismounted and formed up where the aircraft was due to pull up. NCOs ensured all was in order, even cleaning the odd boot with a rag if they saw any mud or water on the highly polished footwear. At 8.55 am the Kommandant inspected the troops and the band himself to make sure all was in order.

Once he was satisfied all was well, he went back to stand by his car. At just after 9 am the sound of an approaching plane could be heard and out of the sky to the east the familiar sight of a Junkers JU 52 appeared low in the sky and made its final approach into Guernsey Airport.

It landed with a bump and once the pilot had bled off its speed the plane turned and pulled up in front of the waiting troops. A young Oberleutnant called them to attention, and they presented arms. As the door of the plane opened the band started to play Preussens Gloria.

Generalfeldmarschall Ernest Rommel appeared in the door carrying his famous red and gold Field Marshall's baton. Steps had been rushed into place and without hesitation he stepped down from the plane on to Guernsey soil.

It was an historic moment. He was the first high ranked German officer to walk on captured British soil. GeneralMajor Rudolf Von Graf could not have been prouder. He marched over to Rommel and saluted, Rommel saluted back with a slight bow and held out his hand which Von Graf shook, amazed at the informality. While the band continued to play, he invited the Generalfeldmarschall to inspect the troops.

As he passed along the assembled troops he stopped occasionally and spoke to awestruck privates and junior NCOs.

Once that was complete he let Von Graf escort him to the car and they drove out of the airport grounds and headed towards Pleinmont, following the route the Kommandant had planned to show off the Island's defences in the best possible light.

As they drove, Rommel asked numerous questions about the island and quizzed Von Graf's on his views on the defences. He was keen to know if there were any gaps that needed filling or if there were any supplies that the Kommandant needed to ensure the Island was protected in the strongest way possible.

Rommel was as focused as any man Von Graf had ever met and was taken in immediately by the aura of greatness that surrounded the Desert Fox.

At Pleinmont Headland they got out of the car and Rommel was given a tour of the bunkers and emplacements that formed the stronghold, including battery dollman. There the troops carried out a practice drill and showed the Generalfeldmarschall how fast they could man and load the gun and how it could be traversed to reach potential targets.

Rommel and Von Graf then took a short walk along the cliff to the Marine Peilstand observation post where he took a pair of binoculars and observed the other batteries in the area and scanned the sea across as far as Jersey. They got back in the car and took the short drive to MP3, one of the tallest observation towers on the island. Rommel climbed to the top and from there took in the view of the islands west coast and the other fortifications that had been built around the headland.

'Impressive,' was all he said as he made his way down again, stopping to talk to the Kriegsmarine personnel on each level.

From there they drove down to the west coast and made several more stops, one of which was Stutzpunkt Rotenstein. This time the troops were as sharp as a tack and a small honour guard was waiting for the Generalfeldmarschall. At their head was Hauptmann Fischer, who sported an impressive scar on his left cheek.

Rommel spoke to him and a few of his men before allowing the proud young Hauptmann to show him round the bunkers and casemates which made up the stronghold.

Rommel shook Fischers hand before they left and as the Generalfeldmarschall was getting into the car Von Graf caught the young Hauptmann's eye. The young man smiled and the Kommandant smiled back and whispered, 'well done.'

Von Graf followed Rommel into the car and the entourage headed off to the next stop.

'You have some fine young men here Von Graf,' Rommel said as they drove through the guard house where the troops were standing at attention. 'Thank you, Herr Generalfeldmarschall,' he replied, 'I am very proud of my boys.'

The rest of the tour seemed to fly by but Rommel seemed particularly interested in Pembroke Bay.

'This is where I would attack if I were the British.' He explained. To emphasise the point Rommel spent more time looking at the defences around L'Ancresse than anywhere else on the tour.

'I think you need another bunker in the middle of the anti-tank wall and more defences on the high ground to the east of the bay. I would also add more Machine gun posts along the top of the wall.' Rommel advised.

Von Graf noted all the advice given by the great man.

They eventually headed back towards St Peter Port where Rommel was taken to Castle Cornet for lunch. They passed the Royal Hotel on the way and Von Graf pointed out his HQ as they drove past. A British Policeman was waiting at Castle Cornet and opened the car door for Rommel.

Cameras clicked to capture the staged moment that would appear in a future issue of Signal magazine. The band had been moved from the Airport and were playing in the grounds of the Castle when the Generalfeldmarschall walked through the gates and into the ancient courtyard.

Rommel was given a brief tour of the Castles newly installed bunkers and anti-aircraft positions before they stopped for a buffet style lunch with several of the Von Graf's senior officers. As they were eating, the Kommandant asked Rommel how long he would be staying.

'I fly back at 4 pm Herr GeneralMajor, so if there is anything else you want to show me, I suggest we make it quick.'

'Very well, Herr Generalfeldmarschall, we shall leave here in thirty minutes and we will visit the main barracks at Stützpunkt Georgefest (Fort George) before we head back to the Airport. Excuse me a moment.'

Von Graf hid his disappointment and summoned two of his aides who were never far away and re-arranged his plans. Word was sent to Stützpunkt Georgefest to prepare for a parade at 2.30 pm and the band was ordered to go back to the airport as soon as they left Castle Cornet, ready for Rommel's departure at 4 pm. The honour guard was also to be ready at the airport to see the Generalfeldmarschall on his way. He made sure the car was waiting outside the castle gate.

The weather was threatening to change and he didn't want Rommel to endure a walk in the rain, if at all possible.

He returned to Rommel's side just as he was talking to the senior officer in the Kriegsmarine on Guernsey. They were talking about a new HQ bunker that they were building and how it would link to all the observation posts around the Island and enable them to report back more effectively to the Admiral Kanalküste who looked after the Channel area.

Their role was to report details of any allied ship movement they could observe from the huge towers.

Once lunch was over Von Graf gave the Generalfeldmarschall a brief visual tour of the harbour and its defences from a viewpoint on the North side of the Castle. They then made their way down to the car just as the heavens opened.

They drove carefully up to Stützpunkt Georgefest, passing the guards standing at attention at the gated entrance. Inside around a thousand Wehrmacht troops were lined up with several Renault tanks and other mobile units, getting soaked in the pouring rain. They drove up and down the lines rather than walk in the rain but at the end of the inspection Rommel asked if he could address the troops.

The Kommandant ordered the driver to stop by one of the small tanks and Rommel clambered up next to the turret. He waved the troops over and they gathered round to try and hear what the great man had to say.

'Brothers, Germans, Heroes of the Third Reich. You are my Atlantic wall, not concrete bunkers. I am depending on you not to break when the waves of British and American forces smash against your defences. You are strong, your Kommandant is strong, together you can face anything and win. I will ensure you are well equipped so you can be ready when the test comes. Be sure, you will be tested. Your Fuhrer himself is watching you. He is proud of you. He is proud of what you have achieved here and of what you are yet to achieve. For your families at home, for the fatherland, for the Fuhrer and for God, we will win this war! For Victory, Sieg Heil.'

The massed troops, despite the incessant rain, were completely captivated and gripped by his words. With one voice they responded 'Seig Heil, Seig Heil, SEIG HEIL!!'

With that Rommel waved his baton at the crowd in acknowledgement, got down off the tank and climbed back into the car.

'Thank you, Herr Generalfeldmarschall,' Von Graf spoke as the car cleared the mass of troops, some still waving, cheering, and running after the car as it made its way back towards the gates of Fort George.

Water was still dripping off Rommel's cap as he turned to Von Graf. 'You organised everything perfectly Herr Kommandant, apart from the weather,' he added with a rare smile. 'But I prefer this to the sands around Tobruk.'

He stared out of the window at the passing houses and the occasional civilian walking in the rain. 'These British, Montgomery and Churchill are stubborn bastards Von Graf. They will come to take this Island back, I don't know when, but I don't think we will have to wait long. We have intelligence that suggests they will attack France from the Pas de Calais and the Fuhrer believes that. I do not. It is too obvious. I will reinforce you as much as I can, but my hands are tied as resources are being pushed to the limit on the Northern French coast. Keep your troops sharp, plan for an attack from the north and try and keep the population happy. We need their hearts and minds. We don't want them hating us and turning on us at a crucial moment.'

The drove on in silence, both deep in thought. They passed through St Martins village and then on towards the airport.

As they were getting close to the Airport Rommel turned to Von Graf again. 'Thank you again for today, I am sure you had planned much more but my travel plans must be top secret. If there is anything you need, contact me direct and I will do whatever I can to help?'

'Thank you Generalfeldmarschall, it has been a pleasure. We did have a meal arranged in your honour for tonight, but I will cancel it and rest assured we will hold the British off if they have the nerve to try and attack Fortress Guernsey.'

'Have your meal Kommandant, in my honour. Your men deserve it.' He shook Von Graf's hand as they were driving through the gates to the Airport. The skies were starting to clear, and the rain had stopped as Rommel got out of the car. The band started to play again and the honour guard formed a line to the Junkers parked on the concrete.

As usual Rommel spoke to several of the troops before taking the few steps up into the plane. At the door he turned and aimed a salute at Von Graf who was now standing at the end of the line of troops. Von Graf saluted back and with that Rommel disappeared into the JU 52.

An Oberleutnant ordered the honour guard away from the plane as the engines started. The band marched away while the plane was turning. It stirred up a flurry of spray from the puddles on the tarmac. Von Graf stood his ground, great coat flapping and holding on to his cap as the blast from the engines caught him, but he was rewarded with a last glimpse of Rommel at the window. The plane moved away to the end of the airfield and without waiting sped down the runway, up into the clouds, quickly disappearing from sight.

Von Graf was in awe at what had just happened. He got back into the car and headed back to his HQ.

Despite the absence of their VIP guest the meal went ahead that night. Someone found a picture of Rommel and stood it on a chair in the position of honour at the head of the top table, next to the Kommandant.

The meal was a great success and at the end they toasted Rommel three times before the final toast to the Fuhrer.

Von Graf slept well that night.

*****

While the Kommandant was enjoying the experience of a lifetime the Heaume family were making plans. The night before they had a meal of potato, cabbage and carrots mashed together into small fritters and fried on the aga. The simplicity did not seem to bother them as they enjoyed the experience of having Mark with them.

Having company for an evening meal had not happened since the occupation began. Laura was determined to make the most of the situation, as dangerous as it was, and the children were so excited to see their parents so happy.

The next morning they started to put their plans into action. After a breakfast of weak porridge Laura started to work on Mark to get him looking as much like Rob as she could. Rob had started to go a bit thin on top and she had kept his hair noticeably shorter than Mark's hair. That meant she had to give Mark the same haircut and shave some of his hairline back to match his brothers. She found some clothes that fitted Mark and as Rob wore glasses found an old pair of his specs and put them on Mark.

She stood back and admired her handiwork. She got out Rob's identification card and a small mirror and showed Mark what he looked like compared to the ID Card.

'That's great Laura, I think I'll pass inspection.'

She smiled at the compliment and squeezed his shoulder. 'Shall we have a walk into town later. We need to leave early as we have to get back before dark and it looks like it might rain later.'

'The sooner the better,' he replied. Laura started to get the children ready as to not have them with them would look odd. Soon they were all wrapped up and ready to go. Laura had her youngest in a pram. Mark carried the five-year-old and Betty, her eldest held her hand.

'Why is Uncle Mark coming with us?' Betty asked. 'Daddy is having a rest love, just pretend Uncle Mark is Daddy for today and we'll have a treat tonight. Betty skipped up and down excited at the promise of a treat.

They walked out of the front door and turned right, walking along Summerfield Road before turning left past the North Cinema and on to the bridge. Mark noted that German propaganda movies were on offer in the cinema as well as an old French film. He later learned that the few English films that had been in the Island in 1940 had been run so many times no-one went to see them anymore.

As they crossed the bridge, he noted that there were German troops everywhere, he wanted to walk towards the end of the harbour but Laura ushered him along New Road and the Grande Maison Road. As they walked, she explained that there were restricted areas that way and they would not have been allowed to pass.

Laura assured him that there were heavy defences at the end of the south side of the harbour and the North side was protected by the Vale Castle. She also mentioned that she had seen the occasional German vessel in the small harbour but as it dried at low tide most vessels used St Peter Port Harbour.

As they reached the end of the Grande Maison Road they spotted a check point.

'That's not normally there,' Laura whispered but it would look too suspicious if they turned around now so they kept walking. When they reached the junction, they were asked for their ID documents and Laura and Mark produced their cards. The guards looked at them both and the cards and gave them back.

'Where are you going?'

'Just out for a walk with the children,' Laura replied confidently. 'We are going as far as town and back before it rains.'

The German sentry smiled at her and waved them through.

'He seemed a bit friendly,' Mark whispered as they walked away.

'They're all like that Mark. They think all local women are fair game.'

As they walked Mark took particular note of bunkers near the halfway and another at the tram sheds, both covering Bellegreve Bay. The small headland at the tram sheds was now home to a large bunker which included manned machine gun posts.

All the bunkers were manned by well dressed, sharp looking troops. Each slipway into the bay was covered in barbed wire making access to the beach virtually impossible. They eventually reached the Royal Hotel which was bedecked with Nazi flags. 'They're not usually there,' Laura whispered as they paused before turning around and starting their way back home.

Betty was getting tired, so Laura managed to perch her on the back of the pram between the handles as they walked back. Mark's arm was aching too so he perched the five-year-old on his shoulders. The baby was sound asleep in the pram.

As they approached Salarie corner Mark noticed a commotion on the bend as a group of troops he had spotted on their way into town sprang into action and formed up on the corner, presenting arms as the family approached.

That's not for us, Mark thought, puzzled as to what was happening. The thought had hardly left his head as two motorcycles followed by two black cars, both flying Nazi flags, came around the corner in the centre of the road. The cars were followed by a half track full of troops and another two motorcycles.

The family stopped to watch the cavalcade drive past and a man in the second car locked eyes with Mark and made a casual wave to the family as he drove past.

Bloody hell, Mark thought as he realised who had just waved at him. 'That was Rommel,' he whispered to Laura as the family carried on walking home. The troops dispersed as the couple approached. Two of the soldiers stayed to keep watch around Salerie Harbour while the others formed up and marched past them towards the harbour.

The only nervous moment on the way back was when they bumped into a family that Laura knew. They wanted to chat, but Laura made the excuse that they needed to get the baby home as they were worried he wasn't well. The other family seemed a bit puzzled but did not question the excuse so after a few pleasantries they walked on towards home, this time over St Clair Hill as far as the Braye Road.

All the way Mark was assessing each junction and making a mental note of any defensive positions and potential defensive positions. Up ahead he could see the Vale Church and decided to try and go that way next time he was out. They got back to Rob and Laura's house just as the rain started.

When he got back, Mark couldn't wait to tell Rob about who he had seen while they were out and they spent the evening discussing why Rommel might be in Guernsey and the reason for his visit.

After soup for tea and a spoonful of macaroni pudding, as the promised treat for Betty, they went to bed at 8 pm. Mark sleeping on the couch in the front room.

THE PARAS

After seeing off Brigadier Mark Heaume, in Weymouth, Colonel Ronnie Krimp had returned to his parachute regiment, which was based on the outskirts of Exmoor National Park. He had set out the training regime he calculated would give them the best chance to fulfill their part of the mission.

He had marked out an area the size of around ten football pitches close to Wimbleball Lake to try and replicate the fact that the landing zone was bordered by the sea.

His plan was to get the men practicing dropping into that area from different heights in different weather conditions. He was proud of what they were achieving. The 600 plus men had not had a chance to drop as a group yet but individually they had all had at least one proper drop over the last couple of weeks, weather and availability of transport planes permitting.

Around 70% of the men hit their target but Krimp knew that meant that he could possibly lose 200 men before they even faced the Germans. The issue was getting all the men out of the planes quickly while they were over such a small target and he was working on ways to improve the way they bailed out; the best option he knew was to have less men in each plane.

The downside of halving the complement in each plane was that he would need something like 60 Dakotas for the mission and with all that would be going on over France he felt that his mission would be unlikely to receive that level of support. He needed to either get the men out quicker, expand the landing area or reduce the number of troops on the mission.

The reality was that the target area was bigger but he wanted his men on the ground in close proximity so they didn't lose contact in the dark and get dispersed around the common land. However, if he could increase the number of target areas and assign each division a separate role, he might solve the problem. He decided to get his team together and discuss the options.

It was a problem he had raised with General Hood but not being experienced in parachute drops, the General could not offer ideas apart from telling Ronnie that he had every confidence his team would come up with an answer.

Krimp had been allocated a small cottage to use as his HQ. It was on the southern edge of Exmoor quite close to Wimbleball Lake. On the morning after Mark Heaume had left on his mission, he called in his company commanders to discuss the issue.

On the trestle table in the small living room which he had made his Ops room were aerial reconnaissance photographs of the north of Guernsey and also the latest ordnance survey maps to try and establish what the topography of the area was like. He knew the area well, but he knew this was all virgin territory to his company commanders.

A Company was commanded by Major Gordon Druce one of the most experienced men Krimp had in his team and who he would be jumping with. B Company was led by Major Robert 'Bob' Bridle and C Company had Major Thomas 'Tinker' Bell in charge. The four men stood around the table as the rain lashed the windows of the cottage.

'There'll be no jumping today gentlemen,' Krimp announced, 'the weather boys have grounded all flying at least until lunchtime so we'll let the men have a day off.'

'I have called you together today to discuss a problem. I know we have been planning on using a single target for the drop zone but it just isn't practical. The specific role we have been given is to prevent reinforcements reaching the German garrison on this hill,' he said pointing to the bunker complex on a hill called La Varde.

'As far as I can determine the likelihood is that troops will come from the south via the Military Road here, L'Islet, here or from Bordeaux via La Fontenelle in the east, here. We also need to harass the troops on La Varde Hill from their rear.'

Each time he used a swagger stick to point to the relevant area.

'That means we will need to divide our forces as we have four goals and just three companies.'

'We could create a 4th Company, sir. That way they can train together for each specific mission.'

'Good idea Gordon. Any objections to that idea?' The other's shook their heads. 'We'll need another Major, does anyone have someone who they think would make a good company commander?'

'Captain Flatterly is a good man sir.' Major Bell suggested. 'The men respect him, and he has a good service record.'

Krimp knew the man in question. 'Any objections anyone?'

'No sir, I agree he will be good in a fight,' Major Bridle replied. The others nodded in agreement.

'That is settled then, I'll put him in for promotion. Now let us divide up the men and create D Company.'

The four men settled down with a hot tea brought in by one of Colonel Krimps aides and worked out how the units would be divided up. They opted to keep as many men as possible in their original companies but pulled out whole platoons where possible to form D Company.

Each company had its own radio operator although A Company would have two. Colonel Krimp needed his own personal Radio Operator to ensure he could keep in touch with each of his commanders in the field as well as with General Hood in his command centre.

All four companies would consist of three platoons of 50 men. Each platoon would be equipped with two 3-inch mortars, two Bren guns and two PIAT's for anti-tank operations. Platoons were led by a Lieutenant or a Second Lieutenant who could call on the expertise of an experienced Sergeant, Corporal and two Lance-Corporals. Each platoon also had a trained medic.

When they had finished, they had full complements for each company marked out on a chart which had been pinned to the wall. The name of each officer taking part in the mission had been added to the chart.

Next, they looked at the proposed battlefield and set out where each company would be based.

It was agreed that Colonel Krimp together with A Company would form up in the grounds of the Vale Church and defend the crossroads and the western side of the church. If possible, he intended to commandeer a cottage near the entrance to the church, the church itself would be used as a medical aid station for the injured.

Krimp and his team had all agreed that the crossroads next to the church was the key to the whole battle from their perspective but he was acutely aware that there was a row of cottages stretching along the Military road which would be in the firing line. He was less concerned about reinforcements from the L'islet side and felt one of his platoons could hold that position if enemy troops came from that direction.

B Company was given the task of attacking the enemy on La Varde Hill. This was one of the most dangerous elements of the mission as the navy would be shelling that enemy stronghold right up until the troops were on the beaches. Any shots going over the top of the hill could fall on B Company.

The last thing anyone wanted was troops killed by friendly fire but they had to take the risk.

C Company was to position itself around the base of the hill at La Fontenelle on the East side of the landing beaches and stop any reinforcements from the east while D Company would hold the crossroads in the centre of the common and provide back up for the other units if needed.

Now they had a plan, Krimp and his officers had a discussion about the landing zones. It was agreed A Company and D Company would stick to the original drop zone. B Company would drop between the primary drop zone and La Varde Hill putting them nearer their target and C Company would drop into the open land between a rocky outcrop called Rocque Balan and the high ground known locally as Bunker Hill.

This was quite a narrow target but again would place C Company in prime position to block the anticipated reinforcements from the east.

A third cup of tea was being drunk, sandwiches had been eaten and the rain had stopped by the time Krimp's team were happy with their plan. He was secretly worried that C Company could be cut off from the rest of the regiment. However, it was the best they could come up with.

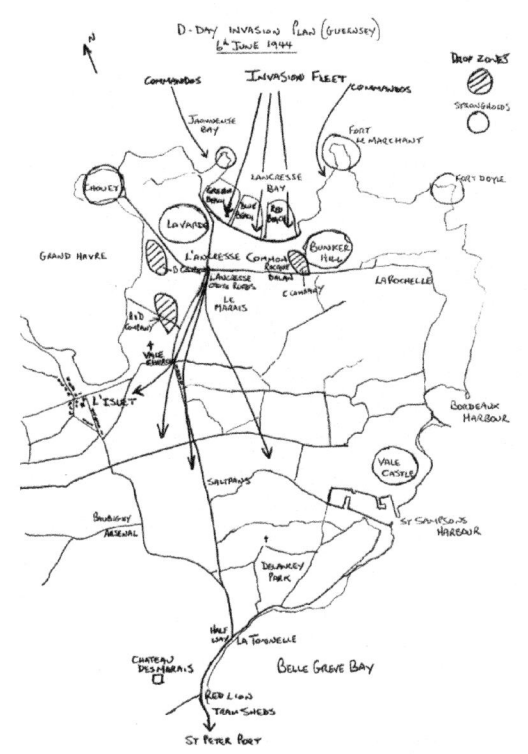

Guernsey Invasion Plan 6th June 1944

The Colonel would run the plan past General Hood to make sure it was appropriate for the overall mission, but he was quietly confident he would get the green light. Now he just needed to adjust the training schedule and include exercises that would hone their skills when they were on the ground. It was vital for the success of the mission that the men could find each other and defend each other as soon as they were on the ground.

*****

In the White Hart Hotel General Hood was looking out of the window at the awful winter weather. He was wondering how Brigadier Heaume was getting on in Guernsey. HMS Sealion had returned from the insertion and reported that all had gone to plan. Hood just hoped his friend had got off the beach safely and had met his brother. He knew it would be 6 days before he knew the answer to his questions. Hood would be waiting when Sealion got back from the recovery mission.

As he stood looking out the window, he sipped a glass of water while waiting for his senior team to arrive. The meeting today was to start formulating a plan of action for the next three months. On the agenda they also were going to work on ideas for the landing itself.

The General needed to take stock of what resources they had and the support they would need to put the plan into action. On the table was a marine chart of the waters surrounding the Island. Joining them would be a senior member of Admiral Ramsay's team so that any ideas that were formulated at the meeting could be taken back to the Admiralty.

On one of the walls the updated aerial reconnaissance photographs had been pinned and a large-scale map of Guernsey was placed next to it. Hood had some ideas but needed to validate them with the team or have flaws pointed out. Arrogance was certainly not a quality that could be assigned to General Hood, and he was more than happy to listen to advice and change his ideas if necessary.

Captain Barlow was first to arrive, resplendent in his dark blue naval uniform, he carried a well-used dark brown leather briefcase.

'The Admiral sends his compliments, sir.' Captain Barlow announced with a crisp salute. General Hood saluted back.

'At ease Captain, you are very welcome here so relax and take a seat.'

Barlow smiled, removed his cap and took a seat at the table, looking around the room at the various maps and charts.

'You seem to have everything we might need General.'

'Everything apart from a decent cup of tea and a slice of fruit cake,' Hood joked. 'The tea will be on its way in ten minutes, sadly we don't have any cake but we might be able to rustle up a biscuit or two.'

'Tea is fine General. If I'd thought, I would have brought along some grog as a winter warmer. Nothing better than a tot in a hot cup of tea to warm the cockles.'

Hood detected the cockney twang. 'Are you from London Captain?'

'Born and bred General. My streets completely gone now mind, gawd knows what they'll build in its place. I lost my Gran in the bombing, she refused to go to the shelter with my parents.'

'Sorry to hear that, but they're alright?'

'Yes sir, they lost everything but have moved in with my Dad's brother in Kent. They were always the posh ones in the family. They've got a big house. My parents will be fine. Dads tough, fought in the trenches, he's known worse.'

With that there was a knock on the door. As he was still standing by the window General Hood went across and opened the door. In came the group of officers that consisted of his senior team.

They consisted of the Brigade commanders of the 69th Infantry Brigade, 151st Infantry Brigade and the 231st Infantry Brigade.

With them was a senior officer from the Royal Armoured Corps who had been invited by General Hood on the advice of General Morgan. His job was to explain how the Armoured Corps could help with their plans for a landing on mine infested beaches.

After all the introductions, the six men took their seats around the table.

'Gentlemen, I have invited Captain Barlow here to get a better understanding of the assets that will be available for us on the day of the invasion. Captain, the floor is yours.'

Captain Barlow stood and went over to the map of Guernsey. He pulled out a folded chart from his case and unfolded it. 'If I may General?'

'Help yourself Captain.'

The Captain pinned his chart over the top of the Guernsey map. What it showed was a chart of the Western approaches including the south coast of England and the bay of St Malo where the Channel Islands were situated. He then got a wooden pointer out of his bag.

'Gentlemen, it goes without saying that what I am about to show you is top secret. Are you all comfortable with that?' He paused as everyone acknowledged his question with a nod.

'Over the next few months, we are planning on building up our naval resources in the south coast ports and in west coast ports as far north as Liverpool. On the morning of Operation Overlord, whenever that is, we will have substantial naval assets available for the invasion. Our main job is to support the invasion fleet which will be following these routes.'

He used his pointer to indicate several dotted lines that started from points on the south coast, converged in the central channel. The lines then followed two paths, one between Alderney and the Cherbourg peninsula. The other route passed to the west of Alderney and then to the north of Guernsey, Herm, and Sark. Once that route had passed Sark it divided into three prongs to land on the coast of France.

'To get past Alderney safely we will be bringing our biggest guns to bear on the German batteries on that Island and will hopefully silence them quickly. The most vulnerable units will be those passing between Alderney and France so we must protect those transports as best we can. Current thinking is that this will be the US invasion force tasked with securing the port of Cherbourg. At the same time, we have to be prepared to support your invasion force.'

Barlow pointed to a separate dotted line which came straight on to Guernsey when the others angled to the east towards France.

'To do that we will allocate at least a cruiser and four destroyers to support your transports and support vessels as they approach the Island. What we need is for you to allocate targets for our guns.'

'You point and we fire.' He added with a smile.

'Thank you, Captain, please take your chart down and let's take a closer look at Guernsey.'

Captain Barlow packed his chart and pointer away and sat back down while the General walked across to the map with his swagger stick in his hand to use as a pointer.

'Again, this is Top Secret as I am sure you will be aware Captain. The capture of Guernsey, with the least amount of collateral damage is, as you know, considered a priority. It can provide the invasion force with a base for close air support and a safe harbour until Cherbourg is captured and secure. The proximity of Guernsey to the invasion beaches will provide us with a bunkering point where supply and demand can be met and could also provide a base for the treatment of casualties. The guns on Guernsey are also a threat to the invasion force and rendering them inoperative is vital to avoid unnecessary casualties before our forces even get to the beaches. The biggest guns are here,' he pointed to the large guns inland from the west coast of the Island.

After a sip of water, he continued. 'We are planning a commando raid to render these large guns inoperable. They are in a populated area so your big guns will be targeting these at a last resort.' He looked directly at Captain Barlow who acknowledged his words with a nod.

'If the commando raid fails, then we will be asking your cruiser to take them out, whatever the consequences. The main targets in the initial stage of the attack are the La Varde stronghold, the sea wall area itself as it includes gun emplacements and these forts on the headlands each side of the bay. We anticipate two destroyers will be able to provide enough cover to severely damage or destroy these defences along with the units we send in to support the landings.'

He looked at Captain Barlow. 'That sounds good to me General.'

Hood continued. 'If the cruiser could station itself along with another destroyer off the West Coast and target the strongholds here at Grandes Rocques, Vazon, L'Eree and Pleinmont that would be ideal. We would hope this would cause not only severe damage to these defences but would also serve as a diversion and cause confusion amongst the German troops on the Island. The final destroyer we would like stationed off St Peter Port to stop any German naval forces that might try and leave the Island. It can also shell the barracks at Fort George if necessary and when our troops arrive in St Peter Port supply heavy guns, if they are needed, as directed by the commander on the ground. We also believe seeing a British vessel off St Peter Port will give hope to the civilian population and demoralize the defenders. What do you think Captain?'

'It all seems achievable General, but I will need Admiral Ramsay to endorse the plan and allocate appropriate assets to meet your needs. I can't promise but I am hoping we may have a second cruiser and a small frigate available to you as well. I think you will need as much firepower as possible, especially around the landing beaches. I'll let you know Admiral Ramsay's reply and the final fleet complement as soon as I can.'

'That would be exceptionally useful Captain. If you can confirm the Admiral is happy then we can get on with our detailed planning for the invasion and the taking back of our Island.'

'Thank you for the tea, General. I look forward to seeing you all again soon.'

Captain Barlow stood and placed his cap back on his head. He saluted General Hood and left the room.

'Gentlemen, that was very encouraging, I think we can count on the senior service to get us to the beaches and cause as much confusion as possible to the defenders.'

He turned to the representative of the Royal Armoured Corps. 'Major Chauvel, the floor is yours.'

Major Colin Chauvel got up and walked across to the aerial photographs of Guernsey.

'As you know gentlemen the plan is for the main landings to take place here at L'Ancresse. If you look very closely, the beach is peppered with hedgehog defences and is probably mined. We have considered different ways of trying to negate the mines, including special forces landing under cover of darkness to defuse them but it is far too dangerous. Any accident would give away the element of surprise. A rolling barrage from the navy may destroy some of these defences but it is more likely the explosions would just move them around. It would also divert precious shells away from the main targets.'

Chauvel paused for a moment. 'We've been working on a few ideas under the guidance of Major General Hobart, and we believe by May, given support from the Chiefs of Staff, we will have tanks that will be able to clear the mines and hedgehog defences from the beach. If some of his ideas prove practical, we may also have ways of getting you off the beaches.'

'That is good to know Major, let me know as soon as you have confirmation that we have access to these machines. We could certainly do with several clear paths off this beach. I am establishing a beach marshalling unit to control traffic on the beach and to manage the area after we have established our beachhead on L'Ancresse Common. The tides here can be our friend, and our enemy, so we need to get off the beach as soon as we can as we can only use it according to the tides.'

'Do you need me any more General?'

'No Major, I look forward to hearing from you soon and maybe we can have a demo of your special tanks in a few weeks' time.'

'I am sure that can be arranged General. Gentlemen.' With that Major Chauvel got up from his chair, saluted the General and left the room.

The General followed the Major out and asked his aide to bring in more tea and biscuits for his team. He also called in Captain Ian Best. Once the tea had arrived, he addressed the officers.

'Gentlemen, we need to decide what resources we will need when we go ashore. Let's get down to business.'

With that, the men spent the rest of the afternoon planning what they needed for the invasion of Guernsey and by the end of the day Captain Best had a long list of support units the team wanted for the invasion.

GUERNSEY

On Monday Rob had to go to work and it was agreed it was too risky for Mark to even consider taking his place. Rob trusted his fellow workers and he knew they wouldn't turn Mark in to the Germans, but they worked too closely with the Germans to believe Mark could stand close scrutiny. Especially if he encountered some of the officers Rob regularly dealt with.

During the afternoon Rob told his colleagues that he felt he was coming down with flu or at least a heavy cold and it was agreed he should take a few days off.

This gave Mark the chance to take the bicycle, and Rob's ID, out for a few days and have a look around. He was especially keen to get as close as he could to L'Ancresse Common to get as much intelligence as possible with regards to troop placements and patrols. On Tuesday afternoon he rode the bicycle to Bordeaux Harbour and followed the main road towards L'Ancresse, assessing how easy it would be to move troops in that direction and what reserves they might have in the area.

He noted that the Vale Castle had been converted into quite an impressive stronghold and the troops there could be pushed to L'Ancresse if required. It would also provide a difficult defensive position to attack, if that was needed. Large searchlights were on the top of the castle walls, and it seemed to bristle with guns. The realisation that he had come ashore so close to such a major stronghold unnerved him as did the thought he had to come back this way in a few days' time.

A few locals were out walking, and he saw several bikes on the road. Occasionally someone would wave to him, and he just waved back. Luckily, he realised very early on in his journey that he had to ride on the right-hand side of the road. That simple mistake would have given him away to the many German vehicles that were using the same roads or potentially could have got him killed.

He saw a mix of trucks, motorcycle, and sidecar units and one halftrack while he rode towards L'Ancresse Common. As he approached the common land the roads got much busier.

The first thing he noticed was a wall of barbed wire which was placed around the base of bunker hill, bordering the edge of the area of common land between Bunker Hill and Rocque Balan. He couldn't see any evidence of bunkers on the hill so surmised it might be some form of barracks area or a defensive position of some kind.

Mark was trying not to be too obvious as he peddled along the road so tended to look over his glasses, glancing towards the common whenever he thought it was safe.

He could see machinery that looked like a giant excavator that was taking sand from the common and he could not miss the bunkers that had been built all over the hill at La Varde. In a passing thought he wondered if the Germans had destroyed the prehistoric Dolmen which sat on top of the hill.

La Varde hill bristled with bunkers and defences, all sporting guns of different types, some of which he believed would cause concern to the proposed parachute invasion, unless they were neutralized in some way.

On his left as he approached the crossroads in the centre of L'Ancresse common, were dozens of Greenhouses. The idea of glass shrapnel exploding everywhere didn't bear thinking about. An old lady in a cottage next to a small block of greenhouses waved and smiled at him as he rode past and he waved back.

Mark stopped when he reached the crossroads and made a point of fiddling with his chain. That was enough to attract the attention of the Germans and a motorcycle and sidecar approached him just as he was getting back on his bike. The guards asked to see his ID and asked him why he was out on his bike. He explained in his broken German that he was looking for wood for his home as his children were cold. He had come to the common in search of gorse branches which he could use for the fire.

The troops looked at each other and then looked again at the man on the rickety bike with tattered clothes and a haggard face. Without hesitation they made a decision.

'Follow us,' they ordered and unbelievably they took him along the Pembroke Road, through a guard post, as far as the rear of the anti-tank wall. He could see the defences on the beach, prepared gun positions on top of the wall and noted the several pathways which led up to the bunkers on La Varde Hill.

There was a pile of timber near the base of the wall. It was a mix of driftwood from the beach and planking left over from the construction of the wall. The soldiers helped him load his bike, tying the wood on with strong cord around the crossbar and on the pannier behind the saddle.

'Thank you so much,' he said, offering his hand and both soldiers shook it. He tried not to squeeze too hard to show any strength.

'Bitte,' they replied and escorted him back as far as the Guard post. He wobbled away down the military road noting a small defensive position by the crossroads near the Vale Church. As he rode a column of four French Char B1 tanks drove past him on their way to L'Ancresse, two seemed to have been modified but he had no idea what their purpose was. He was about to turn down the Braye Road towards home when the rain started again. His hands were bitterly cold, but the cycling was helping to keep his body warm.

There was another small defensive position at the Braye Road, Military Road crossroads and one of the sentries there waved to him as he struggled past. When he finally got to Rob's home it was nearly 4 in the afternoon and it was getting dark. Mark pushed the bike around the back of the cottage where he unloaded the wood into the shed so it could dry out. Once the bike too was in the dry, he went into the house and was welcomed with a cup of weak tea.

He cupped the warm drink in his hands savouring the heat more than the taste.

Laura had spotted him unloading the wood and asked where he had got it from. His brother and sister-in-law were amazed at his good fortune. Laura went off to start to get supper ready.

While she prepared the food, Mark and Rob discussed how well prepared the Germans were and just how much resources they must have invested in this tiny piece of British soil. Secretly he was starting to wonder if this invasion was such a good idea.

Over the next couple of days Mark rode out a bit further. He explored the lanes between the Braye Road and L'Ancresse common, never venturing too close to the headland again. The last thing he wanted was to get caught there twice as the troops might find that suspicious. He went almost as far as the West coast and found a place on higher ground where he could look out towards Fort Hommet.

Even without the benefit of binoculars he could see the headland was heavily defended. Troops were everywhere. During his travels he spotted a communications tower and more defences around Le Guet.

He was stopped once more on the Thursday and this time he said he was looking for somewhere that sold cabbages. That day he came home with two cabbages and a loaf of bread, courtesy of the Germans.

Mark was amazed at how friendly the Germans were, wherever he went. When he thought about it he concluded that they must have some form of standing order to keep friendly with the locals.

He did see one local girl walking out with a German soldier on her arm on the Thursday. The weather had been surprisingly good for January and the winter sun had brought a few more people out from their homes.

When he got home with his cabbages and bread, Laura explained that girls like that were known locally as jerry bags, and she was worried that they might be treated badly once the war was over.

Mark shook his head. 'I hope not Laura, three and half years is a long time and young people are the same the world over. These are ordinary people, just like us, but I am sure not everyone will be as understanding as you. God help them.'

That evening Mark mentioned to Rob that he had not seen any trains on the railway. Rob told him that the railway was not being used in the North of the Island anymore as he believed the bunker building programme at this end of the Island was now over. Rob also believed that many of the tracks in the north of the island had been removed. The bridge and embankment Mark had crawled over when he first arrived on the island was one of the few remnants of the railway system beyond St Sampson's Harbour.

On the Friday, armed with full knowledge of all the places Mark had been and who he had met, Rob went back to work. Mark took the opportunity to begin planning how he would get back to the rendezvous point. He knew it would not be easy.

That afternoon there was a knock on the door. Laura peaked through the net curtains and spotted a German Officer standing on the path. Mark quickly and quietly went upstairs. Laura quickly checked around for any evidence Mark had been there and then, when she was happy all was well, she forced a smile on her face and answered the door.

A German Major stood there with his hands behind his back. He nodded to her and clicked his heels in salute. 'Frau Heaume?'

'Yes.' She replied nervously.

'Is your husband at home?' He asked in perfect English.

'No, he is at work sir.'

'He has been spotted around the Island, scavenging for wood and food. Is everything alright?'

Laura's heart was pounding in her chest. 'It is hard sir, we have three small children and we really struggle at this time of year to keep them warm and fed. My husband wasn't well but he still went out to try and find wood and food.'

'I know,' he replied, 'we are trying hard to keep everyone fed but the winters are hard for us all. I hope this will help.' With that he pulled a bag from behind his back and gave it to Laura. She took it carefully and looked inside. There was a loaf of bread, a lump of meat and eggs, lots of eggs.

'Thank you,' Laura said as she burst into tears, 'this will help so much. Thank you, sir.'

'You are welcome, Frau Heaume. If you need anything else, please do not hesitate to ask. We do not bite.' He added with a smile.

With that the Major gave her a casual salute, clicked his heels again and turned smartly, walking casually down the path and out into the road where a car was waiting for him. He turned to wave before he got into the car which drove off as soon as he shut the door.

Mark came back down from upstairs just as Laura was unpacking the bag. She had a dozen eggs, a sizeable leg of pork and a loaf of bread. Hidden at the bottom were three chocolate bars, no doubt for the children.

Mark was just as amazed as Laura was at the gift and the kindness that the Major had shown her family.

'I can't wait for Rob to get home,' she said truly excited. 'Tonight, we will have a roast to celebrate and to fill you up for your journey home.'

True to her word by the time Rob got home at 5.30 a meal of roast potatoes, cooked in pig fat, cabbage, and pork was waiting for him.

Rob had known something was up as soon as he stepped through the door. The smell was amazing. The family tucked into their treat and the chocolate was shared out between all the family. Mark divided his share of the chocolate amongst the three children.

'There's plenty of American chocolate available in England.' Mark whispered to Laura.

After the dishes were cleared away, and the children were safely in bed, Mark got himself dressed in the same clothes he had worn when he arrived in Guernsey last Saturday. Now he just had to get himself safely back to the same place he had been dropped off by 2 am in the morning.

Keen to give himself plenty of time to get back to the beach Mark decided to leave at 10 pm. After an emotional goodbye, Rob blew out the candles to plunge the cottage into darkness. Mark quietly opened the back door and crept across the back yard to hide in the shed.

Mark sat there for around half an hour until he was confident his night vision was as good as it could get.

This time he decided to take a slightly different route to his rendezvous. The night was dark with low clouds scudding across the sky giving an occasional glimpse of the thin crescent moon. Walking slowly and as quietly as he could down the lane, Mark headed towards the railway bridge. He paused about 30 yards from the Bridge and tried to spot the Guard that he knew would be patrolling that segment of the railway line.

Waiting in the overhang of a copse of trees, he tuned his senses to listen as much as look for the guard. Eventually he was rewarded as he heard the distant crunching of gravel above the rustling and creaking of the trees. The footsteps gave away the guard's position.

Once he was confident that he could tell which direction the guard was walking he waited. When he was sure the guard had his back to him Mark quickly ran the 30 yards until he was safely under the bridge. Again, he waited until the guard had followed his prescribed route and then while he was walking away, Mark made his move down to the main road.

Praying that no vehicles would come his way he knelt against the wall and watched the guard who was patrolling the piece of land above Bordeaux beach. Timing had to be perfect as he needed both guards to be looking away when he made his dash across the road and over the narrow strip of land to the top of the beach.

The patrols took different lengths of time, so he had to wait almost an hour before the timing was just right. He had been studying the wall opposite and was confident he could climb over it quickly and quietly.

Mark could hear waves breaking on the beach and hoped that any noise he might make would be masked by the sea and the wind.

As soon as both guards were looking the other way, he made his move. Crossing the road at a low crouch he vaulted the wall, landing in the thick grass on the other side. He then rushed across the open land, heading for some bushes. Mark was almost there when he tripped on a stone and fell headlong. Somehow he managed to keep moving and crawled under the bushes, but the noise had attracted the attention of the guard who turned around and shone a torch in his direction.

Mark crawled as far back under the bushes as he could as the guard made his way towards where he hid. Moving even further back he felt something move against his back and a cockerel clambered over him and ran out in front of the guard.

The Guard made an attempt at catching it but the brown and white cockerel wasn't about to get caught easily and made a dash for the road. The guard ran after it and disappeared into the dark. Mark waited, trying to compose himself. Eventually the guard came back, the hapless bird in his hand. He shouted across at the guard on the railway line and held up the bird.

'Chicken tomorrow,' he shouted and then rang the unfortunate bird's neck. The guard on the railway line waved back and carried on his patrol. The soldier near Mark tucked the legs of the bird into his belt and carried on his patrol. Mark waited for a few more rotations before easing himself out from under the bushes. Carefully and as quietly as he could, he sneaked down to the top of the beach.

He paused again where the barbed wire met the wall and watched the guard for a while. When the guard was walking the other way, he turned his attention to the barbed wire. Mark couldn't see if it had been mined in any way, but it looked as if it was attached to the virtually sheer rocks at that end of the beach. The coil went up the wall of rock and into the darkness above him.

What he had noted was that where the coil bent up the wall of rock there was a small gap underneath the wire. Getting down on his knees he started to scoop pebbles and sand away until he was sure the gap was big enough to allow him to squeeze underneath.

Mark carefully took off his coat, folded it up, and, pushing it ahead of him, crawled carefully under the wire. Timing was critical and he had around five minutes to spare before the guard turned and started to walk back towards him. He made it just in time. He froze in position once again while the guard followed his patrol.

All the time he waited, Mark was looking out to sea trying to see if he could make out the submarine or the commandos. All he could think about was being safely back on board, but it was so dark he could not see much beyond the small breakers. Once the guard turned away, Mark spent a few minutes refilling the hole he had made and then quickly made his way down to the sea. This had been the moment he had been dreading.

He watched the guard for the final time turn away and slid into the freezing water. The cold caught his breath and he wondered if he could do this. He was so close but still so far from safety.

His plan was to swim out to sea a short way and then angle back toward the rocks where he was due to rendezvous with the commandos. After a few steps he was out of his depth and swimming as quietly as he could out to sea. The weight of the coat was a problem, he had put it back on as he did not want to risk leaving it on the beach. It meant he had to put extra effort into his swimming to keep himself afloat. He also had no idea of the exact time. By the position of the moon, he thought it must be around 1.30 am but he could not be sure.

Using a steady breaststroke, he pushed through the waves and into the calmer water around 50 yards out. He turned towards the entrance to Bordeaux Harbour and swam steadily in parallel to the shore until he was opposite the rocks where he was due to be collected. As he turned to swim back to the shore a hand grabbed his shoulder and unceremoniously dragged him out of the water.

'Thought you'd come to meet us did you sir?'

Mark recognised the hushed Yorkshire accent of one of the commandos that had dropped him off a week earlier.

'Seemed like a good idea at the time. You don't happen to have a tot of rum do you? I'm freezing.' His teeth were chattering as he spoke.

The commandos were already paddling the dinghy quietly away from the shore.

'If you can wait five minutes sir, I am sure the skipper will be happy to give you a tummy warmer.'

He lay back in the dinghy watching as the outline of Guernsey faded into the darkness behind him. His head was full of emotions, elation that the job was done and sadness to be leaving the Island. All the while the commandos paddled steadily out to sea.

About ten minutes later, a couple of searchlights suddenly lit the sky from the Vale Castle and searched the skies towards the south. Anti-aircraft guns opened up from the Castle and also from Brehon tower over his left shoulder. Tracer shells lit up the sky and he was worried the submarine could be seen in the reflected light, but as quickly as the action started it was over.

Probably a false alarm, Mark thought. *These boys are on a hair trigger.*

A few moments later the dinghy bumped into the side of HMS Sealion and before he knew it, he was being bundled down below and into the warmth. When the Captain saw he was soaking wet, he had the crew find him some dry clothes and a blanket and soon he was settled in the wardroom with a warm cup of tea laced with a generous tot of rum.

The comforting sound of the submarine diving put a smile on his face. When the Captain came to see how he was, he was already sound asleep.

The crew let him sleep until around 6am when the Captain woke him with a plate of bacon and eggs. He explained that they were a long way North of Alderney now and in friendly waters.

Happily, he tucked into his breakfast.

'I see you took time off to have a bit of a haircut while you were there?' The captain asked with a smile.

'My brother's not been so lucky with his hair as me,' he replied with a mouthful of bacon.

'Was it worth the risk Brigadier?'

'Yes, it was Captain, yes it was.'

'Good, I'll let you know as soon as we are heading into Weymouth. I am sure your colleagues will be waiting for you. You can keep the spare kit.'

'Thank you, Captain, for everything. I hope we will meet again.'

The captain left him to his breakfast and another cup of tea soon appeared, this time without the rum. He dozed off again for a while until the Captain returned and announced they had surfaced. He invited him on to the bridge just as they entered the harbour. As they tied up alongside the dock, Mark spotted General Hood on the quay along with Colonel Krimp and Captain Best.

Ropes were thrown on board and the deck crew made the ship fast. The gangplank was put in place ready for him to leave.

Mark turned and shook the captain's hand and thanked him again. He made his way down on to the deck just in time to see the commando unit getting their kit ready to go ashore. He shook each of their hands and they stood and saluted him as he walked to the gangplank. The deck crew also stood to attention and saluted as the coxswain piped him ashore. Mark turned and waved back to all the servicemen on the Submarine and then went over to his welcoming party.

He saluted the General who saluted him back.

'Decided to change allegiance and join the senior service I see,' General Hood said with a smile.

'Never sir, I like to keep my head above water.'

'Come on then, let's get you back in a decent uniform and you can tell us all about it.'

Colonel Ronnie Krimp came across and shook his friend's hand and together, the four of them made their way over to a waiting car and started their journey back to Exeter. On the journey, he spoke of how the Island had changed since the occupation had begun. He also mentioned how friendly the Germans were with the locals and how his family were living on the edge of starvation.

Mark also told Ronnie that he had remembered to kiss the granite for him and how a cockerel had saved the mission and probably his life. They decided not to discuss any intelligence he may have picked up until Mark had some time to rest and gather his thoughts.

Hood told Mark that he wanted him to spend at least a day with Ian to put together a report covering everything he had learned. They could then brief all the Guernsey team at a meeting the following week.

Mark was ordered to rest on Sunday and to gather his thoughts before a full debriefing with Ian on Monday.

Mark was grateful for the time off; he needed some good food and some proper sleep. However, he did want to spend some time with a notebook on Sunday to jot down the key findings of his mission. The last thing he wanted was to forget something crucial.

*****

On the afternoon of Wednesday, the 2nd of February the Guernsey team gathered in the White Hart Hotel to hear the news from Guernsey. Ian had put together a top-secret report based on the information that he had teased out of Mark. That report would be delivered to General Morgan after the meeting, with any additions or suggestions that might come to light during the discussion.

Rain was lashing the windows and Colonel Krimp had got soaked just running from his car into the Hotel. The others had been there for a while so had already dried off next to the roaring fire.

General Hood had already read the report, but the information it contained was new to the others.

Brigadier Vaudin and Colonel Mahy hadn't seen Mark yet and both shook his hand, pleased that he had got back safely. Tea and some sandwiches were produced before the General asked Mark to begin his briefing.

He stood and walked over to the map of the Island and the updated aerial reconnaissance photographs that were on the wall. A new detailed image of the L'Ancresse area took pride of place.

'Gentlemen, first can I say how pleased I am to be back. I know some of you will be a bit jealous that I have been home, but don't be. Conditions are not good. Food is very basic and things like clothing and furniture are not available. The people live in a make do and mend culture. Fuel for heating is difficult to find and the people are resorting to looting empty houses to find things they can use or burn for heating and cooking. What surprised me was how well the German occupying forces seem to be treating the local population, supporting them as best they can and trying where possible to befriend them. However, they too have supply issues. My brother is one of a team that works with them to try and secure essential supplies from France to keep the troops and the population fed.' He paused and took a sip of tea.

Colonel Mahy seemed uncomfortable. 'I hate to say this Mark but is there any hint of collaboration in what's going on, in your opinion of course?'

Mark took another sip of tea while he digested the question. It hadn't crossed his mind that what his brother was doing could be viewed that way.

'It never crossed my mind, Harry. From what I could see people were focused on keeping themselves and their families alive. Yes, Guernsey people are working for the Germans and some young girls are walking out with German soldiers. And yes, my brother works with them to help feed the people, but I didn't think of it as collaborating, I thought of it as surviving.'

General Hood could see where this topic could go and stopped the conversation sharply before it got heated.

'Gentlemen, an assessment of whether the Islanders have collaborated or not can be made after this is all over. Let us continue to discuss the matter in hand. Mark, please carry on.'

'Thank you General. While I was on the Island, I managed four reconnaissance missions around Guernsey, three involved bicycle rides around different parts of the north and west of the Island and the other was a walk into St Peter Port with my sister-in-law and her children. To enable me to do that, I borrowed my brothers ID for those excursions, hence the rather severe haircut.' The others smiled easing some of the tension which had filled the room.

'I'll let Ian take you through the defence report but what I will say is that these troops are sharp. We are not faced with a battle lazy army of second-rate soldiers. These boys are on the ball. To emphasise that I saw the Desert Fox himself getting a tour of the Island and you can bet your bottom dollar, as the yanks say, that he has got them tuned to a fever pitch of readiness.'

Colonel Mahy spoke first. 'Are you sure it was Rommel?'

'Bruce, as sure as I am standing here it was him. He looked straight into my eyes and bloody waved at me!'

'Shit.' Brigadier Vaudin muttered quietly.

'Exactly,' General Hood commented, 'but let us not dwell on that for now. Ian, do your worst.'

'Thank you, sir,'

Ian stood and walked over to the maps and took the Guernsey team through everything that Mark had seen. Putting meat on the bones as he put it to the aerial reconnaissance photographs.

He explained how there appeared to be several well-equipped strongholds that could prove an issue to the invading forces, particularly at La Varde and Bunker Hill. Each major junction seemed to have some form of defence works and the anti-tank wall at Pembroke was extremely well defended.

Anti-aircraft batteries were quite widespread and there were several small French tanks, some of which had been identified as being equipped with flame throwing equipment, from the description supplied by Brigadier Heaume.

Troops seemed to be everywhere, well equipped and in good spirits. It was estimated that from the numbers observed by Brigadier Heaume that their estimate of 20,000 troops on the Island could be on the conservative side with anything up to 30.000 troops potentially there at any one time.

It also looked like the Headquarters of the German Kommandant was in the Royal Hotel which had to be one of their major goals once they broke out of the beachhead. It was noted that most of the defensive positions Mark had seen were mainly focused on the sea and beaches, so could be vulnerable from the land.

It was agreed this helped justify the tactic of seizing the open land behind the proposed beachhead using Krimp's paratroopers. By landing behind the coastal positions, they could attack them from the rear or at the very least cut them off from receiving reinforcements. With luck they would surrender when they see the scale of the invading forces.

Each stronghold that was identified through a combination of aerial photography and visual reconnaissance by Brigadier Heaume was earmarked as a potential target for the guns of the navy.

During the discussion it was agreed that General Hood would try and secure air support from the RAF to help keep those defences battened down. Close air support could also be used against any columns of troops and equipment pushing towards the beachhead.

After the briefing Colonel Mahy remarked at how many greenhouses there were on the Island. They all knew there were a lot of greenhouses but seeing them from the air just brought home just how much land was covered in glass. They all realised how dangerous they would be to the troops on the ground and heaven help anyone who parachuted into a greenhouse.

The enormity of the task that faced them was really sinking in and for a moment the conversation stopped. They were all trying to picture their own role in the attack and what they would face. No-one relished the battle to come as they all knew the cost in men had the potential to be enormous. There seemed no doubt that this was quite possibly the most heavily defended piece of Hitlers Atlantic wall.

General Hood tried to lift the mood.

'Gentlemen, we knew this wouldn't be easy but thanks to Brigadier Heaume, we have had eyes on the area we are looking to attack and can be better prepared thanks to his efforts on our behalf. We have the support of everyone, including the Prime Minister, General Eisenhower and Monty so let's not be downhearted. Whatever we need, we can have so let us do this and do it right. Ian, can you prepare some plans based on the Brigadiers observations and the aerial photographs and see if someone could create a model of the headland. They can tap into the combined knowledge of all the Guernsey team and the latest reconnaissance. Let's call it a day but meet again next week to try and put together a draft invasion plan. In the meantime, if you have any ideas, no matter how off the wall, let me or Ian have them. No idea is a bad idea until we all decide it is.'

He paused for a moment. 'Unless there is anything else you want to raise right now you are dismissed gentlemen. Let us also pray for some better weather because training in this is impossible.'

No-one had anything else to raise at that moment so with the scrape of chair legs on the wooden floor and a flurry of salutes everyone left the room.

I need to think of something to lift their spirits, Hood thought to himself and went over to look at the plans again. *This is not looking good.*

OVERLORD

General Morgan was sitting in his office in his HQ in Norfolk House. He had just returned from a meeting with Winston Churchill, General Montgomery, and other key personnel where they had formulated plans for the invasion of France from the British perspective. It was mid-February and the bad weather seemed unrelenting. He got up and looked out of his window. The attack had been scheduled for mid-May and they just needed to decide which units would be allocated to each beach.

Since originally conceived the plans had been developed and now involved an Eastern Task Force as well as the now designated Western Task Force. The Americans would attack the Eastern side of the Cotentin Peninsula along with some Canadian Divisions. The target beaches were between Saint-Vaast-La Hougue and Saint-Martin-de-Varreville the rest of the American troops would join the British in their attack of the Western Beaches of the Cotentin between Beaumont-Hague and Barneville Carteret.

In the hours prior to the attack, which was scheduled for dawn, Parachute regiments and glider troops were scheduled to land in the open fields between Picauville and Beuzeville-la-Bastille. Their job was to prevent reinforcements reaching the landing beaches. They would be equipped to counter the German Tank units which would inevitably be rushed to the scene.

It was hoped some elements of the French Maquis would mobilise to join in the disruption of troop movements towards the Cotentin and help take the pressure off the beachheads. Work had already begun to facilitate this by contacting specific units, deciding on the best ways to disrupt the Germans in the area and arranging coded messages to indicate when the attack would take place.

Once the beachheads were established the Americans on the West Coast would push to take Cherbourg while the Americans and Canadians in the East would push South towards Bayeaux.

The British troops would secure the port town of Port Bail and other units would head for the strategically placed town of St Lo.

Using their experience in Italy, further landings were planned with the aim of cutting off the Brittany peninsula by driving a wedge from Nantes towards St Malo, trapping the German forces in that area and ultimately denying the Germans use of their U Boat bases on the French coast. Once that was achieved, the next phase would be to push East towards Paris.

That was the plan, Morgan thought, *but as someone once said, no plan survives first contact with the enemy.*

He knew he had to trust his commanders in all the various locations to not only deliver on their respective goals but also to support their neighbouring units if they should run into trouble or get bogged down in some way. While they might have specific targets, they also needed to be able to display flexibility and use their best judgment on the ground as to how to achieve those goals.

Every officer had to be prepared to change their plans on the hoof. On the day he could not be everywhere, in fact he would probably be on one of the supporting cruisers until the beachhead was established and he could move his HQ ashore. Morgan knew he would be as frustrated as hell, but Monty wouldn't let one of his key men get too close to the action too soon. If all went well he hoped that by the evening of the first day he could go ashore, but only time would tell.

Morgan looked again at the rudimentary plan, with some hand drawn lines on it and wondered if it was enough. Had they made the right decision to attack the Cotentin, or should they have double bluffed and hit the Pas de Calais or just focused on Normandy?

It was too late now; the die was cast and they had to go with the plan. The Russians were depending on the British and Americans, but Morgan wasn't happy. He felt like they were being rushed, it was only three months away now and he did not feel they were ready. They needed more landing craft, a lot more landing craft. American troops were arriving every day but would they all be here in time. They also needed to ensure they had command of the air by D-Day, as it had been designated.

Air Chief-Marshall Leigh-Mallory had been confident that air supremacy could be achieved by the due date, and he had explained that the RAF were also working on plans to step up a bombing campaign in Northern France. These would target railway lines, boat yards and known German military bases using low level fast attack aircraft. Air reconnaissance was being stepped up, when the weather allowed, so that the invasion forces had the best intelligence possible before they hit the ground.

He looked again at the plan and thought of General Hood and the Guernsey operation. He had seen the report from Brigadier Heaume and the ideas they were putting forward for their own invasion. That too was a hard call. The German defences were strong around their chosen landing beach and he had visions that the attack could result in a high level of civilian casualties to add to the inevitable military losses that would be incurred.

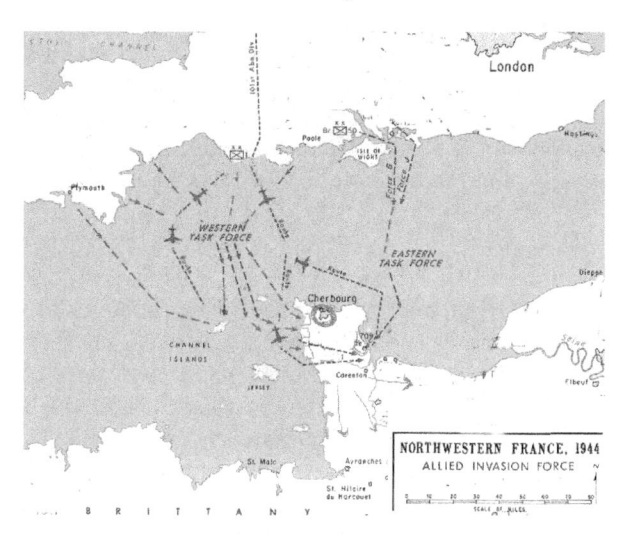

He decided he needed another meeting with Hood to see what his plans were for securing the Island with minimal losses.

On the plan he could see that Commando units would be delivered from Plymouth to the Island, while Hoods Division would form part of the Western task force, peeling off from the main body to hit the north of the Island. A parachute brigade was also assigned to land on the Island not long after the paratroop units were landing in France. What he wanted was a clear picture of how the attack on the beaches would be made.

Morgan knew he was going against his own rules about trusting his commanders, but Hood was new to his rank and to such a vital role. As such Morgan felt it was paramount that he should be confident that Hood was covering every angle and not missing something important. They needed the guns on that Island to be silenced and its harbour and airport to be in British hands. These could then be used to safeguard and support the main attacks in France.

His aides got Hood on the blower and rather than Hood coming up to London, Hood suggested General Morgan come down to Exeter to see what they had been working on. He looked at his diary and realised he had a demonstration of some tank variations by Major General Percy Hobart next week at Slapton Sands so suggested he meet Hood there and then they could drive to Exeter and see the latest plans for the Guernsey invasion. This was agreed.

In Exeter, Captain Best had secured the assistance of some model railway enthusiasts and together with Brigadier Heaume they had been working on a model of the L'Ancresse Headland in a large room at the rear of the hotel. Their brief was to have the model finished in time for Morgan's visit the following week and Ian rarely let people down.

*****

The following week Hood and Ian arrived in Slapton Sands to watch demonstrations of Hobart's funnies as people were calling them. Mainly based on the Churchill Tank chassis, but also able to be used on the Americans Sherman tanks, the vehicles being demonstrated were flail tanks, known as Crabs, which would agitate the beach with chains and take out anti-personnel mines, flame throwers, assault vehicles (AV), which mounted a mortar instead of the standard gun to destroy bunkers and concrete walls. The last variant was the Double Onion, a Churchill tank with two large demolition charges that could be placed against a wall or bunker to destroy it.

These last two were of particular interest, along with the crab, as Hood immediately saw the potential for using them to breach the anti-tank wall. Another piece of kit which was interesting was a centaur bulldozer which could be used to remove beach obstacles. As they knew the Germans had covered the beaches with hedgehog defences, the bulldozers would be useful to clear the beach before the tide came in so that vessels that came in later in the day would be safe.

They were not so impressed when the Duplex Drive tanks floated ashore. They could see little value in using those in the confines of the landing area they were working with and in any case Hood reckoned that in any sizeable waves they would be liable to flooding and sinking.

On the way back from Slapton to Exeter, Hood had the opportunity to explain to Morgan that they could use several of those funnies and it was agreed to allocate vehicles to the Guernsey Division once Hood advised Morgan's office of their total needs.

Once they got back to the White Hart Hotel, Hood took Morgan into his new ops room and then through to the back room where the scale model of the L'Ancresse common headland was located.

The large model was complete with bunkers, pill boxes, anti-tank wall, strongholds, houses, greenhouses, and the Vale Church. Morgan was impressed.

On the diorama were movable tapes indicating the proposed attack vectors, landing zones and initial beachhead boundaries. Morgan was so impressed he told Hood he would investigate if it would be possible to create models of the landing zones in France and Ian offered to send him details of the team he had used to create the models.

After an hour any doubt Morgan had in the capabilities of Hood and his team were thoroughly dismissed and he travelled back to London safe in the knowledge that the invasion of Guernsey was in good hands.

*****

Apart from the vital distraction of Hobart's funnies, Hood and his Guernsey team were working on the troop complements for the invasion. The 50th Division was now widely known as the Guernsey Division and included 12 Battalions from across the army, together with artillery companies, a medical corps and an anti-tank battalion. An anti-aircraft regiment had recently been added to the Division, just in case, as well as Royal Marine Commandos who would be landing on the west coast.

His own Beach HQ group brought the Division up to around 11,000 men. More individual regiments were being earmarked each week as there was a belief that at least 20,000 men were needed to achieve success.

A request by the Americans to add a regiment to the division had been denied as both he and Morgan wanted to keep this a British affair. However, they did allow a unit comprising two specialist platoons to join Hood's beach HQ group. Their task was primarily to report back to Eisenhower and if required provide some security for Hood himself if the beachhead came under pressure.

In anticipation an American Captain had been assigned to Hoods HQ team, in an observation role, and was now based in the White Hart Hotel. Hood had not warmed to him yet, but he had only been with him a few days. What they did appreciate was the seemingly infinite supply of chocolate he had brought with him which now accompanied every evening meal.

Captain Walter Larch was from Missouri, he was a long way from home and trying his best to adapt to life in England. A family man, he was missing Kansas City where he was born and raised but he was dedicated to helping Hood as much as he could.

His main mission was to learn as much as he could from the Limeys who had been fighting the Germans for over four years now. Any expertise that could be shared had the potential to save American lives in the months to come.

Larch was currently with Colonel Krimp who had intensified his training regime based on the revised drop zones that the Guernsey team had come up with. Krimps biggest concern was the sheer number of planes he needed in the air at the same time to get his men on the ground in the right places. The static line drop they would be making had a minimum height for the jump of 400 feet and he was making sure his troops were able to cope with operating at such a low level.

Krimp's plan was for the Dakotas to deliver his troops in groups of four. The planes would fly in pairs in close formation. The front pair at 400 feet with the rear pair 100 feet higher above the tailplanes of the front two. That meant each company would need two groups of four planes which altogether meant the aerial force required two waves of sixteen Dakotas to deliver his 600 men and all their equipment.

Krimp dreaded requesting so many aircraft, especially as he knew there would be pressure to have all available planes ready for the main attack but he couldn't use gliders in Guernsey so there was no other way to get his men on the ground.

He need not have worried, as Captain Larch explained, the allies had 800 Dakota aircraft available to them so his requirement for 32 was considered a drop in the ocean, so to speak. The other positive was that his drop was after the French drop so, if necessary, he could use Dakotas once they had returned from their first mission.

The other members of the Guernsey team would be embedded with the first troops that would go ashore.

It was decided the 231st Infantry Brigade would go ashore first, and Brigadier Heaume would go with the 2nd Battalion of the Devonshires. Colonel Vaudin would be with the 1st Battalion of the Dorsetshires and Colonel Mahy, along with Captain Best would be with the Hampshires.

All were training with their troops on a regular basis unless involved with the Guernsey team planning. The plan was that the Brigades would hit the beach in three different places.

The Hampshires would be in the middle of the beach with the Devonshires on their left and the Dorsetshires on the right. The latter brigades had been given the specific target of getting off the beach and taking the strongholds in front of them during the first phase of the operation. The Hampshires would support the Battalions on their flanks, as required, secure the beachhead and once the strongholds were subdued push on to meet up with the Paras and prepare the way for the push south towards St Peter Port.

That phase would happen as soon as the armoured support had come ashore, and the other brigades had landed in the second and third waves.

The Beach HQ would be established in the second wave of landings and provision would be made to hold prisoners on the beach.

Until General Hood was on the beach, command on the ground would be with the Senior Officer in the Hampshires. That was the charismatic Lieutenant Colonel Roy Phillips.

Never without his pipe, swagger stick and beret and with the weathered look of Montgomery, even down to the same moustache, Phillips was loved by his Battalion and was fearless under fire. Having Colonel Mahy with him did not bother him at all and they had become good friends, sharing the pressure of organising the big show as Phillips called it. He was never far from his men and often shared his meals with them. Roy was looking forward to getting at Jerry and would make sure the Hampshires were ready when the time came.

The Hampshires had already had one full Battalion training session using landing craft at the specially prepared training grounds in Inveraray and Castle Toward in Scotland. More training was planned but there were not enough landing craft available to hold a full practice with all of the 231[st.] Consequently, each Battalion took turns to practice getting in the Higgins Boats from the transports and storming the beaches.

All had agreed that they were looking forward to warmer weather because when they got their boots wet the water was freezing. Without exception all the men had got their boots wet.

Major exercises like these are never held without risk and the 231st had suffered several losses, mostly from drowning.

Phillips spent a lot of time in Scotland watching and supporting his men.

When the troops rushed ashore to take their positions, Phillips would walk amongst them encouraging them to keep their heads down or move up the beach. He knew getting off the beach as fast as they could was key to the success of the landings.

Roys swagger stick was always tucked under his arm. Even when they used live explosions he never flinched. If he saw one of his men was hesitating, he would be there to offer them encouragement and urge them to ignore the nerves and keep moving. The safest place he would say is off the beach, so the quicker we take the enemy positions and get on dry land, the better. The troops loved him for being there, loved his bravado and without hesitation, to a man they would follow him anywhere.

He was counting on that come the day of the big show.

*****

As the exercises increased and the time of the invasion got closer, a ten-mile strip of land along the South Coast was evacuated. Across the southern counties, troops were stationed in commandeered property and millions of tons of equipment and vehicles were stored, mostly under cover.

As the months rolled by, thousands and thousands of American troops, landed in England and by the time D-Day came, two million Americans would be based in the country. There was still a chronic lack of Landing craft. To counter this virtually every town and village in the country with a garage was involved in building parts for the vital landing craft.

It had become such an issue, that the date for the landings was put back to early June to get as many landing craft in service as possible to move the huge number of troops involved in the landings.

People were suffering, the pressures on the country's resources were enormous. Food and materials were becoming scarce as they were directed towards the millions of troops who needed to be fit, healthy and fully equipped for D-Day. The population had to endure several months of hardship before the troops left for France. It was hard for everyone.

While all this was going on General Hood had become firmly of the belief that the 50th needed specific island landing practice. After formulating a plan with the Guernsey team, Hood had a long conversation with General Morgan. Morgan asked him to submit a written proposal which he then placed before Churchill, Eisenhower, and Montgomery.

After due consideration the plan was approved, and Hood received a call from Morgan. He was given the go ahead to implement his detailed training plan.

ST MARY

One of the big moments for the 50th was their first dress rehearsal which took place in mid-March 1944. It was agreed that they would treat the exercise as if it were D-Day itself. In fact, many of the troops did believe they were going to France the build-up was so realistic. The target was St Marys in the Isles of Scilly.

The six square mile island had a small aerodrome where a flight of Hurricanes was based and in 1941 a series of pill boxes had been built around the island to defend it against potential invasion. It was considered by Hood to be an ideal practice ground. St Mary had a garrison of around one thousand troops on it already, so these were designated as the defenders for the purpose of the exercise.

A naval contingent was put in place, partly to escort and protect the troop carriers and different types of landing craft (LCAs, LCIs and LCTs) but also to provide realistic conditions by firing over the troops and creating the cacophony of sound that would accompany the landings.

In the first instance the troops would just focus on getting safely ashore but in the following weeks further exercises would involve live rounds and beach explosions to simulate a real landing. Most of the small population were evacuated to ensure, in live firing exercises, there would be minimum potential for civilian casualties.

The Great St Mary's Tea Party as it would become known was realistic and chaotic. The troops embarked on their troop ships from several south coast ports and from ports in the Bristol Channel. Each troop ship carried LCAs on its davits and had scrambling nets ready to hang down each side.

The troop ships were accompanied by a fleet of LCTs containing several early versions of Hobart's funnies. Some of the LCIs or Elsies as they were known contained large groups of up to 200 soldiers and were heavily armed compared to the LCAs. A few were equipped with heavy guns and were designated LCI(G) as they acted as gun boats. The Navy were heavily represented by some of the ships that had already been designated to the Guernsey invasion. This was to increase familiarity between the navy and the units they were there to protect.

They all departed for the first exercise in the late evening of the 15th March with the landing designated for dawn on the 16th.

This would be at low tide to expose the beach defences that had been planted on the designated beaches. St Mary's on its own did not have a sufficient stretch of beach to replicate the invasion so the three different attack battalions were designated different beaches while the paras were given targets on the island including the airport. The commandos were sent ashore just below the Woolpack Batteries which were their designated target.

The Devonshires and the Dorsetshires were designated to land on Town Beach and Porthcressa Beach respectively while the Hampshires were to practice on beaches on the south coast of Tresco. The troop ships were heavily laden with men for the night voyage but food and drink was still handed out. Many of the troops were struggling with sea sickness while most tried to rest.

Officers and NCOs toured the boats trying to keep the troops motivated, reminding them of their respective missions. Groups of soldiers played cards, told stories of old battles, or just closed their eyes, trying to shut out the hubbub around them. Others wrote letters home or cleaned their kit ready for action. Each man had their own way of relaxing.

The hours passed until 4 am when the first troops were directed towards their allocated LCA (Higgins Boat). It was pitch dark, so no-one could see what was happening, they just followed the man in front. When each LCA was full of their allocated thirty-six men and four crew, they were lowered into the sea. The LCA's then headed away from the troop ships at 7 knots. Several of the LCA's were designated for command and control and they marshalled the Higgins boats into their groups.

As the Higgins boats literally bobbed around getting into position conditions were deteriorating for the troops. They felt like sardines in a can as they were squeezed into each boat with all their kit. Some were sick from the rolling motion and of course they had no idea where they were or how close they were to the shore. Banter was all that kept them going as NCOs and Officers did their best to keep up morale and support the soldiers that were suffering. The jokers tried to lift their friend's spirits, and the medic in each boat did what they could to help the sick.

Fear of the unknown was also rife as they had no idea what to expect when they got ashore. A persistent rumour was that they were going into France and that this wasn't an exercise but every time it was mentioned it was just as quickly smacked down. Each man was under strict orders not to fire their weapons and guns were empty, so it was only the foolish who thought that they were heading south.

The truth was fear of the unknown had resulted in several of the men harbouring a nagging thought that real bullets were coming their way when that ramp went down. They were not that far from the truth.

General Hood and his team had prepared a surprise for the 50th. They had arranged for some local thespians involved in amateur dramatics to be dressed as British troops and to play wounded or dead soldiers on the beach.

The 'bodies' were spread all over the landing beaches, short of a double row of barbed wire that was spread across each landing zone. Hood also had arranged for fixed position machine guns to spray the beach between the barbed wire and the defensive positions. The final touch was explosive charges positioned on the beach and controlled remotely by observers. Each charge was flagged to ensure the observers didn't accidentally blow up their own troops.

The first indication the troops had that the exercise was going to start was when the Dakotas full of Colonel Krimp's paras flew low over the assembled fleet on their way to their drop zones. At that moment, the engines of the Higgins boats were pushed to full throttle and their diesel engines added more smell and noise to the already heady mix of fear and excitement. The Bowman Gunner on the Spears platoon Higgins Boat looked down to the troops from his position and shouted, 'Here we go boys!'.

As instructed, he opened fire with his Lewis Gun aiming onto the sea in front to the landing craft to add to the atmosphere. As the beaches were quite small compared with the Guernsey beach, the LCAs were steered to very specific landing points, while the LCIs and LCTs led the fleet in. Their guns were added to the cacophony which went up another ten notches as the Naval broadsides kicked in.

They were targeting the open sea the other side of the Islands but the sound of the guns and the noise as the air above the fleet was ripped apart by the passing shells was enough to increase the heart rate of even the toughest of the men hidden in their landing craft.

The steernsheetman at the back of the boat had another trick up his sleeve. He had a bundle of grenades and as they went in would lob them into the sea to give the impression that they were being shelled. The troops started to get wet from the fountains of spray. Those that had been feeling seasick were not feeling seasick anymore.

After ten minutes at full tilt, the engine note changed and First Lieutenant Derek Barber, turned to his men, shouting to be heard over the noise.

'Come on you Spears, last one to the top of the beach buys the first round.' His men cheered and steadied themselves as they felt the front of the landing craft hit Porthcreesa beach. With that the Spearhead platoon, known to the men as the spears, hit the beach first. The Bowman Gunner let down the ramp and the troops stormed ashore in three sections, the first led by Barber and the others led by a Sergeant and a Corporal.

The first section stormed straight ahead while the other two fanned out to the left and right. They were shocked to see bodies on the beach and the medic in the third section stopped to attend to the wounded.

The first person he reached had an arm missing and the medic panicked, he looked back but the LCA was already backing away from the beach.

'What do I do?' he shouted but his Corporal was already heading up the beach and out of ear shot.

The injured 'soldier' looked at the medic and winked.

'Nothing you can do for me son; I'm going to bleed out.'

The Medic looked at the man and realised what was happening.

'Cheers mate,' he said as he started forward again, checking the bodies as he went. The spears were dodging explosions as they ran and some of the new members of the platoon fell under the pressure and noise, cowering on the beach. By now Barber and his section were at the barbed wire.

Machine gun fire was kicking up the sand ahead of them as he called for wire cutters and a couple of the specialists in his platoon went to work.

He watched as other platoons rushed up the beach and the tanks stormed ashore crashing into the barbed wire while Hobart's funnies flailed the beach in places, practising their role on the big day. More than one practice explosive was churned up and exploded as the flails did their job. Some troops were following the tanks through, and he quickly realised they would not be first to the top.

He looked back as a second wave of LTAs headed towards the beach and spotted that some of his men were lying in the sand further down the beach.

'Sergeant,' he called out, and Sergeant Mick Wiley crawled across towards him. 'As soon as this wire is cut take the men to the top of the beach and take out that pillbox before the bloody paras arrive. I don't want us to be last off this beach.'

Yes, Sir,' he replied. 'Where are you going?'

'We have a few slackers Mick, I am going to kick some arses.'

The wire was cut at that moment and Sergeant Wiley led the boys through and they rushed up towards the Pill Box. While this was happening Barber ran down the beach and started prodding the half dozen men who were lying on the beach with his rifle.

'Get your sorry arses to the top of the beach. The next wave have orders to shoot anyone slacking so get moving.'

That was enough to get the greenhorns back up on their feet and soon they too were through the barbed wire.

One of the boys in A Section lobbed a dummy demolition charge through the gun slit and their part of the exercise was over.

They walked past the pill box and gathered in a designated marshalling area behind the beach and then marched away towards the airport while the next waves repeated the exercise.

General Hood had been watching from one of the pill boxes and once the guns fell silent, he got in a jeep and headed towards the airport.

Colonel Krimp had almost beaten the troops to the top of the beach with A Company while the other three companies set up defensive positions around the airport. He had been pleased with the drop but there were still too many men landing outside the target zone for his liking, something he needed to discuss with the General at their next meeting.

Observers checked off each platoon on their lists as they entered the airport perimeter, and each was given a spot on which to rest. NAAFI units went around supplying tea and basic rations for all the troops, some of whom had not had anything to eat since the previous evening. Someone suggested it was just a big tea party and the name stuck.

In the centre of the airfield a podium had been erected and at around lunch time, after everyone was ashore and in position, General Hood mounted the wooden steps and called the troops to come forward and gather round. At that moment the sun broke through the clouds and the whole scene was bathed in sunshine.

'Men, if you haven't seen or met me before my name is Major General Hood and I have the privilege of being your commanding officer. Or should I say I am the commanding officer of the finest division in the whole of the British Army.' The men cheered in response.

'I have been observing your landings here today and by and large the whole exercise went quite smoothly but I did notice that some men didn't push off the beach as they should. It might be a nice beach but there isn't time for sunbathing.'

That got a laugh from some sections but there were also several embarrassed faces out there who knew they would be ribbed by their mates for weeks to come.

'You will not be letting your compatriots down again!' Hood said sternly.

'We will be doing this again several times until we all know what we are doing instinctively. There can be no mistakes on the big day. I want you all to think about today and feed back to your officers and NCOs any ideas you might have to improve how we undertake the landings. Mistakes cost lives and we don't want to bring our own mistakes to the beaches.'

He paused as if searching for the right words.

'The Fiftieth is a family, the people around you are your brothers. Look after each other and we will get through this. One day soon you will be able to stand with pride and tell your friends and family back home. I was there. I fought with the fighting fiftieth. I broke Hitlers Atlantic Wall and I helped win this war!'

The assembled troops went mad, applauding and cheering the General. He waited for a moment and then quietened the crowd.

'Now we need to get you back to your bases. Beach Marshalls will direct you back to the beaches and back on board your transports. Over the next few weeks, individual units will train for their specialist missions and then we will come back here and do this again. Keep safe men, I need each and every one of you fit and well for this mission. Officers, look after your men.'

He was just about to step down when someone shouted. 'Three cheers for General Hood. Hip Hip, Hooray! Hip Hip, Hooray! Hip Hip, Hooray!' All the troops cheered enthusiastically, and many applauded him.

From his vantage point he looked above the sea of heads. The six hurricanes based in St Mary's stood in a line, rows of tanks and funnies were formed up at the edge of the airfield and in the distance dozens of ships, troop carriers and landing craft seemed to stretch as far as the horizon.

He smiled to himself and waved to his troops. *This is our time*, he thought proudly as he stepped down from the podium. His senior officers were waiting for him, and they took turns to shake his hand. He made his way towards a waiting jeep and the troops applauded him all the way, some summoning the nerve to slap him gently on the back as he passed through the crowd.

When he was sitting down in the jeep, he became quite emotional at the adulation and the knowledge that not all these fine men would be coming home after the invasion. He shook that negativity from his head and then headed towards the harbour to travel over to Tresco to meet Roy Phillips who was with the Hampshires and their support troops.

He would repeat the same speech to his men all over again.

Later in the day as the troops continued to be embarked General Hood took the chance to speak to Colonel Krimp to see how he thought the paras had performed in their part of the operation. He soon discovered Krimp was not a happy man.

The paras had dropped into the open land to the west and south of St Mary's Church. Once safely on the ground Krimp had joined A Company and had led them across the open land towards Porthcressa Beach. They had been faced with several pill boxes and had dealt with them quite well. But the big problem was that he had been forced to leave several of his men behind as they were judged to have dropped outside the drop zones and as such were voided from the exercise.

He himself had barely made it into his drop zone and this was in daylight, pretty good weather with light winds and no enemy fire.

They had practiced and practiced getting out of the Dakotas as quickly as possible, but he just couldn't achieve the drop rate he wanted using the standard static line method. He had pushed his troops to the point where they had experienced a few injuries with parachutes getting too close to each other and getting entangled. They were lucky no-one had died but he had lost a few troops with serious injuries.

He asked if General Hood could talk to the RAF to see if they had any suggestions on how they could solve this issue and Hood agreed to take it up with the RAF top brass.

This would prove futile, there was no other option, the Dakota was the best plane for the job and Krimp would have to accept a certain level of losses from people missing the drop zone.

The 50th would go back to St Mary's and Tresco three more times before D-Day.

SLAPTON SANDS

Colonel Krimp pushed his men hard. He considered them elite troops and they themselves considered that they were one of the elite units in the British Army.

As a result, they had an arrogance about them that was obvious to everyone who ever met a man from the paratroop regiments.

That arrogance was justified. Paratroopers worked harder and the risks they faced every day were higher than almost any other unit in the army. They wore a different uniform, with camouflage jackets, the precious parachute badge on their caps and wings on their right shoulder. The patch they proudly wore was a silver Pegasus being ridden by the Greek hero Bellerophon on a maroon background.

When they weren't jumping, they were training, the men would run or hike for miles, carrying heavy packs. They were trained in unarmed combat and could all use different types of equipment. Each man carried a sten gun or a Lee Enfield rifle and a handgun. Most had Webley revolvers though some, Krimp included, preferred the American Colt M1911. They were all trained to use the Bren gun, as well as mortars, PIATs and the Vickers machine gun. They were also no strangers to dynamite and regularly practiced demolishing anything from buildings to railway tracks.

The only units that could claim to be better trained were the Commandos or special forces units, but even they could not claim to be as versatile as a paratrooper.

In the build up to the big day the Paras were the only troops who didn't get their boots wet. Krimps men trained all over the country, often with other Airborne units who would be taking part in the French invasion. There was an expectation that once Guernsey was in British hands, the Guernsey invasion troops would move on to France and support the big push out of the Cotentin.

Plans were already in place to collect the Paras from Guernsey airport just two days after the landings and drop them into France.

The 50th would also leave for France within the week and be replaced by units trained to support the local population with their recovery from occupation and deal with the German prisoners of war.

In April, the 50th was working on a major exercise to be held on Slapton Sands. The Americans were running full scale landing exercises over a four-day period and the 50th were taking a slot on one of their flanks. The top brass felt it was vital that the 50th knew how to work with other units just in case the Guernsey invasion was postponed or delayed for some reason.

The 50th loaded up on the transport ships and large Landing Craft as they had during their exercises in the Isles of Scilly. Less men were becoming seasick than before as they got used to the motion and the whole experience. This was another live firing exercise, and the pride of the unit was at stake as well as the pride of Britain. They did not want to lose face with their Yankee friends. Rivalry was good.

On the first day of the Exercise, codenamed Tiger, the Americans had taken some friendly fire casualties so on the second day extra care was being taken to avoid that happening again. What no-one anticipated was the German Kriegsmarine joining the exercise.

A flotilla of German Torpedo Boats managed to avoid a Navy cordon around their base in France and found themselves amongst the convoy of transports and LCTs on their way to the marshalling point. The first the 50th knew about the incident was when they heard gunfire and saw a couple of the LCTs explode and start to sink. Two were lost while others suffered from friendly fire incidents in the confusion.

Despite the setback the exercise continued as planned and not much was said about the losses but the scuttlebutt amongst the troops was that the Americans sustained heavy losses that night. By the end of the exercise the whole episode seemed to have been conveniently forgotten.

The 50th performed well throughout Tiger and proved that the British units could work side by side with the Americans. However, some communication issues had been identified between the British navy and the American ships and efforts were made to ensure that would not happen again.

By the end of Operation Tiger, General Hood was pleased with his troops performance, but his main concern was getting all his troops and their equipment ashore in the confined space of L'Ancresse Bay. In the latest reconnaissance photos that had been taken at low tide, he had spotted a rocky outcrop in the centre of the bay. As they were going in at low tide he was concerned that at least some of the beach would be unsuitable for the landing craft.

Technically L'Ancresse was two bays, Pembroke and L'Ancresse but for the purpose of the invasion they were combined under the one name. Measured together the bay was just over half a mile long.

Hood decided they would return to the Scilly Isles for one last exercise involving the whole of the 50th and this time they would all land on the East coast of Tresco. He wanted all the vessels involved in the invasion to land their troops, as should happen in Guernsey, with the Hampshires in the middle and the Devonshires and Doresetshires flanking them.

Hood decided not to set up defences for this exercise, he just wanted to see that he could get all his men and machines on to a beach of a similar size. This involved meticulous planning by the marshalling teams to arrange how all the boats would be lined up to enter and exit the bay. Timing and organisation were critical for the success of the landings.

The General and his Guernsey team spent hours poring over the model Ian and his team had made. The more they worked on the plan the more they worried about the potential for the L'Ancresse to become a killing ground for his troops. The higher ground all around the bay gave the defender's uninterrupted views of the beaches.

Unless the navy or air strikes could destroy some of those guns, the invasion could falter as soon as the landing craft entered the horseshoe shaped bay. With that in mind they re-jigged the plan to incorporate commando landings either side of the bay to try and take out any defences that the navy and RAF failed to destroy.

This was easier on the East side of the bay as there was a beach of sorts but on the West the commandos would be landing on the rocks, and it was felt local knowledge was needed. Once again, the word went out to search for any Guernsey soldiers in the commando units who could lead a platoon on to those rocks.

Ian worked his magic and it did not take long before two names were put forward to join the Guernsey Division's commando units.

Sergeant Tony Rihoy was the most experienced man they had available. Vitally he had experience of fishing in that part of the bay so he was assigned to the Western assault force. Corporal Frank De La Mare lived in the north of the Island before the war and had often walked around the headlands around L'Ancresse bay hunting rabbits. He was assigned to the platoon designated to assault the East coast of the bay.

The platoon leaders and NCOs of both the platoons were summoned to view the model in the White Hart Hotel. With the help of the two Guernsey specialists the commandos developed strategies and proposed landing points for their assaults.

It was hoped they would not be needed but they planned on the assumption the artillery assault and aerial attacks failed. They realised they faced a stiff task. The commandos would need to land slightly in advance of the main attack as soon as the barrage was over.

The platoons were designated the code names Pembroke and Marchant. The Pembroke team would be landing on the rocks just next to the small beach called Jaonneuse Bay immediately to the West of the main landings while the Marchant platoon would be landing on the pebble beach behind Fort Le Marchant.

Both units would make the assault in small rubber boats and their platoon leaders had the flexibility to vary the plan if they saw a better opportunity to make a more successful assault during the mission. General Hood had emphasized to the commandos that if at all possible, they should not split their forces or go too far off plan as it was vital the main units landing on the beach knew where they were operating to avoid friendly fire incidents.

The RAF officer in charge of the air assault and the Chief Naval Officer in charge of supporting the Guernsey invasion also spent time in the White Hart Hotel analysing Ian's model. Together with General Hood and the Guernsey team they planned which targets to assault.

Overshooting the designated targets was the main worry as that could lead to civilian casualties or in some cases blue on blue situations involving the paratroopers or commandos.

Timing of course was everything and a minute-by-minute plan for the assault was developed. Captain Best had created a top-secret plan for the invasion which was given the top level of security under the codeword BIGOT, which was only for senior personnel on the BIGOT list with specific responsibilities and roles on the day. The troops still had no idea what their specific targets were and when the invasion was going to take place. They would be told their roles in the invasion in the last few hours before the attack.

The final practice took place on Tresco on the 15th May and General Hood was pleased with how their combined units performed in terms of the organisation of the flotilla and how quickly the troops were put ashore. The different types of landing craft worked well together and were able to offload their loads and clear the beach ready for the subsequent waves quickly.

Tresco was soon filled with troops, tanks and dozens of other pieces of kit. The final units of the full 50th Division finally came ashore and the invasion of Tresco was complete. One innovation they had agreed on was a modified assault landing craft which would be positioned in the centre of the bay just short of the rocky outcrop. It would provide fire support for the landing forces and ensure that the waves of LCAs and other vessels had to flow around it, avoiding the rocks.

It was designated LCSC which stood for landing craft support and control and would also be the base for the Senior Naval Officer controlling the movement of the LCAs and LCIs at the beachhead.

After the completion of the exercise, he walked among the men as they enjoyed rations and tea in the afternoon sun supplied again by the NAAFI. Morale was excellent amongst the troops and Hood shook many hands that day.

Everywhere he went he applauded their success during the exercise and expressed his confidence in their ability to be able to achieve the goals on the big day.

That was the last time they would all be together before D-Day.

*****

There were still three weeks to go before the 'Big Show' and it was vital to keep the troops motivated and sharp. General Hood and his team had planned training exercises and fitness regimes for all the units to ensure boredom or frustration didn't set in. The last thing they wanted was to destroy the comradeship and morale they had built up.

Hood wished the date was earlier, they were ready and at their peak.

His job now was to keep them there without wearing them out.

The 50th suffered their first fatalities just after the success on Tresco. It always seems that the moment you reach a high, fate has a habit of kicking you in the guts. For Hood and the 50th it involved a problem with one of the LCAs, which started to take on water on the way back to the LCIs. The Higgins boat rapidly took on water and quickly began to sink. Water gushed through the doors and before any other vessels could get to the sinking boat they were gone. The four naval crew, unencumbered by heavy kit and wearing life jackets, were saved but 36 men from the Durham Light Infantry who formed part of the 50th were lost.

As if that wasn't enough news came back from Colonel Krimp that he had lost one of his men, His parachute had failed to open while on exercise and he had plummeted to his death.

When Hood reflected on the day back in the White Hart Hotel, he strove hard to focus on the positives. Sitting with Ian in his Ops room staring across at the maps on the wall and the charts on the table, he could only think of how horribly and pointlessly those men had died. 'What a waste.'

He sipped a whiskey as they both sat staring into space. The mood was so sombre, Ian struggled to find a reply.

'I know Sir but think of how well the exercise went. We now have a working plan for the beaches.'

Hood downed his whiskey and sat tapping absentmindedly on the arm of his chair. 'Tomorrow I'll go and visit the Durham boys; this must have hit them hard.'

'Good idea Sir. I will arrange a driver for the morning. If you don't mind Sir, I'll get to bed. It has been a long day.'

'Before you go Ian, what do you think our chances are of pulling this off?'

Ian was already halfway to the door when the General asked the question. He paused and turned around to look at the man he now thought of as a friend.

'Never doubt yourself General, you have a great team around you, the finest men under you and the best plan we can possibly come up with. We will do this and then go on to help rid Europe of the Nazi oppressors. You have done and are doing a great job.'

'Thanks Ian,' the General replied quietly.

'Can I make a suggestion?'

'Go ahead Ian, you know you can say what you like here.'

'Get some sleep Sir, and that's an order.'

'Aye aye, Sir,' the General replied with half a smile, and thanks Ian, you are a rock.'

Ian saluted and left the General on his own. Hood looked around the room, he was far from sleepy. *One more*, he thought and gave himself a small measure and sat back down in his chair. He went through the days exercise in his mind and then made his way into their Ops room and looked at the model again.

Half closing his eyes he tried to visualise what he had seen today re-enacted in the confines of L'Ancresse Bay. All he could see where the German positions and the killing zone that they created. *If we don't snuff out those guns……..*, he left the thought unanswered in his mind.

Sod it, time for a distraction, he thought and went off to bed. He was reading 'For Whom the Bell Tolls' by Ernest Hemingway. Probably not the best distraction given the plot but at least it took his mind off Guernsey for a while.

He eventually fell asleep with the book still in his hands.

*****

GeneralMajor Von Graf was standing next to one of the docks in St Peter Port Harbour. A large crane had been installed early in the occupation and as always, the quays were a hive of activity. Supplies were being unloaded from a small steamer that had recently docked and Kriegsmarine sailors were everywhere as a small flotilla of Motor Torpedo Boats had just arrived in the Harbour.

Troops patrolled the Harbour perimeter and the anti-aircraft guns on Castle Cornet scoured the skies looking out for the growing number of RAF aircraft which regularly invaded the skies over the Islands.

A large anti-aircraft gun emplacement had been installed at the entrance to the harbour and as ever the men there were watching the sky for enemy aircraft. That position also provided extra support for the defence of the port.

A large freighter had just docked. The day before the Kommandant had received a message asking him to be at the Harbour when it arrived. The message had ended with the enigmatic line. I am sending you a gift and was signed Rommel.

Curious to see what this gift might be the Kommandant waited eagerly to see what the freighter had brought.

The large crane was brought into use and lowered its hook into the bowels of the ship. Then to his amazement a large German Panzer Tank was lifted out and placed carefully on the quay.

German soldiers started to disembark and as each tank was lifted on to the key, their crews would climb on board and drive them out of the way of the next tank to be unloaded. In all twelve Panzer IVs (2 platoons) of the 21st Panzer Division had been sent to Guernsey to report to Von Graf. He was stunned.

Up until now the Guernsey garrison had only been able to count on the support of a few second hand French light tanks These panzers were a vast improvement on those and would be a huge addition to his defences.

Half an hour after the first tank appeared the twelve panzer tanks were all lined up with their panzergrenadier crews, in their smart black uniforms, standing to attention in front of each vehicle. The Commander of each Panzer stood to attention in the turret.

A young Hauptmann marched over to Von Graf and offered a smart salute.

'Welcome to Guernsey,' Herr Hauptmann, Von Graf replied returning the salute.

'Herr Kommandant, compliments of Generalfeldmarschall Rommel. He has asked me to offer you our services in the defence of your island. May I ask your permission to unload our support vehicles and ask you to assign us quarters.'

He reached into his jacket pocket and pulled out an envelope which he handed to Von Graf.

'A letter from the Generalfeldmarschall for you sir.'

'Thank you, Herr Hauptmann, and your name is?'

'Michael Wagner, Herr Kommandant.'

'Hauptmann Wagner, please unload your support vehicles. We have a facility at a place called Baubigny Arsenal which you can use. I will arrange for someone to direct you. Once you are settled, please join me at my Headquarters this evening, just over there, and I'll bring you up to speed as regards our defences and troop deployments.' He pointed to the Royal Hotel as he was talking. 'I look forward to seeing you later.'

'Herr Kommandant before you go would you care to inspect your Panzer IVs? These are the latest Sonderkraftfahrzeug 161/2's with 75mm guns.'

'Very well Hauptmann, lead the way.'

Wagner led Von Graf along the line of tanks, proudly introducing each Tank Commander as they walked down the row.

The Kommandant was very impressed by the row of superbly presented tanks and when he came to the last one, he clambered up to see what it looked like inside. The commander explained about the side panels and how they had been treated with an anti-magnetic finish to stop magnetic mines being stuck to the tank.

Von Graf was shown how they could all keep in touch with each other by radio and the different types of shells they could use with their powerful 75mm cannon.

The Kommandant asked what experience they had as a unit and the tank commander explained that while they had been together for almost a year they had yet to be blooded in battle. It transpired that the remnants of the old 21st had surrendered after the Battle of Kasserine Pass in Tunisia so the new units were looking to reinstate their damaged reputation in the battles to come.

By the time Von Graf was back on the ground, more vehicles had been offloaded on to the quay. There were halftracks and trucks full of spare parts and other types of equipment. All were designed to keep the Panzers running and support the crew and their mechanics.

Von Graf spoke to one of his aides and soon a motorcycle pulled up ready to lead the convoy of tanks to Baubigny Arsenal.

While the tanks moved away, Von Graf walked back down the jetty to his HQ in the Royal Hotel. He went up to his office where he took out the letter from Rommel. The envelope was marked with the German Eagle above the Swastika and the words Streng Geheim (Top Secret) had been stamped below the emblem.

The envelope contained a single sheet of paper, topped by the same eagle emblem, and had been handwritten by Generalfeldmarschall Rommel himself.

CONFIDENTIAL

18th May 1944

Dear Von Graf

It was a pleasure to meet you a few months ago. I was impressed by your preparations for my visit and trust that your readiness is just as good now as it was then.

We have intelligence that indicates an invasion is imminent. A flotilla of Motor Torpedo boats attacked a convoy of troop carriers a few weeks ago and I believe they were rehearsing for beach landings. Hitler remains convinced the landing will happen in the Pas de Calais region, but I am not of the same mind. I think they will attack the Cotentin and may well look to target Guernsey at the same time. It is what I would do.

My gift is to help bolster your defences. If I could spare more troops I would send them to you but my reserves are being sent towards the Pas De Calais and I am struggling to keep all the troops I think I will need in the Normandy and Cotentin area.

Be prepared. I don't think we will have to wait much longer before they strike.

I trust you will fight with honour, and your men will battle like tigers to retain Guernsey for the Reich.

Keep strong.

Yours

Rommel

Von Graf sat back in his chair, throwing the letter on the desk in front of him.

Guess the good times will be over soon, he thought to himself. He reached for an ornate lighter that he always had on his desk. He picked the letter back up and set fire to the corner, letting it burn in his hand until he was forced to drop it into a bin next to his desk. He made sure the fire was out before he called for his aide.

'Klaus, bring me some lunch, beef sandwiches today and a glass of beer.'

Klaus looked a bit puzzled as had never known the Kommandant to drink during the day but he duly obeyed and five minutes later Von Graf was tucking into beef sandwiches with a glass of beer next to him.

The letter had taken two days to get to Guernsey, so Von Graf knew he needed to move fast. Once he had finished his lunch he called for his driver and drove down to L'Ancresse to assess the defences himself.

They followed a track up to the top of La Varde and there he was welcomed by the Luftwaffe officer in charge of Battery Dolmen. He took him up to highest bunker in the complex which gave him a panoramic view of the whole of the bay.

In the middle of the bay a new bunker was being built, as suggested by Rommel, but it wasn't ready yet. He resolved to send a message to the head of Operation Todt to increase their efforts to finish the bunker as soon as possible.

The hill bristled with anti-aircraft guns and machine gun nests. The anti-aircraft batteries could also be used to fire into the bay if needed. The machine gun nests protected the hill from all directions and a network of Tobruk trenches gave protection to the troops defending the hill.

On both sides of L'Ancresse Bay, casemates were incorporated into the wall and above each emplacement, there were fixed machine gun positions.

On the West side of the bay a small Napoleonic fort had been converted into a fortified position with a large artillery piece. The East side of the bay was protected by Stutzpunkt Marschen at Fort Le Marchant which had been upgraded to hold mortars and searchlights as well as its main guns and machine guns.

Von Graf made a note to issue a standing order that the searchlights of Stutzpunkt Marschen should comb the bay all night, every night, to make sure they weren't surprised by a night attack.

He viewed the common land around the hill and decided on a third order. One report he had recently read was how to install defences to protect open areas from parachute landings. The systems he had seen involved a network of poles and wires attached to explosives designed to explode when parachutists landed on them. The area of gorse and open land between La Varde and the Vale Church would be perfect for these new defences.

Von Graf made a mental note to add that idea into his orders for Operation Todt.

On the high ground the other side of the common he could see the defensive position called Widerstandsnest Dohlenfels (The Doyle/Bunker Hill resistance nest.). He imagined what the battlefield could look like if the troops somehow managed to breach his anti-tank wall. To counter that possibility he decided to reinforce the defences on Bunker Hill to provide more fire into the lower ground between the two hills. Machine guns and mortars were already there but he made a note to establish more.

He then looked back towards the Vale Church and thought if by some miracle the British survived his killing ground how could he stop them moving out of the L'Ancresse area. He thought of his new Panzers and where they were to be stationed. He could see the Baubigny Arsenal from where he stood. It was about a mile beyond the Vale Church.

He had deliberately picked Baubigny for its proximity to L'Ancresse and decided to propose to the young Hauptmann he was meeting that evening that his tanks be brought up to the Vale Church as soon as the attack came to prevent any British troops or tanks getting off L'Ancresse Common. Once the attack was halted, they would lead the push to drive the invaders back into the sea.

Pleased with his plan, he left the hill and went to visit the sea wall and see if he could urge the men working on the new bunker to increase their efforts. Once there he walked along the top of the wall, noting the Loophole towers that were dotted around the headland.

They had not changed since Napoleonic times and were looking quite derelict. The Kommandant decided they would make good defensive positions and added another order to his list to see if his engineers could create machine gun slits in each tower. He also wanted to see machine gun positions on top of the wall and instructed the troops there to build positions using sandbags, each to be armed with MG42s.

He looked out across the bay and noted the beach defences. They seemed more than adequate to him, and he felt no action was needed there.

Next, he drove up to the Doyle resistance nest and surveyed the defences. He met Major Balzer there who happened to be carrying out his own inspection of the resistance nest. Balzar was in overall charge of the L'Ancresse defences.

Together they walked around the hill and they agreed to dig more Tobruk trenches around the headland, starting with the beach and L'Ancresse common sides. They also agreed to add strength to the barbed wire defences that were already in place.

Von Graf also told Balzer to build another six machine gun positions and that he would send him extra MGs over the next couple of days. Satisfied with the work they had scheduled for the Doyle resistance nest; he drove with Major Balzer down to Fort Le Marchant to inspect the positions there.

At the end of the inspection tour Major Balzer invited him back to his office in a commandeered Guernsey granite-built farmhouse just below the defence point. Von Graf accepted and once the car had pulled up outside, they walked up the path into the farmhouse through a rose covered arch over the door.

It was a typical Guernsey farmhouse and the Major had done a good job of converting it into his HQ. His quarters and those of his aides were upstairs and downstairs he had turned the lounge into his Ops room while the kitchen still provided catering for him and his staff. In the Ops room they pored over maps of the common area, firming up where the extra defences would go.

They drank coffee while they talked and a plate of sandwiches appeared.

Von Graf realised he hadn't eaten for some time and was very hungry. He asked if some food could be taken out to his driver and the kitchen staff happily obliged.

A picture of Hitler hung above the fireplace, and he looked at the familiar face for a moment, Major Balzer noticed the Kommandants distraction and stopped eating.

'Do you think he is confident we can win this war?' Von Graf asked Balzer.

'No doubt at all Herr Kommandant, he shall lead us to victory.'

'Given the choice who would you follow, Rommel or Hitler?' He knew the question was unfair and wondered why he had even asked it, but he was curious to see what the response might be.

The young Major cleared his throat while he weighed up what to say.

'On the battlefield Rommel has no equal but in leading a country, Hitler is the man to follow.'

Von Graf smiled. 'Good answer Herr Major. Rommel thinks the attack will come here while Hitler believes it will be in the Pas de Calais region. Who should we believe?'

Balzer paused for a moment. 'I would believe whoever is right. We must be ready for whatever eventuality for as sure as night follows day the fight will come to us one day.'

Von Graf laughed, something Balzer had never seen. 'Well, right now I believe the attack is coming soon and it is coming here. We must be ready. I will get you those guns tomorrow and you will receive detailed orders for the defences. Right now, I need you to believe in me and be ready. Expect an attack any day now, there will be no down time, no rest. Are you with me?'

'Yes Herr GeneralMajor, you can count on me.'

'Good. Now if you'll excuse me I have a lot to do.' They saluted and Von Graf went back out to his car. Before getting in he stood looking up at the resistance point on the Doyle and smiled. *We are ready,* he thought.

Satisfied he drove back to his HQ to write up his orders.

Hauptmann Michael Wagner arrived at the Royal Hotel at 7.30pm. After an exchange of salutes, GeneralMajor Von Graf invited Wagner to sit down. Wagner reported to the Kommandant that he had set up a service and repair station in the Arsenal and that all his troops were now barracked in the surrounding area. He was keen to carry out exercises as soon as possible.

Von Graf took stock of the young man before him. He could not have been more than 21 years old and the stubble that was starting to grow at the end of a long day was blond and wispy.

'Relax Herr Hauptmann,' he said smiling. 'I do not bite, unless I am upset,' he added with a wink.

He unrolled a map of the German defences which was on his desk and weighed down the corners with a paperweight, his lighter and a couple of glasses and went through the various strong points and bunkers around the island, finishing with the cluster of defences at L'Ancresse.

'This is where the British will land; if they come. I have carried out another inspection today and have some plans to increase the defences around this bay and I want your tank platoons ready to play their part.'

He took his pen out of the ornate pen stand at the front of his desk and put a circle around Baubigny Arsenal. 'This is where you are based and as you can see there isn't much in the way of buildings between you and the Vale Church here.' He put a cross over the area where the church was sited.

'I want you to be able to move your Panzers from here to here as quickly as possible in the event of an attack. I am confident we can pin the attackers down on the beach or on this Common land but under no circumstances should we let them break out towards the rest of the Island.'

The Hauptmann nodded his head to show he understood and agreed with the summary of the situation from the Kommandant.

'I want you to inspect this area and decide the best places to position your tanks to stop any enemy advance here.'

With that Von Graf drew a line between the Vale Church and the small crossroads at the end of the Military Road. If you need to make any changes to the environment here, like demolish houses or Greenhouses, let me know and we will do what we can to accommodate your needs. Is that understood?'

'Yes Herr GeneralMajor.'

'And Wagner, keep your tanks hidden, no exercises for now, do your scouting in one of your other vehicles. There are planes in the skies above us almost every day and I don't want the British to know we have your Panzers on the island. It will come as a nasty surprise,' he added with a smile.

'Yes Herr GeneralMajor, there are some Greenhouses opposite the Arsenal which I can hide the tanks in. We can simply smash our way out of those when we get the call.'

'Excellent idea.' He sat back in his chair. 'Any questions?'

'No Herr GeneralMajor.'

'Good, would you like to join me downstairs for a drink in the bar?'

The young man thought for a couple of seconds. 'Forgive me Herr GeneralMajor but if you don't mind, I would like to get back to my men and make sure the Panzers are well hidden before dawn tomorrow.'

'Understood Herr Hauptmann, no offence taken. Maybe another day. You're dismissed.'

'Thank you, Herr GeneralMajor. I look forward to it.' He stood and saluted before turning to exit the Kommandants office.

'*So green,*' he thought to himself, *but I admire his keenness. I wonder if he will still be so enthusiastic when the shells begin to fall.*

With that he made his way down to the bar which had become an Officer's mess and joined some of his senior officers for a schnapps, or two, before retiring to bed.

THE QUIET TIME

For the troops of the 50th and the many other allied divisions holding in England, the last few weeks before D-Day seemed to drag by. The veterans of Africa and Italy were grateful to not be on the front line while some of the new troops could not wait for action.

Friction began to build amongst the men despite the best efforts of Officers and NCOs to keep them busy. In areas where the Americans and British were closely stationed rivalries were rife whether it be over a girl or a pint on rare leave days. At the beginning of June all leave was cancelled and preparations were stepped up, as was training. Troops were also uprooted from their temporary barracks and moved closer to their launch points.

Reconnaissance flights were stepped up. Naval and Air patrols were increased in frequency to stop the chances of a German plane spotting the build-up. Attacks on targets on mainland France also increased.

The RAF now had unprecedented air supremacy and they hammered home the advantage at almost every opportunity. One of the main targets for the air attacks were German radar stations along the French coast from the Pas de Calais to Guernsey. One of the targets for Leigh Mallory's forces were the Freya Radar masts at Fort George.

On the 2nd June and the 5th June, Canadian Typhoons attacked the structures losing one of their planes in the process. The raid was unsuccessful.

In the Pas de Calais region the raids were deliberately unsuccessful as the Allies stepped up their efforts to create a diversion. Shipping in that area increased as did air strikes and the Germans retained the belief that if an attack came it would be in that region.

Von Graf remained firmly not of that mind. He had been invited to a conference in Rennes of Senior Officers in the region to discuss tactics in the event of an allied attack but declined, citing ill health. The Conference was due to start on the 5th June and the raid on the 2nd convinced him that being away from his post at that time was not a good idea.

The weather in the last two weeks of May had been excellent and the troops around the country were frustrated not to be able to spend as much time out in the nice weather as they wanted. When they had been on their frequent training and exercises, they all suffered from the heat. Flaming June did not live up to its name however and the weather in the first couple of days of the month was very unseasonal.

Wind, rain, and low cloud blighted the landscape but those still tending their gardens gave thanks for the water. The clouds did however make reconnaissance difficult for both sides and the Allies took the opportunity to move troops in daylight. shifting men nearer to the south coast ports and their jumping off points.

Then as suddenly as the bad weather came, the sun returned, and on the 5th of June it looked as if the dry spell had returned. While ordinary folk were looking forward to the fine weather, thousands of fighting men were being crammed into their boats as quickly as possible to make room for the thousands more that were arriving at docks and harbours across the south coast.

Ships put to sea to allow others to take on their eager cargoes. A quarter of a million men prepared for their big day. Paratroopers sat polishing knives and cleaning guns as they waited to board their planes. Gliders were hitched to planes ready for their assault on France and Naval forces converged on the Channel. It had been four years since so many boats had been in one place but this time, they were going the other way, full of men desperate to revenge the retreat from Dunkirk.

Colonel Krimp had a bit more time than the paratroopers who were destined to land in France. The French attack was going in soon after midnight on the 6th and it had been decided that he would be using planes that had already made the drop in France.

His big day would start at around 4.30 am when they bailed out over Guernsey. The moon was already high in the sky, visible between the clouds, and the first wave had taken off when he gathered his 600 men in one of the hangers at Exeter airport. Krimp knew his men were nervous because he was too.

Not the tallest of men, he stood on an ammunition box so he could see all their faces, most now sporting black camouflage paint.

'Boys, we are almost ready to go. When we get to Guernsey, we have jobs to do, you all know what your job is. The first waves on the beaches will be depending on us to protect them from reinforcements reaching the beachhead area. Some of you are going to capture the high ground or at least distract the defenders from targeting the boys on the beaches. Expect tough resistance, we know Jerry will be ready for us. Expect chaos, despite all the training and rehearsals, no assault ever goes to plan just work to regroup when you are on the ground and remember your code words. Are we ready?'

A few voices muttered, 'Yes sir.'

He looked across at them. 'I am not convinced! ARE YOU READY!' This time he shouted and got a rousing response in return 'YES SIR!'

'Better. Now as soon as our rides get back let's do this job so we can all go home and put our feet up!'

That got a laugh and, satisfied they were ready, he stood down from the box and walked out of the hangar.

He looked at the sky and then his watch. It would be at least an hour before the first planes returned. He wished the hands would move a bit quicker so they could get this waiting over with.

*****

In the control room for the Freya Radar station in Fort George on Guernsey the operators were monitoring their radar sets and could not believe their eyes. Their screens were full of blips, and they all seemed to be heading to Guernsey. They were about to contact their HQ when the radar targets turned to the East and vectored away towards France.

A call came in from Alderney to say they had heard what sounded like hundreds of planes, but they were now disappearing towards France. The Radar operators agreed it must be another bombing raid and they wrote up a report to be sent through to HQ the following day. However, it was not long before they began to receive reports from France that there appeared to be Paratroopers landing in the Cotentin area.

Despite the reports, there was uncertainty as to whether this was the anticipated invasion. Some believed this was just a spate of Guerrilla style activities, designed to cause confusion and diversion from the main attack in the Pas de Calais.

In the Pas de Calais area the Radar stations were overwhelmed with reports of planes and ships. Given the apparent huge level of activity, troops in that area were put on maximum alert

The Naval HQ based in a bunker in St Jacques on Guernsey started to receive messages concerning a potential convoy to the North of the island and called that into their central command. It was soon clear that the convoy was moving slowly to the East but there was concern enough that a call was put in to the Kommandants HQ at the Royal Hotel.

The duty officer took the call and weighed up the information in front of him. Given the heightened state of readiness in the Island he made the decision to wake the GeneralMajor.

Von Graf rubbed the sleep from his eyes and considered the report in front of him. His mind went back to an incident a year ago, when there had been a false alarm involving a barrage balloon. He had received some criticism about wasting ammunition following their over response to that report and therefore it had been agreed that engagements were not to begin unless confirmation of an enemy target was verified by at least two sources.

The duty officer explained to Von Graf that they had received reports from France of potential parachute drops and the Islands radar stations had spotted an aerial armada to the north of the Island seemingly heading towards France.

He was instantly awake. 'Sound the alarm, Gunther. This is it and we need to be ready.'

Within minutes, all over the Island, troops were being awoken by alarms and running to their stations. At their Headquarters in Baubigny Arsenal, Panzer tank engines were warming up as Hauptmann Wagner prepared his platoons for action. By 3.30am the defenders were ready and waiting.

About 7 miles North of the Island the Guernsey Invasion forces paused as the troops scheduled to land on the Cotentin sailed on. General Hood was on board a British Cruiser that had been designated to provide fire support for the Guernsey attack.

Hood had wanted to be in the first wave but had been ordered by General Morgan to hold back until the beachhead was secure.

The landing craft involved in the Guernsey invasion were organised into three columns. Tank Landing Craft, LCT, were in the lead and they contained Hobart's Funnies as well as some standard Churchill tanks. The beach had been divided into three zones, Red, Green and Blue. The three strike regiments, in the leading troop-carrying Landing Craft (LCIs) were each designated a zone.

On the west coast, 47th Commando were approaching the headland on the southern edge of L'Eree bay. They had been dropped off from LCIs over a mile off the coast of Lihou Island and were steadily paddling towards shore in a flotilla of Goatley boats. Each of the collapsible vessels held ten men.

Two large landing craft had been designated to head towards the entrance to Grande Havre Bay and were slightly ahead of the invasion force. LCA's containing Frank De La Mare and Tony Rihoy were also ahead of the group ready for their special missions.

Despite the noises of the sea and the whistling of the wind the scene was eerily quiet. The odd moan from a soldier was quickly shushed away and only whispers could be heard as the troops guessed at how long it would be before they went into action.

In Guernsey, the quiet of the night was shattered as the guns of the Mirus Battery opened up, firing their enormous shells across the Island towards the invasion fleet that was approaching France.

People across the Island woke up wondering what was happening as their windows rattled and the air above them was ripped apart by the huge shells.

None anticipated an invasion.

THE ATTACK

Exeter Airport was a buzz of activity as the Dakotas returned from France. They also brought back the first casualties of the invasion.

Several of the Dakotas had been hit during their missions and had brought back injured paratroopers or in some cases injured pilots or co-pilots. Ambulances buzzed around the base as Colonel Ronnie Krimp and his men jogged out to the Dakotas that had been refuelled, and were waiting for them. As they crossed to the planes one Dakota came in without its undercarriage and slewed down the runway in a cloud of sparks, eventually ending up on the grass where it was quickly surrounded by fire engines.

Of the thirty-two planes designated to transport Krimp, and his men only twenty-seven were ready. A request went out for volunteers and five crews quickly came forward, ready to fly again. No-one mentioned where the five missing planes might be.

Soon they were loaded up and ready to go.

All was set.

At 3.50 am they took off from Exeter Airport and headed south.

The first guns of the Guernsey invasion weren't aimed at the Paratroopers, nor at Guernsey, they were aimed at Alderney. At 4.15am while the Paratroopers in France were struggling to become a cohesive force, blow bridges and capture key towns and crossroads; and the Germans dithered, lacking leadership at this crucial moment, the guns of the British Navy opened up on Alderney. The German garrison there had spotted the invasion fleet on radar and visually, during moments when the moon broke through the clouds, but they hesitated.

They sent reports to Guernsey and France and asked for orders. The orders they waited for did not come in time. Massive shells from battleships, cruisers and destroyers ripped into the defences around Alderney, gouging huge holes out of concrete bunkers and emplacements. One lucky shot blew up a gun emplacement completely when it found its way through an embrasure and ignited stored ammunition.

With no more need for orders, the defenders fired back as best they could amid the confusion, but the shelling did not stop and within half an hour Alderney's defenses were all but silenced. Leaving a single cruiser to target any defiant gun positions, the fleet sailed on to France while those designated to support the Guernsey invasion carried on South and took up their positions.

Meanwhile, the Mirus Battery in Guernsey continued to lob its huge shells in the direction of the invasion fleet as it assembled off the coast of France. With no visual targets they relied on their radar and blind luck to hit anything. Eventually they did get lucky, and one support vessel took a direct hit and sank within five minutes of being struck by the massive shell.

In the various landing craft north of Guernsey the sound of the shells being fired on Alderney and the fire from the Mirus Battery on Guernsey shattered the eerie peace that had lain over the fleet. For many it was their first experience of guns fired in anger and it brought home the reality of what was coming. At the appointed time, in one cohesive unit, the fleet started to creep forward towards Guernsey.

While all this was happening to the north of Guernsey, off the west coast of the Island the commando units that had launched from their transport were getting closer to L'Eree Headland. They could see the flashes from the Mirus Battery and knew the defenders would be ready and waiting for them, but they had to silence those guns as quickly as they could.

They paused and took stock, it would soon be light, so they needed to get ashore as quickly as possible. It was agreed to go with the original plan, and they paddled towards the rocks below L'Eree Headland. Above them was one of the main strongholds along the West Coast of Guernsey, Stronghold Fort Saumarez.

47 Marine Commando had reluctantly been forced to split its 420 men. Two platoons would be attacking the headlands with the main force at L'Ancresse while the rest were under the command of Colonel Alan Willcocks. Alan was an extremely strong and fit man and would never expect his men to undertake any task he could not do himself. The three hundred and fifty men who were with him off L'Eree would follow him into hell if necessary and that was pretty much what he was asking them to do over the next few hours.

L'Eree Headland and its surrounds was one of the most heavily defended areas in Hitler's Atlantic wall. It was dominated by the huge lookout tower which had been built on top of a former Napoleonic tower. The headland bristled with bunkers, barbed wire, Tobruk pits, trenches and machine gun posts. In the corner of the bay a gun emplacement watched over L'Eree bay itself while other bunkers on the northern side of the headland covered the area in front of the shingle bank which protected Guernsey's former aerodrome from the sea.

Willcocks and Hood had planned that the Commandos should get off the headland as quickly and as quietly as possible and make their way up the hill towards the Mirus Battery. If that mission was completed successfully, they would push on to try and secure the airport.

Both men had acknowledged it was a huge task and General Hood had met Alan many times before D-Day to discuss the plans to give their mission every chance of success. Despite the enormity of the task Hood had every faith in Willcocks and the men of 47 Commando. Embedded with his men Willcocks had two locals, Lieutenant Jeff Bishop and Lieutenant Michael 'Mick' Riley.

Each led four platoons of men plus several specialists in demolition. Alan of course was in overall command.

Alan had been gutted that he had to split 47 Commando, but he trusted all his men and knew the commandos attacking L'Ancresse were in safe hands. The evening before they had embarked, they had all met one last time to go over the plans. At that meeting they had all sworn an oath to meet in the Royal Hotel in St Peter Port after this was all over and drink German Schnapps and burn ever picture of Hitler they could find.

They had toasted their success with a tot of rum before heading to their embarkation point.

As they paddled quietly towards Guernsey each man was dressed in black with their faces covered in black camouflage paint. It was hard to see anything but the glint in their eyes. If you were lucky or unlucky enough, depending on which side you were on, to lock eyes with one of his men, all you would see was determination etched in every line around those fierce eyes.

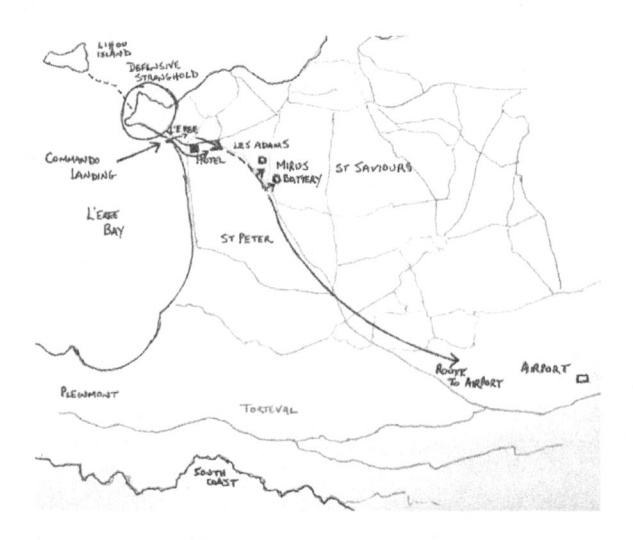

Commandos Plan for 6th June 1944, West Coast of Guernsey

As the Mirus battery continued to fire, the clouds above L'Eree Bay were good to the Commandos. Nearly every guard on the headland was also looking at the spectacle rather than out to sea as instructed.

Whatever was happening the German troops felt it was far enough away not to be an issue for them.

The codeword for the Commandos attack was Glenn Miller. Call Glenn and friends would reply, Miller. They also carried clickers. If you click and hear two clicks in return, that would be a friend. The Paratroopers just used passwords.

Alan personally had bagged a few hundred clickers from US paratroopers when he had beaten a US Captain in an arm wrestling match a few weeks earlier. He was sure the Americans had enough to go round and would not miss a few hundred of the little gadgets.

With the tide almost at its lowest the Commandos had to cross quite a stretch of rocks, and they were slippery. One man slipped and broke his leg and had to be left just above the high tide mark. A couple of his platoon helped hide the distraught Commando as best they could. He was gutted to be missing the action. They left him fully armed. Despite the pain he never made a noise.

A single guard was patrolling the headland above where they landed and as he watched the Mirus Battery fire its guns he died. A Commando knife cutting his throat. He was the first man to die in Guernsey on that fateful day and his body was unceremoniously rolled off the grass on to the top of the rocks, and tucked out of sight.

The Commandos had to cut their way through barbed wire to reach the top of the beach and as soon as that was done, they swarmed across the ground behind the bunkers heading towards the L'Eree Hotel. There, they had to cut more barbed wire to get off the headland and two more guards manning a post at the entrance died, their bodies hidden under gorse bushes.

Willcocks checked his watch, he had to get off the headland by 4.45 am at the latest.

More barbed wire and a defence line had been stretched across the old aerodrome and behind the L'Eree Hotel which Willcocks and his men had to cross. Half of 47 Commando crossed into the old aerodrome behind a line of cottages, led by Lieutenant Bishop while the others swept around the back of the L'Eree Hotel.

On their way they had to silence a couple of sentries patrolling the top of the L'Eree anti-tank wall while being careful not to alert the troops in the bunker at the top of the beach. They had just reached the open land when at 4.45 am precisely the guns of two cruisers started to pound several West Coast strongholds, L'Eree included.

At the sound of the explosions, German troops poured out of the L'Eree Hotel where they had been barracked but hesitated as they saw the headland erupt under the guns of the British navy. One of them happened to look across at the field to his right and in the half-light saw shadows running across the open space towards the barbed wire.

'Achtung, Achtung,' he shouted, pointing to the vague shapes in the field. Having just left their beds the soldiers were yet to get their eyes used to the weird dawn light and to add to the confusion a low mist lay across the fields. The German soldiers ran across the road, taking cover behind a wall and started firing into the field.

One shadowy figure immediately fell with a grunt and the Commandos suffered their first casualty of the night due to enemy action. Willcocks had been with the group working their way around the south of the hotel when he heard the shooting above the explosions on the headland and the guns of the Mirus Battery.

Calling for the Bren, he and a dozen men doubled around the back of the hotel and found a way into the road. He could see the German troops firing into the field and without hesitation took the Bren under his arm and walked into the road firing at the line of troops sheltering behind the wall.

As his fellow Commandos joined in the Germans had no chance and all were killed or wounded within a minute of the start of the engagement. All the action had been noticed by a check point further up the hill and a German MG entered the fray, firing down the hill into the British troops in the road.

Lieutenant Mick Riley had continued his mission with the rest of the Commandos, creeping through the open land on the south side of the road. He arrived just in time to lob two grenades into the checkpoint, snuffing out the resistance and silencing the MG.

A gap in the shelling of the headland created an eerie silence apart from a few moans from the wounded. A call of Glenn was answered by Willcocks with Miller and Lieutenant Bishop climbed over the wall and joined Willcocks in the road.

Willcocks grabbed one of his NCOs and told him to run up the road to Riley and order him to continue up the hill while the rest of his men were sent to root out any troops that may still be in the Hotel. Their room by room search resulted in the capture of half a dozen prisoners.

The Germans had several wounded as did Bishop's men, Willcocks himself had suffered a flesh wound when the MG had opened up on the road and he had two wounded who couldn't continue with their mission. Corporal Mick Taylor who also had a flesh wound on his leg was ordered to gather the wounded, British and German, and utilise the restaurant in the Hotel as a holding and treatment area for the prisoners and the wounded. Two commandos who doubled up as Medics were left with him. One of the captured Germans was also a medic and he volunteered to help treat the injured.

A dozen troops were left with Taylor to set up a defensive position to protect the hotel and the rear of the Commandos as they advanced up the hill.

Once he was satisfied with the position around the L'Eree Hotel, Willcocks joined Bishop and his commandos and followed Riley's men up the hill towards their main target. It was 5 am and getting quite light as the early morning sun tried to break through the clouds.

*****

As the main landing force moved slowly towards Guernsey, they could hear approaching aircraft. At 4.25 am, 32 C-47 Dakotas carrying Colonel Krimp and his Paratroopers passed low over the fleet, heading towards Guernsey. Pathfinder Mosquito aircraft overtook them on their approach and dropped flares on the landing zones. The defenders were alert and anti-aircraft guns opened up as the planes flew over. The fire was intense and one Mosquito was hit and crashed into the open land to the south of the Vale Church, the slower Dakotas were easier targets but at 400 to 500 feet they made targeting awkward for the gunners. Nevertheless, two of their number were hit and fell out of formation one crashing into the sea another crashing into Greenhouses South of Rocque Balan.

Some shells ripped through planes killing several of Krimp's men before they had even bailed out.

The whole attack took under five minutes as that was all the time they had over the Island. Sticks of paratroopers appeared in the morning half-light, many of them way off target thanks to the pressure brought on the planes from the ground. The best outcome came in the Eastern zone where 120 men managed to land in a cluster between Rocque Balan and the Bunker Hill resistance point. Twenty missed that zone landing amongst greenhouses and fields south of the Rocque Balan.

Krimp and most of the men of A and D Company landed South of the Vale Church thanks in the main to the pathfinders missing their target. One flare had hit its mark and the Dakotas on the right of the formation unfortunately did hit their target. Seventy-two men of Company B parachuted straight into the newly created minefield on the common designed to counter parachute drops.

Immediately mines started to explode as paratroopers landed directly on wires and set off the charges, three more exploded as the men of B Company tried to find each other in the low mist that lay over the common. Those that survived froze, realising they were trapped in the middle of a minefield.

Major Bell assembled what was left of C Company at the base of bunker hill. The Germans in the resistance point had spotted the drop and were already directing fire down the hill towards the paratroopers. Men died before they had even reached the ground. Bell quickly organized his men in a semi-circle from the road to the south of the hill across the common towards the anti-tank wall and began to return fire. The 3-inch mortar began sending rounds into the defences while the 2 inch mortar was loaded with smoke rounds and aimed short of the newly constructed defences to try and blind the defenders.

In his Guernsey farmhouse Major Balzer was already dressed as he read the reports coming in from HQ. The windows of the farmhouse rattled as the guns on La Varde opened up at the aerial attack. He checked in with the various strongholds around L'Ancresse by radio and learned that paratroopers had landed across the headland, many of them in his newly laid minefield on the common.

That news made him smile and he looked forward to telling the Kommandant how successful his idea had been. That would have to wait, however, as he decided he needed to get out and check how the defences were holding out.

Without thinking he rushed out of the front door and into the road, straight into Major Bell's right flank and was gunned down before he could cross the road. Under cover of smoke the paratroopers crept up the hill under blind fire from the newly installed MGs around the resistance area. Despite taking casualties they managed to cut through the barbed wire and once they were close enough lobbed grenades into the trenches and then stormed the defences.

In the marshy land to the south of the Vale Church, Colonel Krimp did his best to assemble his forces and took stock of his situation. He had lost touch with B Company and knew they were in trouble. Major Bell had been in touch as soon as they had landed but had been quiet since.

Krimp had around 200 men with him from A and D companies, but some men were missing as was their heavy mortar. Krimp had a quick discussion with Major Druce and Captain Flatterly. They decided to push towards the common and capture the gun emplacement next to the Vale Church. For that task he went with Druce and A Company while he entrusted Captain Flatterly to head to the Western side of the Vale Church and secure that area and the Church itself.

'Still no news from B Company sir,' his radio operator reported as their quick meeting came to an end.

'Keep trying, Sparky, and try and make contact with Major Bell. I need to know how they are getting on.'

'Aye aye skipper,' Terry 'Sparky' Sparkes replied and headed off into the mist.

Krimp looked at his watch, it was 4.55 am and getting light and he needed to achieve his objectives as quickly as he could.

'Gentlemen let's get this done. Captain, I'll meet you in the Church at 5.30.'

Flatterly nodded and went back to his men and together they headed off to the West of the marshes just south of the Vale Church. On the way he gathered a few more men who were floundering in the marshy land and large pond. Sadly, not all of them had survived the drop into the marshes.

Druce and Krimp led their men to the East of the marsh land towards the military road. He left a section to guard the road and protect their rear. They had a PIAT in case any armoured vehicles came down the road.

Another section went into the road, splitting up to use cover on both sides of the road while the rest crept over the fields south of the Vale Church. The realisation soon came that they were quite a bit lower than the road and Krimp cursed his memory of the area.

Sending Druce with a platoon and a radio operator to join the section on the road he sent men to scout a way out of the sunken field. They were not successful.

He called Sparky over and contacted Druce.

'Gordon, this one's on you. Let us pepper the position with a few mortar rounds and grenades. As soon as you hear the third mortar round go in, attack and we'll get back to the road and come in after you.'

'Roger that sir, give me three minutes, I am going to try and establish another point of attack.'

'Three minutes and no more Major.' Krimp wanted to say more to his friend, but this was not a time for needless well wishes, they just had to get the job done. He looked at his watch and got his men to set up the light mortar and counted down the seconds.

Major Gordon Druce had seen the row of cottages at the end of the Military Road and realised they had a very narrow point of attack. He sent a section under Sergeant Eric Archer to try and work their way around the back of the cottages and see if they could bring some fire on the German defensive position from the East to vary the point of attack.

Sergeant Archer led his men around the back of a small chapel and into some scrubland behind the cottages and headed North until they found the small road that went East from the small defensive position. He popped his head over the wall just as the first mortar round exploded behind the German position. Druce by this time had edged up the road in the lee of the granite wall. His men had the Bren and they nestled down at the base of the wall where they had a good view of the German position. They had just set up when the first mortar shell exploded.

The second round exploded quickly after, adding to the confusion in the German position. The defenders had hunkered down and were hoping they did not get a direct hit. Two grenades, thrown by Archer's men went off just short of the sandbags protecting the defenders and then the third round exploded right next to the position, dislodging some of the sandbags and stunning the six men inside.

At that moment the Bren opened up and Sergeant Archers men opened fire with their Sten guns and pushed towards the position.

Druce began moving forward on the opposite side from the Bren gun but the defenders had regained some composure and their MG started firing down the road. One defender threw a grenade towards Archer and his section, and two men went down as did two of Druce's men under fire from the MG.

The cacophony of sound was devastating as rounds were ricocheting off the granite walls, some impacting on the cottages, breaking windows, flaking concrete and breaking slates on the roofs. Seemingly oblivious to the chaos around him, Druce threw a well-aimed grenade which fell just in front of the defensive position, causing enough damage to the sandbags to push the MG back and give the Paratroopers the opening they were looking for.

Archer's section was closest and stormed the position killing all but two of the defenders. The two injured men surrendered to Archer.

By then Krimp and his men had moved back to the Military Road and jogged up to the position. All the British casualties were still alive, and medics were working on them in the road.

Sparky reported that Captain Flatterly was in position at a junction in the road, West of the Church and had met little resistance. Two sentries patrolling the end of Grand Havre Bay had been captured and another killed.

'Good,' Krimp said to no-one in particular.

'Gordon, secure this position and set up the Bren where the MG had been. If you can get the MG working, use that too. Get one gun pointing along the Military Road and the other towards the beaches, we can maybe take out some stragglers if any try to retreat from that direction. I'll get up to the Church with the wounded and the prisoners and set up a field station there and then I'll be back after I have check on D Company.'

Krimp took a section and headed up the long path to the Church. As always Sparky was by his side and on the way, he reported that C Company had secured Bunker Hill and had taken up defensive positions.

Captain Flatterly met him at the church on the dot at 5.30 and from his vantage point, Krimp looked back towards L'Ancresse common. As the light improved, he could spot the parachutes of B Company on the common land and could see the rows of poles that had been put there. Gaps in the rows told him where mines had exploded, and men had been lost. Parachutes were tangled in the gorse and the occasional sound of machine guns told him that the troops on La Varde were trying to pick off the troops trapped below them.

In some of the open areas he could see large craters. He could only imagine what B Company were going through and mentally wrote them off from any plans for the rest of the day.

That should have been us. He thought to himself.

He said a silent prayer for the men of B Company and hoped that some of them could extricate themselves from the minefield. A and D company had been very lucky.

The door of the church was locked so one of his men forced it open and they went inside. Krimp had been there once before for the funeral of a friend, and it was much as he remembered. Some of the prayer books were in German and he guessed correctly that the occupiers had been using the church themselves for their own services.

Away from the madness outside the church a sort of peace came over him as he walked down the aisle towards the alter. He wasn't a religious man, but he knelt in front of the alter and said a quick prayer for his men and asked for God's support to help them succeed that day.

He looked around the Church and decided what had to be done.

Sergeant Archer from A Company was with him, and he called him over. 'Sergeant, can you get the wounded in this central section, use the pews as temporary beds for them and I want the prisoners held over there on the right of the entrance below the bell ropes. Just make sure they don't start ringing the damn bells.'

Sergeant Archer got to work and soon all the injured and prisoners were being sorted in their respective areas in the church. He also sent a man to see if they could find a good lookout spot in the spire or on the roof.

Krimp then ran with Captain Flatterly down to the Western side of the Church and checked on their defensive positions. They had made the most of the cover they had there and had positioned a Bren behind the Church wall to counter any approach from the West and had also set up a mortar to provide additional firepower in that direction.

Flatterly also had men watching the open area they had just come from in case of reinforcements from the south. Happy all was well, Krimp returned to the crossroads and checked on the defences there. Major Druce had done a good job and the East side of the Church was well defended.

Altogether his men seemed in good spirits, some were evening trying to brew up and take on some rations as they prepared for the next phase of the operation. As he looked down the Military Road a man edged out of one of the cottages, holding his hands up. It was the first civilian Krimp had seen, all had sensibly kept their heads down oblivious to what was going on.

Colonel Krimp jogged down the road and met the man by his gate.

'You can put your hands down mate, we're British.'

'Thank God,' was all the man could say and he threw his arms around the Colonels neck and burst into tears. The man's wife was in the doorway looking out, but Krimp urged her to stay there with a free hand.

'I need you to get back in your cottage and keep your heads down, Sir.'

The man finally let Krimp go. 'Are we free now?' He asked.

'Not yet and not by a long chalk so keep indoors and we'll let you know when it is safe to come out. The worst is yet to come so stay inside please.'

'Thank you,' the man said, and walked back to his wife. 'God bless you and keep you safe,' his wife added as they went back in and closed the door.

A sudden noise from the south made the hairs on the back of his neck stand on end. The rattling and squeaking sound was unmistakable to anyone who had ever been on exercises with the armoured divisions.

Tanks.

He ran back up the road to the defensive positions by the crossroads and shouted to Major Druce. 'Gordon, tanks approaching from the south. Get all the PIATS we have here as quick as you can.'

Druce nodded and soon men were scattering to accumulate all the PIATs they had available and bring them to the crossroads.

*****

While the Paratroopers were undertaking their dangerous mission, another unusual mission was taking place in L'Ancresse Bay.

After the Dakotas had cleared the area four Lancaster Bombers from 617 squadron swooped over the fleet and settled at their optimum bombing height of 60 feet. They swiftly approached the beaches of L'Ancresse Bay and dropped their bouncing bombs while still over the water. The bombs took one bounce on the sea, ploughed into the sand but with enough momentum to bounce them up the beach until three hit the anti-tank wall and after a pause of ten seconds, exploded.

It had taken a lot of practice and experimentation to achieve the exact amount of spin and the timings needed to set the bombs for this mission and it was almost a complete success. Part of the planning had involved Commandos kayaking into the bay a month earlier to take sand samples so they could work out just how much resistance the sand would cause.

The fourth bomb, deflected by one of the beach defences, bounced over the wall and rolled across the common to explode against a cottage and greenhouses near the crossroads in the middle of L'Ancresse common. 92-year-old widow, Edith Le Page died in the explosion and became the first civilian casualty that day, sadly she wouldn't be the last.

Once the Lancaster's had finished their mission. fighter bombers followed them in and started to pound the strongholds around the Island. Typhoons and Mosquitos attacked the various forts and gun positions on Guernsey's headlands and cliffs, avoiding built up areas. German Anti-Aircraft batteries fired back and started to take their toll and the second mosquito of the day was shot down, falling in flames into Vazon Bay. Despite the losses, the attacks started to reap rewards and German guns around the Island started to fall silent.

Other attacks were made on the Radar station at Fort George, Vale Castle, the anti-aircraft position on Brehon Tower off Guernsey's East coast and Guernsey's airport. This time the rockets of two typhoons found their target in Fort George and one of the large towers fell to the ground rendering the system inoperative.

At the airport six Messerschmitt Bf 109s and an aging Junkers transport fell to an attack by rocket equipped Bristol Beaufighters, while the guns on Brehon Tower were shattered and the top of the tower was left a smoldering ruin.

Naval guns continued to pound the defences as the pressure on the defenders mounted and the clock ticked towards zero hour.

The last act before the troops reached the beaches took place at the entrance to Grande Havre Bay. Two specially equipped large landing craft began to generate a huge smoke screen. With the light winds from the Northwest they positioned themselves so that the clouds of smoke they were producing drifted across the headlands and beaches of L'Ancresse obscuring the beaches completely from the surrounding headlands.

The stage was set.

*****

GeneralMajor Von Graf looked to organise his forces. From radio reports he knew that his Coastal strongholds were under fire from both sea and air all around the Island and that paratroopers had landed in the North.

He had not been able to get in touch with Balzer and had received reports from the stronghold at the Doyle that they were under attack.

Working in his Ops room he read the steady stream of reports and studied the maps setting out his troop dispositions and considered his options. The attacks on the West Coast had put doubts in his mind as regards the anticipated point of attack.

The fighting around L'Ancresse could be a diversion, he thought to himself, and he started to believe the main landings might take place at Vazon, which was the biggest of the West Coast beaches. He contacted Hauptmann Wagner at the Baubigny Arsenal and ordered him to send one platoon of Panzers North to support his beleaguered forces there, keeping the other platoon in reserve to move West should the landings come from that direction.

Still conflicted, he contacted Fort George and ordered Oberst Volker to mobilise his regiment. One battalion, he ordered to head West to Vazon Bay to bolster the defences in that area. The main body of the regiment was ordered to head for St Peter Port.

All troops in the North of the Island, not manning guns or defensive positions, were ordered to move to Bordeaux or L'Islet, depending on where they were based, and hold there until the picture was clearer as to what was happening at L'Ancresse.

The German army in Guernsey was not blessed with much in the way of transport but two companies were loaded on to trucks and headed North and West from Fort George while the rest marched out into the early morning air.

*****

The Commandos that had landed at L'Eree Headland were making their final approach to the Mirus Battery. The L'Eree Headland behind them had been battered by the Navy and the RAF while they worked their way towards their target.

One motorcycle and side car had come down the hill as they had doubled up the road and the lead Commandos had made short work of the two soldiers it carried. The road was called the Route des Adams and the Commandos had designated it as Adams Road in their planning for the mission. Their target was in an area called La Hougette but had been given the code letter H.

The loud report of the Guns which were now quite close caused Riley to hold a fist in the air and the troops hunkered down along each side of the road. Houses were sparse in this part of the Island but there were dozens of greenhouses. They had passed a couple of farmhouses on the way up the hill and they saw one set of net curtains twitch as they doubled past and Riley swore he had seen a women smile before the curtains had been straightened.

Riley had four platoons with him, and he knew Willcocks would soon follow with another one hundred and fifty or so men.

The Mirus Battery was made up of two huge Gun Emplacements, so Riley planned to allocate two of his platoons to each emplacement.

Each platoon included two men with satchel charges and the plan was to disable the guns in the initial attack, then hold the positions until the guns were destroyed or made permanently inoperable.

If they were successful, the Commandos would move on to their secondary mission - the Airport. Riley sent two men ahead to scout the land around the Mirus Battery and waited until Willcocks and the rest of the Commandos caught him up. They did not have to wait long. Willcocks had avoided the road and had worked his way up through the fields on the Mirus side of the road.

The first Riley knew Willcocks had reached them was a click which he answered with two clicks of his clicker. A voice whispered Glenn from the other side of the hedge and Riley replied with Miller. With that Willcocks climbed over the wall and dropped down alongside the troops in the road.

'I've got troops out scouting the lay of the land Colonel.' Riley reported.

'Good man, as soon as they are back, we need to silence those guns.' Less than a minute had passed before the two men returned.

They reported that each emplacement was surrounded by several layers of barbed wire and they could see some slit trenches nearer the guns. They had not seen any guards. All the troops seemed busy with the guns or were in their defensive positions. They could not see any way through the barbed wire on this side of the emplacements.

'There must be a way in, the troops have to get in and out?' Willcocks mused half to himself.

'Must be around the other side as that's where the barracks are.' Riley replied.

'But that's the way everyone will be looking, we need to attack from this side.'

'We'll have to do this the hard way then with the wire cutters.'

'Maybe not,' Willcocks replied with a smile. 'Those clickers were not the only thing I obtained, shall we say, from the yanks.'

He called up four of his men from the back of the unit who were carrying larger packs than everyone else. 'Jonesy, you and your mates get the kit out.'

With that the four men produced what Riley instantly recognised as Bangalore Torpedos, something he hadn't seen since their time in Italy.

'Bloody hell skip, good call.'

Once the kit was ready to put together, they decided that Riley and Bishop would attack one emplacement while Willcocks himself and Jonesy would attack the other. They set a time to start the attack and Riley and Bishop with half the men headed off towards the second gun.

Willcocks and Jonesy climbed over the wall and crawled towards the wire with their Bangalore Torpedoes. They slid the pipes under the wire, pushing them forward as far as they could, and then connected the wires. Once they were set, they quickly ran the cables back to the road. Jonesy connected the switch and Willcocks looked at his watch. At the agreed time Willcocks gave a nod. Jonesy gave the switch a twist and simultaneously the devices went off.

One of the Germans in the slit trenches had seen Willcocks and Jonesy running back and was running to raise the alarm when the explosions came, creating a wide gap in the wire and blowing the man off his feet.

Willcocks and Riley knew they had to be quick and were up over the wall in a hurry, followed by their men who put down suppressing fire as the two officers ran through the gaps firing into the trenches as they reached them. The commandos threw grenades at the gun positions either side of the gap and soon they had broken through the perimeter and were working their way towards the gun emplacements.

Individual battles took place across the gun emplacement as German troops emerged from their positions to try and fight off the invaders. But weight of numbers told in the attacker's favour and soon they were next to the pits which held the massive guns.

Satchel charges were primed and thrown into the pits, resulting in massive explosions which killed or stunned the gunners and seriously damaged the mechanism of one of the guns.

Riley's attack had the more impressive result as stored ammunition lay alongside where that satchel landed and the resulting combined explosion lifted the gun off its emplacement, depositing it on its side, half in and half out of the gun pit.

German troops were now swarming up to the emplacement from their barracks in the valley below and Willcocks knew time was against them.

'Cover me,' he shouted and ran around to where the barrel of the undamaged, but immobilised, gun pointed out above the pit.

Machine gun fire from the commandos was keeping the Germans pinned down as Willcocks pulled the pin out of a grenade and threw it at the open end of the massive barrel. It missed and the grenade fell into the pit and exploded. He had one last grenade and taking aim lobbed that one towards the barrel. This time he was successful and the explosion, though disappointingly quiet, was he hoped enough to prevent the gun from firing again.

One last satchel charge was thrown into the pit for luck and then, job done, Willcocks ordered his men back to the road and together they began to withdraw towards the airport.

*****

Hauptmann Wagner took control of the lead Panzer and led his platoon of six tanks north through open fields and grassland. A few greenhouses were on his route, but he just drove through them on his way to the open marsh land south of the Vale Church.

Wagner had scouted this ground over the last couple of weeks and knew the safest approach for his heavy tanks was along the Military Road or by heading to L'Islet and approaching the Vale Church from the East.

It was not the best tactic to split his forces, but he had his orders. His second platoon would have brought the extra force he felt he might need. It would have also given him an option to direct his panzers along both routes but with such a small force he could not afford to split his forces further.

Wagner decided to use the Military Road and approach L'Ancresse from that direction. With a wave of his arm and an order through his throat microphone the tanks swung right and ploughed through the low walls that lined the road swinging on to that long straight thoroughfare.

As a column they headed north, with the Vale Church about a mile ahead and slightly to his left. Wagner erred on the side of caution as he didn't know what lay ahead. The best tactic would have been to have support troops with him but as his hero, General Heinz Guderian had done 4 years earlier, he decided to press on and let the troops catch up.

Krimp could see the Panzers and was shocked. The intelligence had been that the Germans only had light French tanks, not these monsters. One shot from one of these would destroy his small defence point on the crossroads and he was not convinced the PIATs could penetrate the side armour of the latest Panzers. He knew his troops had brought demolition charges with them and sent his NCOs to round up anything useful they could bring to bear against the giants bearing down on his position.

Seeing the futility of the small defence work he had built at the crossroads he pulled his troops out of the position. The Bren and MG would be useless against the tanks. Krimp was worried on another score too. There were civilians in the cottages. If he halted the first tank at the crossroads the rest of the tanks would stop right alongside the cottages. They might choose to disperse to the right and crash through the buildings, killing the people who lived in them.

His best choice was to let them pass and attack them next to the common land to avoid civilian casualties. There was no time to warn the people in the cottages. He called Major Druce over.

'We must let them pass Gordon, but we can't let them get to the beaches. What have we got to stop them?'

'We have six PIATs and four satchel charges, sir.'

He looked up the road towards the beaches. As soon as the tanks reached the open common land they could spread out and that area offered virtually no cover.

'This is a mess Gordon, where can we stop them?'

'I could take some men to those walls over there with a couple of the satchel charges and take out the lead tanks. Then when the rest of the tanks look to pass the disabled tanks, you can attack the middle two with the PIATs and use the rest of the satchel charges for the last two tanks.'

Krimp thought for a moment.

'Right, let's do that but take a section with you in case the Panzer crews bail out looking for trouble.'

Druce didn't wait, he grabbed two men with their satchel charges and the nearest section, and they doubled across the grass towards the beach and then crawled across the road to the last low wall before the open common beyond. The half-light and the slight bend in the road protected them from the eyes of the tank crews. Two men with satchel charges hid behind the empty defensive position and the PIAT operators found cover behind some rocks and bushes as the tanks approached.

Hauptmann Wagner had been looking ahead with his binoculars from his position in the lead tank. He was surprised that they had not been challenged by the German troops in the defensive position by the Vale Church.

As he passed the position and rounded the bend, he could see what looked like a pall of heavy smoke across the headlands and beaches. From time to time allied aircraft could be seen attacking the defences, dropping bombs and rockets on the entrenched defenders.

Sporadic anti-aircraft fire erupted as each aircraft flew over and as he watched, one was hit, peeling away trailing smoke. It looked like hell was on the horizon. He scanned the surrounds for any sign of danger and shrank lower down into the tank to give himself some protection.

As they continued towards the beaches, they approached the end of the walled areas and the common land opened up in front of them. Suddenly a package was thrown under the tank from behind the last piece of wall and a machine gun started firing, bullets bouncing off the metal of the tank.

Instinctively he ducked down into the tank but there was no escape what happened next. The satchel charge exploded beneath where he was standing lifting the floor of the tank and crushing him against the roof, killing him instantly along with all his crew.

Behind him the second tank fared little better, this time the charge exploded near the rear of the tank and the crew had the opportunity to bail out. They did not get far.

The first few men out were felled by machine gun fire. The last two clambered out carefully with their hands in the air, one holding a white handkerchief.

One of the tanks at the end of column brewed up in front of Krimps defence position. The two men hidden behind the sandbags had thrown their charges as the last tank was adjacent to where they were hiding but one charge failed to explode.

PIAT crews fired their projectiles and the middle two tanks started to take damage, one catching fire. The tank second from the rear started to return fire from its machine guns as the main turret traversed towards the attackers. One PIAT crew were killed as they tried to reset the awkward spring mechanism of the PIAT. The Panzer gunners searched for the next target.

Four of the tanks were now out of action and any surviving crew were clambered out of them fully armed taking shelter behind their vehicles.

The third tank in the column was damaged but continued to move forward into the open common land trailing smoke. The second from last tank was the main problem for Krimp. The PIAT that had been operated by the crew that had been killed was lying abandoned. From where he hid it seemed undamaged.

He broke from his cover and grabbed the PIAT and the case with the two remaining charges and ran across the open ground towards the defence position.

Machine gun bullets chased him all the way but his men did their best to give him covering fire. He lay down behind the sandbags and put all his effort into resetting the spring. Despite his lack of stature, his strength enabled him to reset the mechanism. After loading the charge into the front of the PIAT he crept to the edge of the sandbags. Judging his moment carefully he edged around the cover and from a kneeling position at point blank range fired the PIAT into the tracks of the tank.

He flung himself back behind the sandbags as the shell impacted the tracks and managed to ignite the satchel charge under the tank at the same time. The explosion lifted the tank in the air and deposited it on its side.

Krimp was buried in sandbags as the explosion destroyed the defensive position.

His world went black.

From his position up the road Druce watched the damaged tank rattle north towards the beaches.

He won't get far, he thought to himself, deciding to let it go. More important right now was the dozen or so Panzertruppen who were hiding behind their tanks and trying to return fire. From his position on the other side of the column of vehicles he could see some of the men who were pinned between the burning panzers and the wall. Druce was convinced they would run out of ammunition soon but wanted to stop them as a fighting unit as soon as he could to avoid further casualties.

His section were all armed with grenades so he ordered his men to work their way behind the German troops and lob a couple of grenades over the wall. As they did that he began firing into their position to keep their heads down. Less than a minute later two explosions ripped into the troops and those who were not killed or wounded, surrendered immediately.

Leaving his section to escort the captured Panzertruppen up to the church he ran over to see what casualties they had taken. A medic with half a dozen men was sent over to tend to the German casualties. He noticed men frantically digging with their bare hands through a pile of sandbags. He rushed over to see what was going on and to see if he could help.

'It's the Colonel Sir,' one desperate Lance Corporal said as Druce arrived on the scene. Without thinking, he started to help shift sandbags until they finally reached the body of the Colonel. Druce was sure he was dead. Blood had oozed from his ears and nose and he was covered in sand. One arm seemed to be bent in an unnatural position.

'Does anyone have some water? And get a medic over here.'

A Lance Corporal rushed off to find a medic while someone produced a water bottle. Druce knelt next to his friend and carefully washed the sand off his face and once that was done poured some drops into Krimps mouth. Nothing happened for a few heart stopping moments, then Krimp started to cough as he regained consciousness.

'Bloody hell, Ronnie, I thought you were a goner for sure.'

Krimp looked at him and could see he was talking but all he got was a loud buzzing in his ear. He tried to point to his ear, but his left arm wasn't working, and his right arm was still under a sandbag. The pain from his arm hit him suddenly and viciously.

'Shit, get me up Gordon.'

Druce put a hand on his chest. 'You stay there Ronnie, you've done your bit for now, let the medic take a look at you. You've bust your arm pretty badly.'

Krimp heard some of that as he started to regain his hearing.

'Got to get the defences back Gordon, we are vulnerable here.'

'I'll sort that Ronnie, no-one is getting past the Paras, just look after yourself for now. That's an order.'

With that a medic appeared. He strapped Ronnie's damaged arm in place so it couldn't move and then together with the help of a couple of soldiers they cleared the rest of the sandbags away from his legs and right arm. Thankfully, they all appeared to be in one piece. Together they lifted him on to a stretcher and took him up to the Church to tend to his shattered arm.

'Druce looked around. 'Well, this is a bit of mess,' he muttered to himself.

He called over his NCOs. 'OK, we've taken a bit of a hit, but we need to rebuild this emplacement and get the machine guns set up as we did before. Someone pop over to Captain Flatterly and see if he has any PIATs or satchel charges he can share with us just in case more tanks appear. Tell him we have been busy while he has been enjoying his breakfast,' he added with a smile.

In the distance he saw the last tank suddenly brew up in a huge explosion.

'What the hell was that?' He muttered to no-one in particular. In the silence that followed the tank explosion it suddenly registered that the constant bombing had stopped, and it had become eerily quiet.

'This is it boys, I think we have visitors coming let's be ready.' With that they all got to work.

THE BEACHES

The thick white fog had seemed to be going on forever as the fleet approached L'Ancresse beach. The last fighter bombers had peeled away after one final attack on the forts on both sides of the bay.

Landing craft carrying the Commando units had turned towards their targets, or at least where they thought they were, as the smoke screen was making things difficult for the fleet as well as the defenders.

On shore the German troops were trying their best to rebuild their defences. Three large holes had been blasted in the anti-tank wall and they had taken several machine gun positions with them. Men were hastily building defences with sandbags and new MGs were being moved into position.

Up in the forts and strongholds medical teams were tending to the wounded gunners and troops and what guns that had survived were being manned and munitions brought up ready for the expected attack. The loss of Major Balzer had been a setback for the defenders but stronghold commanders had taken control and thanks to the strength of the bunkers hundreds of troops emerged unscathed. The main damage had been to the large guns which were set in their emplacements but some large mortars had been well protected and were ready for action, as were the two emplacements tucked away in each corner of the beach.

A few anti-aircraft guns were also still serviceable, and these were re-purposed to target the beach now the bombardments were over.

A slight movement in the breeze moved the smoke away from the top of the beach and one of the men working on building a new defence work for an MG noticed a strange shape emerging from the white cloud. The giant grey bow of one of the LCTs crawled out of the smoke and approached the beach.

'Alarm, alarm,' he shouted and with that, men across the top of the anti-tank wall dropped their tools, collected their guns, and readied themselves for the attack. The anti-aircaft guns opened up on the Landing Craft as did every other gun and mortar the Germans had available. The machine guns held their fire.

By now two LCSs had emerged from the smoke and had begun firing back. Guns zeroed in on the two bunkers at the head of the beach while rockets were launched at those defences on La Varde that were still capable of firing. The sound was deafening.

As the guns exchanged fire the ramps on the LCTs dropped and Hobart's Funnies rolled down on to the beach. Flail tanks and bulldozer tanks lead the way and began clearing the beach obstacles in front of them.

On the headlands on either side of the beach, Commandos, guided by Frank de la Mare and Tony Rihoy swarmed ashore and, in a target rich environment, soon began to engage the enemy.

To the East of L'Ancresse Bay around the stronghold at Fort Le Marchant the Commandos engaged the stunned troops streaming out of the devastated fortifications. Frank de la Mare had led his platoon around an old quarry to reach the Fort but as soon as the engagement had started it was over. The defenders had little fight in them and a soldier carrying a white flag with a bandaged head stumbled out of the badly damaged fort. Fort Le Marchant was in allied hands and the fighting in that area was over.

The Commandos took 24 prisoners and then had the problem of what to do with them. They found an area of the quarry with a small ledge where the prisoners could be held and assigned two men to guard them.

Up on the hill, one bunker seemed to be untouched by the bombardment and as the Landing Craft emerged on the beach it starting to fire down on the assembled fleet.

The Commandos, wary of mines and having to cut through the inevitable barbed wire pushed slowly up towards the position.

Two men made the mistake of approaching the rear entrance to the bunker and came face to face with an MG and were killed instantly in a hail of bullets. Grenades were thrown down into the narrow entrance but the heavy metal doors and a sliding door across the aperture for the MG protected the troops inside from the effects of the explosions.

The main gun continued to fire towards the beach while machine guns rained fire into the commandos from the main gun slit whenever anyone tried to approach. The commandos swarmed around the emplacement, but they struggled to work out how to take out the gun.

Frank De La Mare, using his local knowledge, managed to get alongside the bunker and called up two men to help him. Between them they had a satchel bomb and grenades but could not get in front of the gun slit to lob anything inside.

They managed to heave Frank and another man on the roof of the concrete structure with the satchel charge. Laying down over the front of the bunker with his colleague holding his legs, Frank eased himself over the edge, set the charge and waited a couple of seconds. The gun fired one more time just as Frank arched himself back and with an athletic swing of his body lobbed the satchel beneath him, through the gun slit, right next to the gun barrel. His mate pulled him back just in time to avoid the explosion. Both were lifted off the concrete by the huge blast but most of the flame and debris was directed out of the slit.

Stunned the soldier let go of Franks legs and he fell to the ground in front of the bunker, breaking his arm in the process.

There was no sign of life from inside the bunker.

With Frank out of the action, the rest of the Commandos, led by their Lieutenant, continued south towards Bunker Hill to try and join up with the paratroopers. They left one man with Frank to escort him back down to where they were holding the German troops.

Across the bay, Tony Rihoy was guiding his commando platoon ashore in Jaonneuse Bay. They had landed on the rocks to avoid the barbed wire and potential mines on the small beach. After carefully cutting through the barbed wire around the top of the rocks, they approached the small fort at the end of the headland. All they found was a smoldering ruin.

There were a few German troops, most wounded to varying levels, sitting on the grass and they put up no fight, surrendering to the Commandos as soon as they appeared. Lieutenant Terry Wise took stock of the situation looking for targets. Across in L'Ancresse Bay the Landing Craft were emerging from the smoke screen on to the beach below where he stood.

As he watched the bunker in the corner of the bay opened up with its big gun. On top of the bunker an MG added its wicked sound to the gunfire. Wise was about to order his men to attack but the LCS nearest to where they stood opened up on the bunker sending fierce fire into that defensive position. Soon it had disappeared into a cloud of smoke and Wise realised just how exposed they were.

He pulled his men back from the land immediately above the beach in case they were mistaken for German troops.

Wise was not a man to sit on his heels. He looked at his map and knew there were bunkers and the big observation tower on Chouet headland further to the West. If he could secure the headland, it would prevent the potential for any attacks on the beachhead from that direction. With that goal in mind, the men set off with Rihoy in the lead, to secure the invaders right flank.

Their first target was the observation tower.

Wise and his platoon came under fire from gun slits in the tower as soon as they began their approach. Despite the thinning smoke screen, in the gathering light they were too easy to spot from the top of the tower.

Finding a convenient granite wall which offered some protection they set up the Bren and began to return fire, aiming for the gun slits.

Men with sniper rifles tried to take out anyone looking over the top of the tower and they too aimed at gun slits to suppress the enemy fire. At a signal from Wise, a section rushed to the bottom of the tower and made their way to the tower entrance. As on the other headland the first men to arrive fell to an MG firing through a slot positioned next to the heavy steel doorway.

Next two grenades were dropped from the tower and exploded amongst the men killing and wounding everyone in the section. Wise was devastated but he needed to get to the wounded, and he needed to secure the tower.

Grabbing two men with satchel bombs and with a shout of 'Cover me!' Wise and the two men rushed to the entrance to the tower. Bullets impacting the concrete above him caused a cloud of stone fragments and dust to erupt over their heads.

Both satchel bombs were armed and thrown against the heavy metal door.

Despite taking cover to one side of the entrance, the massive explosion deafened the men and knocked all three of them over, but the heroic act had done the trick. As the dust settled, they could see that the heavy metal door had been blown in. Wise and his men ran in before more grenades were thrown from above and took stock of the devastation inside.

It was not a pretty sight. The remains of three men were literally splattered around the walls and rubble lay everywhere. A runged ladder went up the centre of the tower and offered the only access to the higher levels. Wise lobbed a grenade up to the first level and as soon as it exploded followed it up. On that floor he found two gravely wounded soldiers. They were dressed in the uniform of the Kriegsmarine which gave him hope that the tower might not be filled with fanatical defenders.

That quickly passed as two grenades dropped down from the floor above, passing where he was positioned but exploding on the ground floor level killing the two commandos who had entered the tower with him.

Wise was stuck.

He had one grenade left, his Sten gun a handgun and a knife. Above him he could hear excited voices. He did not speak much German but it sounded as if they were having a full blown argument.

Taking a chance, he climbed a few rungs and lobbed his last grenade up to the next level, quickly jumping back down as the explosion wreaked havoc on the floor above.

Wise quickly took a glimpse up the tower and saw a face looking down at him.

He fired his Sten gun up towards the face which quickly pulled back.

A voice shouted 'Ich gebe auf!' (I surrender) and when he next looked a white scarf was being waved at the top of the ladder.

Wise drew on his smattering of German and shouted' Herunter kommen!' (Come down) up the tower.

With the guns silent, three more of his men were about to enter the base of the tower. They were surprised when eight Germans from the Kriegsmarine, with their hands on their head, were led out of the tower by Lieutenant Wise.

Assigning two men and a medic to guard the prisoners and look after the wounded, Wise and the remains of his platoon pushed on to engage the bunkers which looked out over Grand Havre Bay. Rihoy led the way.

*****

On the sands of L'Ancresse Bay the Hobarts had done a good job and though under fire had cleared large areas of the beach. Paths had been laid out to the gaps in the wall.

A few of the tanks had been hit and lay smoldering on the beach but they now had the support of some regular Churchill tanks. The issue was that the breaches in the wall, while sufficient for men to climb over, were not suitable for tanks to pass through - yet.

One of the Hobarts had a bobbin and approached one of the breaches to lay a path over the remains of the wall. Another equipped with a flame thrower attacked the bunker at the West end of the beach, finally putting that one out of action in a flash of orange amidst the white smoke and grey early morning light.

It was 5.45 am.

In the LCAs and LCIs approaching the beach, tension was reaching fever pitch. The smell of sweat, urine, fear and tension filled the boats, but no one was being sick anymore. In one LCA the whole platoon was singing Roll out the Barrel to raise spirits but their voices were drowned out by the gunfire.

The guns on each vessel chattered away as they emerged from the smoke, aiming at MG positions along the sea wall. With the tide out there was a lot of beach to cover and the men all knew they would have to sprint across a hundred yards of sand while the enemy did their best to stop them.

Anti-aircraft guns around the La Varde strongpoint fired down into the bay and several LCAs were in trouble, one sinking in the shallow water, another hit and turning off course, their crew having succumbed to the heavy fire from above the beaches.

Other's trailed smoke and were riddled with bullet holes from the heavier anti-aircraft guns. Inside those unlucky boats were scenes of carnage.

The three LCIs in the lead columns each included one of the Guernsey team amongst the 200 men they held. Colonel Bruce Mahy was in the centre LCI with four platoons of men from the Hampshires. One of them was Captain Ian Best.

Around the LCI, twelve LCAs had started the journey to the beach, each holding a platoon. Now ten made the final approach alongside the Hampshires mother ship.

Almost 1800 men in the first wave were ready and eager to get out of the tin cans as some men called them, where they had been cooped up for too many hours.

On Green beach to the Hampshire's right the Dorsetshires were taking more of a pounding as they were nearer La Varde Hill.

The LCI containing Colonel Harry Vaudin had taken several hits from the hill and had many casualties before they even reached the beach. They too had lost LCAs but the destruction of the bunker by the flame throwing tank and the demolition of the small fort on the headland by the aerial bombardment gave them a clearer route ashore. They just didn't know that yet.

Across on Red Beach the LCI containing Brigadier Mark Heaume was intact as was all but one of their LCAs. In the lead LCA was Lieutenant Derek Barber who was keen, almost desperate to get his Spears ashore first. They huddled down almost like 36 sprinters at the starting blocks ready to run a race. They just had no idea of what the track looked like.

The Spears didn't have long to wait as two minutes behind schedule at 5.47 am, Barber felt the LCA ground and heard a shout of 'Ramp down!'

The ramp at the front of the boat dropped on to the soft damp sand of L'Ancresse Bay.

The Spears piled out, taking in the devastation in front of them and the 100 yards of beach they had to cross to get to the sea wall. Smoke drifted across the bay as more smoke shells were fired from the landing craft but men fell almost as soon as they hit the beach.

Barber leapt on to the beach and shouted, 'Come on the Spears!' The men ran after him as fast as could with their heavy packs and guns, more than one stumbling in the sand.

Across the beach other Landing craft were disgorging their troops on to the sand and shouts and whistles joined the cacophony of sound as the men raced as fast as they could towards the wall.

Behind the anti-tank wall German gunners were petrified to see the sheer number of men and machines heading their way but most stood firm and fired into the mass of men on the beach taking a heavy toll.

On Blue Beach Lieutenant Colonel Roy Phillips was the first senior officer to walk out on the sand from the Hamphires LCI.

Wearing his trademark beret and smoking a pipe he carried his swagger stick and nothing else as he stood in the middle of the beach taking stock of the situation. Troops ran past him and one fell right in front of him. He walked over and helped him up.

'Come on son, no time for a lie down now.'

'Yes sir,' came the frightened reply, and the young soldier continued his run up the beach.

Nice place for a stroll, Phillips thought to himself and started his leisurely walk across the beach as bullets, explosions and sand flew all around him.

When the ramps went down to let the spearhead platoons of the Dorsetshires on to Green beach they quickly realised that the best place for them to be was in the lee of the wall. The rocks to their right offered no protection so they rushed as quickly as they could towards the gap that the Lancasters had created.

One of Hobart's bulldozer style Funnies was busy clearing the area near the breach when two grenades were thrown over the wall and blew one its tracks off. With no gun the tank was helpless. The crew had no chance of getting out safely so just had to sit and hope that they survived until after the wall was taken.

Five minutes after the first ramps had gone down men were starting to gather at the base of the wall and exchanges of grenades started to take their toll on the defenders as well as the attackers. Most of the MG positions were still intact as men naturally shied away from running straight at the guns.

Those now in the lee of the wall tried to make their way to where the guns were based and when they could threw grenades in their direction but the sand bags around the temporary emplacements offered protection against anything except a direct hit.

One tank on Red beach pushed through the gap using the reinforced base created by the bobbin and German troops protecting the breach scattered. It had just cleared the gap when more grenades and a round from a Panzerfaust, the German equivalent of the PIAT, put the tank out of commission. The crew bailed out into a fusillade of rapid fire from the defenders who had regained their composure as soon as they saw the tank billowing smoke.

Seizing the opportunity some of the Spears pushed through the gap and returned fire at the German troops who were out in the open. Using the still burning tank as protection they cleared the immediate area around the breach and using PIATs took out the temporary positions on either side of the gap in the wall. The anti-tank wall was breached and the Devonshires were the first regular infantry on L'Ancresse Common.

*****

On the common, Company B of the Paras had been devastated by their drop into the minefield but they weren't finished. They had lost several men in the initial drop but Major Bridle had survived and he had done his best to assess the capability of his unit.

Bridle had to be very careful as did all the survivors in his unit as wires and mines were everywhere. They had established a few safe paths through the minefield and around a hundred men had been accounted for. They had eventually found a way out on the eastern side of the maze of mines just as the Panzer, smoking from the encounter with Company A trundled towards them.

Bridle called for their surviving PIAT and one of his Paratroopers crawled out into the open to get as close as he could to the approaching tank. When the Panzer was parallel to where he lay he got up into a kneeling position and from less than 30 yards away hit the Panzer just rear of centre.

The machine exploded in a ball of flame knocking the Paratrooper flying on to his back. Bridle raced over to check he was OK and was rewarded with a smile.

'That went up a treat Sir!'

The Paratrooper was shouting as he had been deafened by the blast. Bridle held him down as he wasn't convinced the lad was OK to stand.

'You rest there for a minute son, you did a great job. How's your head?'

'Ringing like a bell Sir!' Bridle checked him over and smiled. 'You'll be fine son, just stay there until the headache goes down a bit.'

With that he crept back to the edge of the minefield and waved his men out. He sent a Lance Corporal to stay with the young PIAT operator. Bridle ordered a Corporal with a couple of men to double back to the Vale Church and let Colonel Krimp know they were back in the game and were heading to La Varde.

Bridle led one column up alongside the minefield and ordered one of his two Lieutenants to take two platoons and cross the road and secure the crossroads in the centre of the common, if it hadn't been secured already. Lieutenant Geoff Ayling saluted and led his men across the road and worked his way towards the remains of Edith Le Page's cottage.

Once there he set up a defensive position with his Bren team and their one remaining PIAT. The cottage was totally devastated, and they found Edith's remains in what must have been the bedroom of the property.

Carefully they pulled down some tattered curtains and gently covered her body.

The bouncing bomb had left quite a crater when it blew up the cottage and the men worked hard using rubble from the cottage walls to create a defensible position and settled down to see if any business came their way.

Major Bridle reached the bottom of the hill alongside a track that led up to La Varde. The guard post was unmanned though a barrier of barbed wire had been dragged across to block the road. All the action at the top of the hill was being directed at the beach so few positions that were undamaged were facing the Paratroopers. Two of his men were sent forward to drag the barrier to one side but as they struggled to move it, an MG in a Tobruk pit near the top of the hill started to fire at them. They both fell, one dead and the other badly wounded.

Bridle was horrified to see the gun fire continue as the wounded man tried to crawl behind the guard house. Eventually the gunner found his target and the young paratrooper didn't move again.

Most of his troops had seen the man die and their thirst for revenge welled up to fever pitch. Bridle looked around. There was precious little cover up the hill and just a few rocky outcrops to give them some protection. He was currently behind one of those, not that far from where Lieutenant Ayling was setting up his defensive position.

There was a hundred yards of open land between him and the crater where Ayling was based. He called over his second in command, Lieutenant Brian Budwin and told him his plan.

'Brian, if I can get over to Ayling's position and get him to give us covering fire with the Bren it might give us the chance to get up to that position. Can you get half the boys to cover me as I make a dash for it and get the others to spread out towards the West and see if they can find a blind spot to get through the wire and up the hill?'

Budwin protested straight away and offered to make the run himself, but Bridle was insistent. He dumped his pack and rifle and headed as close as could to the edge of the rock while Budwin organised the troops.

Budwin turned and nodded to Bridle when he was ready. Bridle waved and with that Budwin ordered his men to open fire. The ground around the Tobruk pit erupted with shells from Company B's best shots as Bridle set off like a hare towards the crater.

At the same time a platoon advanced along the road which ran parallel to the base of the hill towards the headland where Lieutenant Wise and his Commandos were mopping up the last of the bunkers.

The troops at the top of the hill ignored Bridle and tried to bring their MG to bear on the troops running along the road but the covering fire was so good they had little chance to find a target.

Bridle jumped into the crater. By then Ayling's men were adding their guns to the covering fire from Budwin's troops. Once the flanking troops were out of sight of the MG on the hill firing stopped. Ayling repositioned the Bren to sight it on the MG's position and produced a pair of binoculars to see exactly what was happening on the ridge. He passed them to Bridle who also scanned the ridge.

The whole hill was a scene of devastation, but they could hear some guns on the far side of the hill that were firing down towards the beach and were certain the landings must be taking place. As if to remind them that the fight wasn't over the MG sent a few rounds in their direction and one man ran from the Tobruk pit back towards the bunkers to alert his commander of the attack on their rear and get more ammunition.

Bridle picked up the binoculars again and looked to the left of La Varde. He could just make out some of his men working their way through the barbed wire, getting ever closer to the top of the hill.

Looking across to the position he had just left he could see Lieutenant Budwin waiting for his orders. He checked the Bren gunners were ready and gave them the nod. At a range of about 300 yards the Bren was quite accurate. The gunners laid a few rounds on the position as sighters, they were ready.

Seeing they had the range correct Bridle gave the word to open fire, as he did so he waved to Budwin and half of his troops opened fire. As they were firing, Budwin and the rest of his men rushed the guard post, dragged the barbed wire gate away and then spread out into the open ground below the gun position. They began crawling up the hill towards the MG.

The two remaining troops in the Tobruk pit threw grenades down the hill and two more of Bridle's men were instantly killed Grenades were thrown back and exploded just in front of the pit. Suddenly gun fire from the flanking troops started to pepper the emplacement and the Germans realised they would be overwhelmed and put up their hands in surrender.

But furious with the way their wounded comrade had been treated no quarter was given and the firing didn't stop until both men in the pit were killed.

The third member of the team came running back carrying ammunition boxes but slid to a halt when he saw the Paratroopers standing over his colleagues.

He tried to turn to run but was too slow and was gunned down before he had covered ten yards.

Lieutenant Budwin was the first officer on the scene. He looked down at the men in the pit and then at his men. They were waiting for some type of admonishment, but none came.

'Well done boys,' he said quietly and moved on over the brow of the hill to scout the position. He had to keep low as shells from the beach were still peppering the top of La Varde. He reached a position where he could see the beaches and watch the battle unfold. Major Bridle scampered up alongside him and together they discussed what to do next.

From where they crouched, they watched as clouds of smoke drifting across the beaches. In breaks in the smoke, they could see dozens of Landing Craft in the bay with more coming in all the time. Men were streaming up the beach but German defenders behind the anti-tank wall were still creating havoc.

They could see a burning tank that had just made it off Red Beach and around it soldiers were starting to pour through the gap in the wall. The other gaps were still being defended by hastily built gun positions.

Looking around the hill, they could see anti-aircraft guns that were still firing towards the beaches and noted there were more trenches around the top of the hill that were well defended.

Fighting by the anti-tank wall was getting desperate as the defenders took steady casualties and were not being reinforced.

Bridle and Budwin agreed it was too dangerous to try and attack the emplacements on the hill now as there was so much fire coming in from the vessels in the bay, they were just as likely to fall to friendly fire as from enemy fire.

It was decided to set up a perimeter around the top of the south side of the hill in case any German troops tried to retreat to the south. If a ground assault was made from the beaches, they would then be able to attack the enemy from the rear.

Bridle sent a couple of runners back to Ayling's position and to the Vale Church to make sure everyone knew that Company B had reached the top of La Varde. He wished he still had his radio operator.

Bridle didn't like the idea of sitting on his hands but without a radio he felt unable to get involved in case he and his men put themselves in the wrong position. All he could do was watch and wait.

*****

In his Headquarters in the Royal Hotel GeneralMajor Von Graf was furious. Information was sketchy and he had lost touch with the Northern strongholds, the Mirus battery had stopped firing and many of the West Coast strongholds had been heavily damaged. He had a report from the Baubigny Arsenal that the reserve platoon had lost touch with Hauptmann Wagner.

Von Graf assumed the worst. The British must have invaded at L'Ancresse, just as Rommel predicted.

The Kommandant looked out of the window and could see smoke billowing from Brehon Tower. Below him trucks and troops from Fort George were lined up awaiting orders. They looked fresh and invincible. He decided to push them North to link up with the remaining Panzers, then together they would push on towards L'Ancresse and regain control of the North of the Island.

Walking quickly downstairs and out of the front of the hotel he walked across to meet Oberst Volker. Volker saluted smartly as Von Graf approached. Von Graf quickly appraised him of the situation.

'You must regain control of the North, Volker, at all costs. We must push these invaders back into the sea where they belong. I will divert the second regiment to give you support. Meet up with the Panzers and bring all your forces to bear on the invaders. We are mustering troops to the West and East of L'Ancresse and together you will push the British on three sides and force them back on to the beaches. Is that clear?'

'Yes, Herr GeneralMajor.'

'God speed Volter,' Von Graf added and with a quick salute walked back into the hotel. Orders were given and trucks started their engines. By the time he returned to his Ops room the trucks were approaching Salarie Corner to the North of St Peter Port and his troops were marching away.

Von Graf watched them until they had all disappeared. As he looked North, he noticed the flash of guns and realised a British Destroyer was approaching, firing on gun emplacements on the North of the Island as it sailed towards him. He could see the odd shot was being returned but largely the fire was light and ineffective.

The ship moved on, sailing past Brehon Tower. Keeping well offshore it slowed down opposite where he stood and started flashing a message.

He called to one of his aides and asked if he could find someone to read the signal.

One of his radio operators was brought into the Ops room. Von Graf offered him his binoculars and the Aide spelled out the message.

'S U R R E N D E R'

The aide offered the glasses back to Von Graf. 'They are just repeating the word Herr Kommandant.'

Von Graf smiled and turned to his Aide and the Radio Operator

'Contact the commander on Castle Cornet and tell him to engage with that ship. That will give them my answer.'

'Yes Herr GeneralMajor.' Together the two men hurried from the room as Von Graf waited to see what the answer would be to his reply. He was confident the ship would not fire on the town of St Peter Port because it would endanger the civilian population but he wasn't sure about the Castle and Harbour which had both escaped unscathed from the earlier bombardments.

Guns on the Castle opened fire and the sea around the destroyer erupted but no fire was returned. Instead, the Destroyer headed further away until it was out of effective range and then waited. The simple message was repeated every 10 minutes.

S U R R E N D E R.

For the first time Von Graf had doubts about the outcome of the battle.

He sat down and started to write reports to be sent to Jersey and France, appraising his Commanders and the Kommandant of Jersey of the situation. He did not appeal for help as he knew the invasion of France was under way and support of any kind would not be forthcoming. All he could rely on were the resources he had on the Island.

Even if they won the day in Guernsey, if France fell, he realised they would be left on their own. Already his forces were battered and bruised from the aerial bombardment, could they recover sufficiently to hold on until the British and Americans were pushed back out of France, if they were pushed out of France?

Not one to normally doubt himself the reality was that food would soon run out, injured men would die through shortages of medical supplies and they would be vulnerable to further attacks as there would be no replacement guns or munitions.

Sitting back in his chair he looked up at the portrait of Hitler.

Remembering Rommel's words, he asked the empty room.

'Are you the best man to run our country? We should have never invaded Russia then all this wouldn't be happening.'

Angrily he picked up a glass from his desk and threw it at the portrait.

Hearing the crash an Aide knocked on the door and put his head around to see if Von Graf was alright. 'Get out!' was his reward and he hurriedly shut the door and returned to his desk.

The clock on Von Graf's desk ticked its way past 7 am.

*****

In France the beaches looked similar to L'Ancresse in Guernsey. Dead bodies lay everywhere as well as burned out tanks and landing craft. Troops had made the dash across the sand and were engaging the defenders on the four main beaches. Three on this side of the Cotentin and one on the Normandy side. Paratroopers fought for their lives to stop the scattered attempts at reinforcing the defences around Cherbourg.

The Americans on East Beach suffered the worst. They did not have the support of Hobart's Funnies and had suffered as a result from the minefields on the beach and the barbed wire defences. Air and Naval support had done their best, but many bunkers were still intact and caused the troops serious casualties. Their bravery was undeniable as men battled their way towards the defences and by 7.30 am a small beachhead had been secured but many men were still stuck on the beaches sheltering from enemy fire.

On West Beach for the Americans and Brighton Beach and Blackpool Beach for the British, the Funnies had done their job brilliantly and a much larger Beachhead had been achieved. Armour was already in the fields and scrub land behind the beaches and by 7.30 am troops were pushing on towards Cherbourg. More troops were heading South and East to make contact with the Paratroopers to cut off the headland completely. Overlord was working, albeit at a heavy cost.

Commander of the British Naval forces, Admiral Ramsay, had noted that the shelling from Guernsey had stopped and had reported that back to General Morgan who in turn let General Hood know. Hood was on a Cruiser off Guernsey's North coast and had been desperate to know what was happening on the Island. Hood was glad to hear that at least part of the plan had worked.

Hood stood on the Bridge of the Cruiser with the Captain who was peering through a large pair of binoculars focused on the beaches. He was trying to get a glimpse of the action through the smoke.

'Any news from the beaches yet?'

It was a rhetorical question as if there had been any news, Hood was sure they would have passed it on.

'Nothing by radio Sir, but the smoke is clearing and from what I can see the men are just clearing the beach but are still under fire from La Varde Hill. The forts on either side of the bay seem quiet but the defenders at the top of the beach are putting up quite a fight.'

He passed the binoculars to Hood who studied the beaches as best he could, but it was hard to tell what was happening.

'I need to get closer. Can you transfer me to one of the LCIs?'

'Orders are that you stay here until the beachhead is secure Sir.'

'I know, but this is war Captain, and situations change.'

The captain thought for a second and smiled. 'Guess if I were you, I'd be itching to get closer to my men too. I'll arrange a transfer.'

He nodded to one of the bridge crew who escorted General Hood off the bridge and down to the deck as one the larger LCI's was called across. He was tied into a breeches buoy and as soon as the line was secured Hood was zip lined across to the LCI.

Within minutes he was safely aboard the large Landing Craft and moving towards the beaches with what was scheduled to be the last wave of landings.

*****

Lieutenant Colonel Roy Phillips walked up to the top of Blue beach where over a hundred of his troops were sheltering in the lee of the wall.

Two machine gun emplacements protected by sandbags, housing half a dozen men in each, were located either side of a small breach in the anti-tank wall caused by one of the bouncing bombs.

A large crater was at the base of the broken wall making access difficult. The German troops had been throwing grenades over the wall as well as using their MGs and dozens of dead or wounded were laid out in front of the two positions. A tank had also tried to support the troops, but a Panzerfaust had put paid to that effort and it sat silent on the sand with a dozen or more men hiding behind it.

Standing seemingly impervious to the bullets flying around him Phillips spoke to a Sergeant.

'Are we waiting for a bus Sergeant?'

Some of the men laughed while the Sergeant shook his head. Phillips puffed on his pipe, but it had gone out. He bent down and tapped it on a rock and then took some tobacco from his pocket and filled the pipe bowl.

'Anyone got a match?' One soldier eased himself down the pebbles which lay against the base of the wall and pulled out a box of matches and struck it, sheltering the flame with a practised hand. Phillips bent down as bullets sprayed into the sand behind where he stood and sucked the flame into the pipe producing a satisfying cloud of smoke.

He looked around and spoke to the men in front of him.

'Well, we can't stay here all day. He pointed to one of the men. 'Son, can I borrow a couple of your grenades?'

The soldier unhooked them from his belt.

'Here you go Colonel, I don't want them back.' This got another laugh from some of the men. Phillip handed his swagger stick to the Sergeant with a 'hold this for a minute will you' and started to practice a rather exaggerated bowling motion as if he was warming up for a Sunday afternoon cricket match.

He then took the pin out of the grenade and took a short run towards the defensive emplacement to the left of the breach and bowled the grenade straight over the wall into the middle of the sandbags. He immediately repeated the feat and the MG position fell silent.

His men looked at him stunned. He took back his swagger stick from the Sergeant.

'Well come on then lads, up and at 'em!'

The small breach in the wall was still being protected by German troops and the men in the emplacement on the far side of the breach but now the fire had been halved by the Colonel's action. The Sergeant led his men along the base of the wall and then tossed a couple of his own grenades through the breach. The resultant explosions put a stop to all resistance around the gap in the wall and the remains of his platoon clambered through.

The gun emplacement on the far side continued to put up some resistance and more men, including the sergeant, fell to persistent rifle fire, but grenades soon silenced that emplacement too and the way was clear.

Phillips ordered some of his men to work on filling up the crater with stones and sand. Once he was happy with job, he waved the rest of his men through and with a cheer the Hampshires poured into the open ground behind the wall.

Down at the water's edge, empty Landing Craft were pulling away to make room for the second wave which was already coming ashore. Troops, tanks, and assorted vehicles swarmed across the beaches under the watchful eyes of the beach marshalls. Fire from the East of the beach had ceased all together but the stronghold on La Varde stubbornly continued to target the beaches. The rate of fire was a lot less than when they first hit the beaches but from time to time the gunners got lucky and men and vehicles would falter and fall.

The Devonshires pushed off the beach and met up with the Paratroopers of Company C on Bunker Hill as well as the Commandos who had come ashore at Fort Le Marchant. Together they set up a perimeter ready to face any attack from the East.

Churchill tanks headed towards the crossroads in the centre of the common with flail tanks in the lead to make sure that the area was clear of mines. There they met Lieutenant Ayling who updated their commander on the current situation.

The Lieutenant also explained that the Paratroopers were holding a line around the Vale Church and the remains of Company B were at the top of La Varde hill on the South side ready to attack the remaining emplacements as soon as the shelling from the beach stopped.

With resistance along the wall at an end the Dorsetshires pushed off the beaches and spread West, meeting up with Lieutenant Wise and the remains of his Commando unit that had taken Chouet Headland. The result was that La Varde was surrounded.

Troops were moving into position to assault the hill and Lieutenant Colonel Phillips, after taking stock of the situation, radioed the Naval contingent and called for a ceasefire from the LCS's in the bay. Reacting to the ceasefire the guns on La Varde fell silent too.

Phillips obtained a white cloth and attached it to his swagger stick and started to walk up the hill towards the German defences. The only sound was the noise of tanks moving off the beaches behind him and a skylark, which despite all the death and destruction around it, decided that was the moment to soar into the air above the yellow gorse and grassland at the base of the hill.

He walked past the first gun emplacement watched by the German soldiers in that position and before getting much further was approached by a young, injured Hauptmann who had walked down to meet him from the top of the hill. The man had his arm in a sling.

Phillips saluted the young man who was unable to salute back. He smiled.

Recognising the insignia, he spoke to him in German.

'Herr Hauptmann, you have fought bravely but your men are surrounded. We have overwhelming force and are ready to attack. No more men need to die here on this beautiful day. If you surrender now your men will be treated with honour and respect and your wounded will receive medical attention. Do you agree to surrender now?'

The young Hauptmann looked around at his shattered defences. He had around 100 men still alive on the hill, many of them wounded. He looked down the hill at the approaching tanks and the continuous stream of men and machines coming ashore from the Landing Craft. He knew they were finished.

Many of his men were coming out of their bunkers and he saw several throw down their guns. They had done their best and they had no fight left in them.

The Hauptmann came to attention as best he could. He had a Luger in a holster attached to his belt. He carefully took it out and turned it around in his hand and gave it to Phillips. In English he replied.

'You have our surrender, Herr Colonel.'

Phillips tucked the pistol in his belt and shook the man's good hand.

'Good man, good man. Now get your men to leave their weapons and lead them down the hill and we'll get you off this Island to somewhere safe. You put up a good fight Herr Hauptmann. Maybe we'll have a drink together after this is all over.'

'I'd like that Herr Colonel, thank you.'

Phillips turned and left the Hauptmann to organise his troops and soon a column of German troops walked down the hill towards the beaches, some men supporting injured colleagues, others bandaged and bleeding. As they walked, they passed the men of the Devonshires who looked fresh and fit. A few offered the Germans cigarettes which were gratefully received.

Across the beaches and on La Vardes the British had captured over 200 men and they were being organised and loaded into an empty LCI to be transported away from the Island.

On the common, Phillips and the commanders of the Devonshires and Dorsetshires established a Head Quarters near the L'Ancresse crossroads. An observation point was set up on top of La Vardes hill to look out for any German troops moving in their direction. The defences put in place by Krimp near the Vale Church were reinforced. His exhausted Paratroopers were sent back from the front to regroup and rest until the next push began. Krimp himself had fully recovered, apart from his broken arm.

It had just gone 8am.

Seeing the danger, the residents of the cottages along the military road were in, Colonel Bruce Mahy of the Hampshires arranged for them to be moved from their houses. The people living in the cottages between the Vale Church and L'Ancresse common were asked to take them in until the battle moved on into the interior of the Island.

They were not the only ones to realise that the British had landed. Across the Island the local population were woken by the gunfire and air raids and they had guessed an invasion had begun.

In his cottage near Bordeaux Harbour, Rob Heaume and his family were saying a quiet prayer for his brother and all the other troops who were risking their lives to bring freedom back to the Island.

Rob and many others wished they could do something to help but without weapons and seriously weakened by years of occupation there was little most people could do except keep out of the way.

However, some defiant gestures were made with trees being felled to try and block roads and hinder the German troop movements. Even a couple of telegraph poles were chopped down to impair their communications. But the main show of defiance came as British flags were flown from hundreds of windows across all the Islands parishes.

In the cottages behind the Vale Church men and women offered what food they had to the troops and in some cases helped treat the wounded. Smiles abounded amongst those few that were already freed, but all knew there was a long road ahead.

In his hastily erected HQ, Phillips and his colleagues looked at maps of the Island and considered their next move. Colonel Krimp, arm in a sling, was with them and Phillips asked if his men were good to carry out another mission.

'They've just had some tea and dog food Colonel so are ready and willing, just point us in the right direction.'

'We need intelligence, and we need to get to the seafront here.' Phillips said pointing to the Northern end of Belle Greve Bay which was the other side of Delancey Park.

'If we can cut off the whole of the Northeast of the Island along a line roughly centred on the Military Road, over this hill and down to the coast, St Sampsons Harbour will be ours. We can then push towards St Peter Port and cut the head off the snake.'

He drew a line from L'Islet straight across the map to Belle Greve bay.

There were a lot of nods around the table.

'We'll be your eyes Sir,' Krimp offered, and Phillips shook his hand. 'Good man. Are you sure you are OK to lead your men?'

'I'll be fine Sir; I still have one good arm and over 400 good men.'

Phillips took a big puff from his pipe and savoured the taste.

'OK, once you are on your way we'll advance slowly down the military road and across towards the Gigands, here,' he added, pointing towards the Baubigny Arsenal area.

'Once you have reached the coast and have given us the nod, we'll then push to the coast near these Gas Works.'

'You can rely on us Sir. Happy hunting.'

With that Colonel Krimp headed out to rejoin his men.

THE BIG PUSH

General Hood waded ashore and looked around.

'Bloody hell,' he swore as he scanned the devastation on the beaches.

The scene looked like his version of Armageddon. Acrid smoke still drifted across from the burning bunker on the West side of the beach and from several burning vehicles. Medics tended wounded men where they lay while some were being stretchered back on to the Landing Craft. Men were checking the bodies which lay everywhere, and the dead were being lifted on to vehicles and taken back to the vessels for repatriation to England.

Columns of men and vehicles were still moving ashore under the strict control of beach marshalls who were using whistles and flags to move vehicles and men off the beach. He went over to the nearest marshall and tapped him on the back.

Without looking around the man shouted. 'What do you want? Can't you see I'm busy!'

'If it's not too much trouble I'd like to know where I could find Lieutenant Colonel Phillips?'

The beach marshall looked round and saw the Major General's lapel badges and snapped to attention. "Begging your pardon Sir. The Colonel is in his HQ on the common Sir. Shall I find you a guide?'

General Hood smiled. 'Just point me the right direction Corporal and I'll find my own way.'

'Yes sir. Head for that gap in the wall and keep walking straight ahead. You can't miss it. There's a field station next to his tent.'

'Thank you, Corporal, carry on.' Hood saluted the corporal and marched up the beach in the direction the Corporal had indicated.

When he passed through the breach in the wall, he could see British bodies and German bodies lined up along the base of the wall. Craters were everywhere, as were the burnt stains caused by explosions. Patches of blood were smeared on the wall. For a moment Hood stood taking it all in, it seemed eerily quiet.

Next to a lost battle, nothing is so sad as a battle that has been won, he thought to himself paraphrasing Wellington after Waterloo.

Looking across to the western end of the bay he could see a column of German prisoners being guided into one of the large landing craft.

'The lucky ones', he muttered to himself before turning and striking out across L'Ancresse Common towards what was obviously the centre of all the activity.

Jeeps, trucks, and tanks were buzzing all over the landscape around him as he walked across towards the tent. Two guards were standing outside and went to block him but stood back when they saw who it was.

'Knock, knock.'

The men inside looked up from the maps they were pouring over and smiled.

'General, welcome to Guernsey.' Phillips said, walking across to General Hood shaking his hand. 'Couldn't wait, eh?' He added.

'Didn't want to miss out on all the fun Roy. How's it going?'

Phillips invited him over to the table and talked him through the current position.

'It was tough General, make no bones about it, but the boys did well, especially the Paras, but we'd expect nothing less. I have just sent Colonel Krimp on a scouting trip towards the East coast. We've got observers on the hill and on top of the Vale Church over there.'

'I know where it is Colonel, I was christened there.'

Phillips smiled.

'Well, you'll be pleased to know it is one piece, for now, and we have some wounded in there. The people from those cottages are making the boys at home and helping the men where they can. We are also seeing if they have any useful information for us about Jerry and where they might be coming from.'

The radio operator interrupted the discussion.

'Sir, the observers on the hill report movement. We have six or more Panzers supported by trucks full of troops heading towards us from the South. The trucks are on the Military Road.'

'Thank you, Sergeant.'

Phillips turned to General Hood. 'Do you want to take over General?'

'No Roy, you have done brilliantly, you carry on. You are closer to the men right now and know your dispositions. I'll be here if you need a sounding board.'

Phillips turned back to the assembled officers. Colonel Harry Vaudin, Colonel Bruce Mahy and Brigadier Mark Heaume of the Guernsey Team where in the tent along with Major Colin Chauvel of the Royal Armoured Corps. The commanders of the three Infantry Brigades were also present and for a moment Hood wondered about the group dynamics.

On the way to the tent Hood had happened across Captain Best who had come in with the second wave. Best had told him about the way Phillips had secured the surrender of the garrison on La Varde and how he was an inspiration to the troops.

'Gentlemen, one last thing. I am pleased to announce that with immediate effect Lieutenant Colonel Phillips is promoted to Brigadier and is now the officer in charge of the campaign. He will report directly to me.'

'Thank you General, but if I may...' Phillips pointed at the map and puffed at his pipe, ignoring his field promotion.

'Sorry Roy, carry on.'

'If I was the German Commander I would try and pin us down in this pocket. That means we should be expecting company from the East and the West as well as from the South. I would like the 69th Infantry Brigade to take over the position on Bunker Hill and protect us against any attacks from the East. I want the 151st to secure our right flank and establish defences here at the base of Grand Havre.

The 231st with the Hampshires, Devonshires and Dorsetshires will confront the attack from the south. Major Chauvel can you bring your tanks and guns to bear on this advance now and I'll get the Navy to supply some extra firepower into this area to back you up.' Phillips pointed to the open land towards the Braye Road.

'Gentlemen let's get this job finished. I want to be in St Peter Port by early afternoon.'

The members of his team headed out to get their forces into position and the coordinates for the Naval strike were radioed to the Navy.

Phillips asked the Guernsey team to stay behind.

'Once we get into St Peter Port, I will be depending on you Gentlemen to meet with the local officials and make sure we control the population as much as we can until we have the German surrender. Be ready to step in whenever you can. Is that clear?'

'Yes Brigadier,' Vaudin replied with a smile. 'But the first drink in the Royal Hotel is on you.'

They all laughed and left to join their units.

Captain Best walked into the tent as the others were leaving. 'General, I have someone here who is keen to see you.'

With that Captain Walter Larch, the American Liaison Officer, entered the tent and saluted General Hood.

'Captain, welcome aboard,' Hood came over and shook his hand. 'I trust your trip was comfortable?'

'Tolerable General, thanks to being last to arrive on the beach but my men are outside and ready to help where we can. I see the first wave took a bit of a battering.'

Captain Larch was introduced to newly promoted Brigadier Phillips and Roy took a minute to bring him up to speed with the plan. As they finished, they heard a report from one of the tanks and soon after the air above them was ripped apart as the Navy opened fire.

'Roy we'll leave you to it, Captain, I suggest we get up to La Varde and observe the battle from the top of the hill. Bring your men and they can assess the German fortifications while we are there. That might come in useful in other places.'

Phillips barely looked up as Hood left the tent with the American. His aides and radio operator took their places bringing reports from the various sectors to the Brigadier and soon the tent was a hive of activity. More shellfire and gunfire came from the south of his position; he knew battle had been joined.

*****

Major Chauvel had mustered half of his available tanks on the common land just north of the Vale Church and was waiting for orders. He had also brought forward some artillery pieces.

Brigadier John Hart overall Commander of the 231st infantry Brigade was standing on the sandbags where Colonel Krimp had overcome the former German position. He was looking down the Military Road at the German column heading his way. Major Chauvel stood with him using his binoculars to watch the enemy movements.

In the open land to their right, Hart could see a row of Panzers supported by half a dozen Renault tanks. As he was watching the tanks opened fire. He just had time to shout take cover as the ground in front of where he stood erupted with explosions. In response one of Major Chauvel's two pounder guns opened fire quickly followed by five more that he had lined up along the road to the south of the Vale Church.

One of the shells dropped in front of the column of trucks and they ground to an immediate halt, German troops spilled out of the trucks into the road and into the land behind the tanks. Seconds later the air above where they stood reverberated as the massive shells of the Navy flew over them and fell amongst the advancing tanks.

Hart turned to Colonel Bruce Mahy who had walked up to stand next to him. 'One hell of an opening gambit eh Colonel?'

'Not bad sir, not bad at all.'

'Guess we'd better get ready to dance. Are the Hampshires in position?'

'Aye, Brigadier, raring to go.'

'Good, let the big guns have their fun and then we'll send your boys in as soon as I get the go from Brigadier Phillips.'

He turned to his Radio Operator, 'Jack, get the 151st on the blower. I want them to push the 6th Battalion of the Durhams on to Jerry's flank as soon as the shelling stops.'

'Aye Sir.'

He turned back to Bruce. 'Is there open land behind those cottages on the left?'

'Yes Sir.'

Hart thought for a moment. 'We should push some men into that area in case they try to flank us. Jack, call up the Devonshires, I want some men in the fields behind those cottages.'

'Righty oh Sir,' Jack replied and was back on the Radio.

Soon men from the Devonshires started pouring past their position and into the land behind the cottages.

Shell fire was being exchanged all the time and one round from a Panzer exploded against a wall about 20 yards in front of where they were standing.

Hart shouted across to Major Chauvel. 'Colin, let's invite the Churchills to the party shall we.'

'Yes Sir!' he shouted back.

Chauvel turned and ran back to the twenty Churchill tanks that were waiting opposite the cottages to the North of the Vale Church and gave them a wave. Engines started across the group and the lead tank rolled forward, avoiding the burnt-out panzers and past where Brigadier Hart stood. They then turned right, breaking through the wall opposite the cottages, veering off the Military Road and rolled into the open land.

As they were effectively below the two pounders in the road they created the opportunity for a combined fusillade against the approaching German tanks. As the range narrowed both sides started to take damage.

The Naval bombardment ceased as the British tanks rolled south and the Hampshires and Dorsetshires were moved forward to provide close support for the Churchills, and engage enemy infantry when in range.

A tank battle ensued as Panzers took on Churchills. Amongst the tanks, men fought, sometimes hand to hand. Greenhouses caused as many injuries as bullets and shells as some of the fighting took place in and around many of the vineries as they were known on the Island.

The battle was at a stalemate for at least half an hour as casualties mounted on both sides, but the superior number of Churchills started to tell and when the Devonshires who had been unopposed on the enemies right started to move in to flank the German troops the momentum briefly moved in the attacker's favour. It was then that the German troops who had walked to the battle arrived, and Von Graf sprung his pincer movement.

His second regiment arrived from the West supported by troops that had survived in the West Coast strongholds while troops from the Vale Castle and the Bordeaux strongholds arrived through a variety of routes making a big push against 69th on bunker hill. In places they surprised the troops on the common by appearing between greenhouses and from the many small lanes that ran through that area of the North of the Island.

General Hood, from his place on the hill, spotted the threat and led Captain Larch and his men down the hill to help defend the HQ tent and the Field hospital.

Troops resting on the common after their landings were quickly mobilised and pushed towards the fast moving and often vague perimeter. Across the North of the Island battle was joined by virtually every unit now in Guernsey.

On the far side of Bunker Hill German troops were streaming forward from Fort Doyle on the Northeast tip of the Island, joined by troops from the East coast strongholds. They had little mechanical support, just two small Renault tanks, but they did have several PAK 36 mobile guns that had been hastily hitched to trucks and sent to the front line.

These were set up quickly and started to pour fire into the defences that were now manned by the 69th on Bunker Hill. Mobile artillery was still being brought up by the 86th Field Regiment of the Royal Artillery who had brought with them eight quick firing 6 pounders. That meant in the initial stages of the battle the 69th had to fight with what they could carry.

The small Renault tanks spearheaded the attack from the North East, pushing across the common land, firing at the hastily built defences. PIATs did their best to take out the tanks but they were a small target. Three of the six pounders were man handled to the top of the hill with a lot of effort while the other three were positioned to counter any attacks from the East via the road from La Moye.

Men laboured and cursed as the guns on top of the hill were rolled into position. One fell to a PAK 36 before it had fired a shot but the other two were positioned successfully and were soon living up to their quick firing reputation and the PAK 36's were soon destroyed.

German troops following the remaining Renault tank reached the allied lines and soon hand to hand fighting broke out on top of the hill. The British Brens took their toll on the advancing troops and the appearance of Bren carriers helped stem the tide. Bunker Hill was held. Just.

The German troops pulled back and regrouped taking up positions to harass and pin down the British lines.

At the same time to the South of the hill more troops moved forward to try and flank the defenders, but the six pounders destroyed a truck full of troops and halted the main thrust from that direction. The German troops were not about to give up and spread out to attack in loose order, firing when they could. The six pounders were well protected by several platoons of the Green Howards and try as they might the German troops could not get close enough to silence the guns. They tried to use Panzerfausts but could not find their targets.

German troops, working their way through the maze of lanes and tracks started to engage the beachhead from the marshy land to the south of the eastern side of the common. Bringing up MGs they caused chaos in the unprotected ranks and were threatening to engulf the HQ tent.

Troops in the crater where Edith Le Page's cottage had stood tried to engage the Germans that were attacking them while more German troops swept around the back of her cottage to try and flank them. At the height of the battle bullets ripped into the HQ tent.

Captain Larch arrived in the nick of time. He and his men pushed past the tent to take on the closest of the German troops. General Hood ran into the tent expecting to find Brigadier Phillips in a pool of blood. Instead he found the Brigadier still pouring over his maps and relaying orders to his radio operator who was sensibly lying on the floor as he sent out his messages and received reports.

'Bloody hell Roy, I thought you were a gonner!'

'It would take more than a few bullets to put me out of action General.'

'The Americans are providing some security Roy, but we need to fall back and get you to safety.'

Just to emphasise the point a mortar shell exploded close enough to the tent to shower earth and sand all over the roof.

'I'm not pulling back from here, General, we have worked hard to earn this ground and I don't intend to give up a yard to Jerry today.'

He turned to his Radio Operator.

'Sergeant, get on to the Cheshires, and get them over here. I want them to push these troops back from our perimeter and create a new one.'

'Yes sir.' Sergeant Dory got on to the 2nd Battalion, Cheshire Regiment who had recently arrived on the beach and spoke to their Commanding officer.

'Brigadier Phillips invites you to the party sir and it's starting now.' There was a pause as he listened to the response.

'We need you to secure the open land behind the crossroads in the middle of the common.'

Again. there was another pause and Sergeant Dory finished his conversation with a 'Thank you sir.'

General Hood looked across at where the Sergeant lay in a corner of the tent. 'What did he say?'

'He said they had just brewed up and he didn't want to waste the tea so he would ask the boys to drink up and they'll get over here pronto!'

'Bloody Buffs.' General Hood muttered.

Another mortar shell landed close to the tent.

Phillips smiled and puffing his pipe enthusiastically walked out of the tent and shouted. 'Will someone shut that bloody mortar up, I can't think with all the noise!'

Men were sheltering all around the HQ tent but seeing their commander so unconcerned some started to move towards the crossroads. This gained momentum and dozens of troops including the Americans and a couple of Bren Carriers were soon moving towards the main points of fire.

Behind the tent the 2nd Battalion, Cheshire Regiment were moving up in quick order and swept past the HQ tent and straight into the action. As they passed their commanding officer, Colonel Laurence Derham popped his head into the tent. 'Watcha Roy, thanks for the call. We've been looking forward to getting stuck into Jerry.'

Roy walked across and shook Derham's hand. 'Larry, long time no see. How have you been?'

'Fit as a fiddle and frustrated as hell. This is pay back for Dunkirk. Best get cracking, I told the boys the last one across that road buys the drinks. Tally ho!'

With that he swept out of the tent and rushed after his troops.

The Cheshires' arrival pushed the Germans back and soon all firing from that direction ceased as the Young Buffs cleared the area and established a perimeter line beyond the marshes as far as the lanes across the Marais as it was known.

Meanwhile across towards L'Islet the 151st were facing stiff opposition from the 2nd German regiment that had arrived from Fort George. They were supported by another thousand men that had come from the West coast strongholds and several barracks' facilities.

These fresh troops hit the Dirty Little Imps as the Durhams were known, hard. But they were not called Dirty for nothing. The Brigade was a long way from their home in the Northeast of England where a history of coal mining and ship building had earned them a reputation for being a tough, hard-fighting unit.

The Durhams were in fact one of Montgomery's favourites, and Hood had needed to fight hard to get them on his roster for the invasion.

The Germans pushed against their flank and were repulsed immediately. The Durhams had some artillery support, and this was brought to bear expertly and soon several trucks and a Renault Tank were burning under their accurate fire.

Brigadier Jim Reddish could see that the German troops were spilling to his left and threatening to enter the desperate battle being fought by the tanks and the 231st.

Jim was determined that they shouldn't join up and sent his 9th Battalion to try and drive a wedge between the two German forces, keeping them on his front.

His Radio operator interrupted his train of thought.

'Sir, HQ wants us to try and flank the Germans in the centre.'

Jim thought for a moment. They were hard pressed across the whole of their front. In some places the Germans had occupied local houses and were putting up a stern resistance, using upper windows to bring fire down on his troops. Sadly, he knew that some of those houses held frightened local families, but he had no option but to use force to take out some of the snipers with heavy weapons.

'Tell HQ, we're happy to oblige.'

He then ordered the 8th to relieve the 9th and the 9th to continue East to flank the Germans in the centre. He then contacted Colonel John JP Day and spoke to him personally. 'JP, the 231st are in a bit of bother and we need to support them. Can the 6th hold fast?'

'No bother Brigadier, they'll not get passed the 6th.'

'Good stuff, I know I can depend on your lads.'

As the 9th moved off East to attack the German flank, the 8th Battalion not only plugged the gap but began to squeeze the Germans back towards the guns of the 6th Battalion by sweeping around towards Le Martins and pinning the Germans into the more densely populated village around L'Islet Crossroads.

The Germans still had a route out towards Le Picquerel to the Northwest but this also saw a steady stream of reinforcements filling the L'Islet pocket as it became known. It was obvious they were determined to break through the Durhams if they could.

The battle in the West degenerated into house to house fighting as ground was won cottage by cottage and house by house. In virtually every property that the Germans left or died in, the fighting 6th found locals, some alive but many dead. It was a heart rending and tortuous battle for the men from Durham as most came from humble backgrounds just like the people they were striving to rescue from occupation.

*****

In the centre, the fighting in front of the 231st was intense as the battle weary Hampshires struggled to hold the line as more and more German troops seemed to join the battle as each minute passed. Hart could see the enemy troops streaming down the Military Road from St Peter Port and spreading out into the land either side of the main thoroughfare that joined the North of the Island to the East Coast.

The Greenhouses on both sides of the Military Road were damaged beyond repair as tanks, explosions and troops ripped through them, spreading shards of glass everywhere. There would be many troops that survived the battle that day that would carry a scar or two from flying glass for the rest of their days.

The 9th Battalion of the Durham Light Infantry moved from Oatlands along the Braye Road towards the battle, spreading out into the fields either side of that road. A small pillbox at the crossroads near Oatlands was given short shift with a PIAT round and the troops pushed on.

A larger defensive position at the crossroads where the Military and Braye Roads crossed was at the centre of the battle and had been manned by the Germans throughout, sending withering MG fire into the Hampshires to their front.

Hart considered it key to the battle and wanted it destroyed. Burning tanks were piling up on all sides but new Churchills, fresh to the battle began to turn the tide. One of Hobart's funnies took on the task, battling, through the heavy fire and thrown grenades.

As it approached the Pillbox it let fly with a long stream of flame, incinerating the troops behind the sandbag and concrete defences, exploding ammunition and killing all the defenders.

The last Panzer died spectacularly after ramming a Churchill and trying to push though the British lines, but a desperate attack by one of the Hampshires with a demolition charge launched the tank into the air, the turret spinning off to land over twenty yards from the smoldering hull.

The Devonshires had come up against fresh German troops who were working their way through the land to the East of the Military Road. Their battle line started to spread East towards St Sampsons Harbour while the Dorsetshires on the right of the Hampshires were under heavy pressure from German troops that had worked their way through from the Baubigny area.

At that moment the outcome of the battle hung by a thread. That was when the 9th Battalion of the Durhams arrived, perfectly placed behind the left flank of the German troops. Instantly the situation changed as the stunned Germans on that flank were forced into a partial retreat.

Bitter hand to hand fighting, using knives and bayonets in places, was common as both sides refused to give quarter. In places where there were buildings or sheds the German troops took possession and used them as defensive positions. Troops hid behind walls, ambushes on both sides were frequent but mechanical superiority began to tell.

More mobile guns, Bren carriers and tanks were being pushed forward and these were making the difference as across the line the Germans began to gradually fall back until a rough front line between L'Islet and St Sampsons Harbour was established. Both sides exhausted by their efforts rested and recouped for a moment.

It was 9.30 am but it seemed an eternity since the landings had taken place.

*****

Colonel Alan Willcocks had pushed up from the coast with the remainder of his men. Working his way across fields and between greenhouses he finally found himself on the outskirts of Guernsey Airport. There was little opportunity to find a vantage point as the airport was situated on the highest point of the Island, but he did find a water tower in one adjacent vinery. He climbed to the top which gave him a good view across to the airport buildings and adjacent sheds that the Germans had erected. Aircraft were still burning in places and at least two of the gun emplacements around the perimeter had been severely damaged.

He could see troops trying to put out fires. A Messerschmitt 109 that had been in a shed when the attack came had been wheeled out and men were working on it to try and get it ready to take off. There was a thick pall of smoke from what looked like a burning fuel tank on the far side of the grass runway.

Alan realised there was no way he could send his men across the open ground which constituted the aerodrome as they would be picked off too easily. However, he did want to keep that plane on the ground and secure the airport. While the aerodrome was in German hands, he knew it provided a way to bring in more troops if any were sent to help the defenders.

The gun emplacement nearest to where he was perched was still intact. Willcocks had the idea that if he could capture the emplacement and use the 88mm gun to take out the other emplacements he could keep the Germans occupied while some of his troops circled around the aerodrome. They could then take out the troops that were clustered around the airport terminal and associated buildings.

At the same time, he could use the gun to destroy that fighter before it had the chance to take off. Ideally, he wanted to capture the emplacement quietly so it would not arouse the interest of the rest of the aerodrome.

It was time for a diversion.

After clambering back down from the water tower he spoke to Lieutenant Jeff Bishop.

'Jeff, I need a diversion. On the Southeast corner of the Airport there is a gun emplacement that was damaged by the RAF. There are a bunch of troops over there trying to rebuild it. Can you take a platoon and engage them but not from too close? I want to draw Jerry's attention to that corner of the airfield while we take the nearest emplacement and turn their own gun against them.'

'Can do skipper, once you've captured the gun, what do you want us to do next?'

'Once you see us engage them with the 88mm, capture that position and then work your way along the southern edge of the airfield and engage with any troops you come across. Be ready to take those buildings as soon as you see us approaching from the North.'

'Just one thing skipper, do you know how to fire that gun?'

'How hard can it be?' Alan replied with a laugh.

Bishop smiled and with a thumbs up called over B platoon and together they crept away to the south. Alan and his men crept forward under the cover of some hedges to around 50 yards from the emplacement and waited. Some of the commandos took the opportunity to take on some food.

They had barely managed a mouthful when a burst of gunfire from the south of their position brought them back to full readiness. Willcocks had primed his men to make sure they knew they needed the gun, so it wasn't a case of lobbing grenades into the position.

The gunfire increased in intensity as Bishop pressed his attack and the commandos with Willcocks spread out moving as close as they could to their target without breaking cover. From his vantage point on the water tower Willcocks had identified three men in the emplacement and from where he was now, he could see at least two of them looking across at the action taking place some 200 yards away to the south. Both had binoculars up to their eyes and had their backs to most of the Commandos.

Willcocks held his fist in the air and when he judged the time was right, he dropped it and broke cover scurrying across the 50 yards as quickly and as quietly as possible. The men were virtually on top of the emplacement before the Germans realised they were under attack, but Willcocks was nimble as well as fast. With one step on the sandbags, he threw himself into the emplacement clattering into the two men who had been standing up and watching the action.

His men followed him in and found the three Germans flat out on the ground with Willcocks lying on top of them. They were quickly overpowered and tied up.

One of his men who luckily had a little artillery experience quickly worked out how to move the gun and soon he was traversing the 88mm around and down until the barrel was pointing towards the other undamaged gun across to the Northeast of the airfield.

In terms of range and accuracy this was point blank for the German 88mm and once it was sighted on his target, he looked around to Colonel Willcocks.

'How do we fire this thing, Colonel?' Willcocks picked up a shell and shoved it in the breech, it shut so fast it nearly took his hand off. He looked around the gun and saw a small leaver on the left-hand side.

'Cover your ears boys and stand back.'

He pulled the lever and across the airfield the other gun emplacement erupted at the impact of the high explosive shell.

'Bloody hell, that was fun.'

One of his men picked up another shell and reloaded as the man on the dials swivelled the gun until it was pointing at the Messerschmidt 109 they were prepping for action.

'Fire!' Willcocks shouted and pulled the lever again. The plane disappeared in a ball of flame.

'Now we know what it's like in the artillery boys. Cushy number if you ask me.'

The men laughed and Willcocks took a pair of German binoculars and looked for his next target. He decided on some wooden sheds and soon they too were being smashed to pieces by the 88mm.

Across to the south Bishop and his men took the opportunity caused by the fire from Willcocks to storm that position with grenades. After seizing the gun emplacement, they moved on to skirt the Southern side of the airfield, heading towards the airport terminal buildings.

Willcocks had taken a shine to the excellent German binoculars, so he commandeered them for his own use. He left a crew to man the gun and mind the prisoners. They were instructed to take out any targets of opportunity as they saw fit.

Willcocks then took the rest of his men and worked his way around the Northern perimeter until they were opposite the airport buildings.

On a signal from Willcocks, they sprinted towards the Airport terminal building. In response to their advance an MG opened fire from the roof of the building and his men immediately dropped to the ground. The firing did not last long as the 88mm manned by the commandos fired again and that part of the roof of the building disappeared in a cloud of smoke and concrete dust.

The commandos out in the open immediately started to run forward again and Willcocks, barely breaking stride, kicked down the front door of the building and rushed inside, Sten gun chattering away. His men followed him in and within five minutes the building was theirs. A few German troops had broken out of the back of the building, but they fell to Bishop's men who had arrived just in time to prevent their escape.

Willcocks ran up to the roof and waved across to his men in the last surviving gun pit who waved back. The airport was secure.

There were a couple of walking wounded and the commando's medic went about patching them up while one of the men pulled out a Union Jack from his backpack. Together with Willcocks and two of his NCOs they pulled down the Swastika which was flying above the building and hoisted the Union Jack.

The man who had carried the Union Jack quickly stuffed the Swastika in his pack to keep as a souvenir. Meanwhile, Lieutenant Riley had found a rather nice Leica camera in the building, and he got Willcocks and Bishop to pose in front of the newly hoisted flag, proudly saluting their achievement.

That picture would go down in history as the first Union Jack to fly over an official building in Guernsey in over four years.

Job done, the men took up defensive positions and in time honoured tradition, brewed up a strong mug of char.

*****

Colonel Krimp had pushed his paratroopers up towards Delancey Park through the lanes between the Military Road and St Sampsons harbour where they were confronted by a network of bunkers and gun emplacements mainly covering Belle Greve Bay. The old monument he remembered was gone, to provide a full field of fire for the batteries situated there.

As he looked across the park from his vantage point near the top of the Pointues Rocques he could hear the intense battle taking place behind him.

Krimp knew that if he could take out these defences and those down on the coast it would help with the inevitable push out from the beachhead, which was scheduled for before noon.

He looked at his watch. It was 9.30 am.

He assembled his commanders.

'Bob can you and Captain Flatterly take B and D Company around the North of the park and work your way into a position ready to attack from that side. We will work our way into the grounds of St Sampsons School and approach from this side. I am sure the school will have been used as a Barracks of some kind, but it seems quiet, so maybe many of the troops here have been moved North to counter the invasion. Our aim is to clear this area then get down to the coast and take out the bunkers there. Have we plenty of demolition charges and grenades?'

'We re-armed sir before we moved out so no worries on that score,' Captain Flatterly replied.

'Good, I think we are going to need all the explosives we can get looking at these bunkers. Drop a few down any tunnels or vents you can find and that should flush the buggers out.'

'Once we are secure on the coast road, we will establish a defensive position at the end of the Vale Road and stop further reinforcements heading North. It will also put us in a good position to attack any troops retreating from that direction.'

He had a small map which he had placed on the ground and using his one good hand he pointed to the junction of the Vale Road and the Coast Road at La Tonnelle.

'There Gentlemen we will make our stand. Now let's get this done. Alan, can you be ready to go in 15 minutes?'

'We'll be ready, Sir.'

'Good, off you go and happy hunting.'

Major Bridle and Captain Flatterly quickly left to gather their men and headed off around the North of the Park. The park had been left in a sorry state and was very overgrown in places. This provided some good cover for the paratroopers as they entered the park grounds from the North.

They found two guards near the North gates. They had been sitting in the early morning sun enjoying a cigarette and put up no resistance to the fierce looking Paratroopers. They were taken prisoner and tied up.

Entering the park, the Paratroopers made their way south until they found a good position from which to assault the bunkers and look out points. There they waited.

Krimp, with Druce and Bell from A and C Company moved their men down towards the school entrance. Civilians from some of the houses came out to welcome the troops but were ushered back.

One man insisted on speaking to someone and advised the Paratroopers that there was a defensive position at the bottom of the hill and urged caution. With that useful bit of intelligence Bell led a section down the hill to attack that position as soon as the action started. The action came sooner than they had planned as a soldier in the school spotted the paratroopers working their way around that building and raised the alarm.

Men began pouring out of the building straight in front of the paratroopers who were quickest to open fire, but they were exposed outside the building and once the Germans had recovered from the shock the Paras started to take casualties.

Krimp and his men threw grenades through windows to try and disrupt the defenders and looked to break into the building by throwing grenades through the door. It wasn't pretty but it worked and soon a platoon from A Company were working their way through the building taking care of any last defenders.

Several were not prepared to fight on and surrendered to the Paras who rounded them up and secured them in one of the classrooms leaving two men to guard them.

As soon as the firing started, one of Bell's men ran under the gun slit of the emplacement they had been warned about and threw a satchel demolition charge through the gap. It exploded killing all the defenders, the size of the explosion was so huge in the confined space it lifted part of the roof off the position. The men then streamed into the park running back up towards the bunkers.

As soon as he heard the firing from the school, Bridle led his men towards the rear of the bunkers. At the same time Krimp and the main body of paratroopers swarmed out of the back of the school, bringing a three-pronged attack to the defensive positions. One MG managed to swivel to meet the attack and two men fell before a grenade silenced the position.

The Germans hunkered down in their positions, sealing doors and gun slits where possible and the Paratroopers stood on top of the positions, frustrated as to what to do next.

Then a call from one of Flatterly's men brought Krimp across to the edge of an old quarry. Below him German troops were streaming out of what must have been a large tunnel, just like ants swarming on a sunny day. Some were heading north towards St Sampsons Harbour, while others turned right towards the coast.

The men of D Company started firing down at the fleeing soldiers. One soldier threw a demolition charge over the cliff down to where the tunnel entrance must have been. The explosion halted the stream of men.

Leaving D Company to target any more troops that might try and escape the rest of the Paratroopers set charges around the various entrances to the bunkers. Where gun slits were open the Paratroopers pushed charges through gaps to destroy the guns.

This was choreographed by Krimp so that all the charges exploded together. At the prescribed moment the German defences around Delancey park erupted in clouds of earth, concrete and flame.

Colonel Krimp walked to the southern edge of the park and looked across the expanse of Belle Greve Bay towards St Peter Port. Spotting a British Destroyer to the south of the Island of Breqhou he smiled. Things were going to plan.

Krimp left Captain Flatterly with two platoons to hold the hill, look after the wounded and deal with any troops that might venture out of the many holes in the ground. After sending a message to HQ to let them know that Delancey park was secure and that he was moving to the coast, Krimp and the rest of the Paratroopers left the park and moved south.

It was 10.15am.

*****

The British had established a firm foothold in Guernsey. Apart from isolated pockets of resistance in the Northeast, the whole of the Northern part of the Island from L'Islet to the North side of St Sampson's Harbour was in British hands.

There were also no escape routes left for the Germans. As Krimp's keen eye had spotted from Delancey park, the British Navy patrolled the seaways out of St Peter Port and of course the Airport was now under the control of the Commandos.

In St Peter Port the Kommandant of all the Guernsey forces, GeneralMajor Von Graf was struggling to keep up with all the reports that were coming in. He had lost touch with the Airport and that annoying British Destroyer was still outside his window, repeating that infernal message over and over again.

On his map, using the information Von Graf had available, he had drawn a line between L'Islet and St Sampson's Harbour. He had also drawn circles around the Airport and the Mirus Batteries.

His forces on the South side of St Sampsons Harbour were hastily creating defensive positions and covering the many small streets and lanes in that area to stop the British filtering through his lines.

Worryingly he had now lost touch with the forces on Delancey Park which he could not understand. He drew another circle around that area.

Troops defending the Vale Castle which had been bypassed by the invaders could see Delancey park though their binoculars and reported explosions and now smoke billowing over the park. Fort Doyle had not been attacked but troops there were now surrounded by elements of the 69th who had pushed out from L'Ancresse to the East.

An observation tower at the Vale Mill was still in contact with Von Graf and was reporting any troop movements they could see, but they too were surrounded.

All troops not in defensive positions had either pulled back to the front line, were in hiding or in many cases had surrendered feeling they had no other option.

There was a knock on the Kommandants door and his Aide announced that the Islands Bailiff was waiting to see him.

That's all I need, he thought to himself. 'Send him in.'

The head of the Guernsey Government, Ambrose Sherwill, came in and without waiting to be invited, sat down in front of the Kommandant who was sitting at his desk.

'Good morning, GeneralMayor. How are you on this fine sunny day?'

'Busy Mr Sherwill, as you can imagine. How can I help you?'

'I just wanted to offer my services GeneralMayor. If you wish to discuss surrender terms with the British forces, I am happy to act as an intermediary?'

Von Graf was furious, but he kept his calm. 'You are a little premature Herr Sherwill. There will be no surrender. Now if there is nothing else, please let me get on with my business.'

Sherwill looked across and raised an eyebrow. 'Are you sure GeneralMajor, there is no disgrace in an honourable surrender?'

Von Graf lost his composure and thumped his desk with his fist.

'There will be no surrender Herr Bailiff. We are here to protect your people from the invaders, and we will do that to the last man. Is that clear?'

Sherwill paused for a moment, unimpressed by the Kommandant's tantrum. As he stood up he made a point of looking at the map of the Island Von Graf had been working on.

'Well, if you change your mind, I will be in my office. Good day.' He smiled at Von Graf, which only infuriated the Kommandant further, and then left.

As he walked back to his office he couldn't help smiling. *This will be over soon*, he thought. Then, like a cloud crossing the sun, the realisation that hundreds, maybe thousands of people were going to die before it was all over struck him and sent a shiver down his spine.

I hope he calls and puts an end to this waste of life, he thought.

When Ambrose Sherwill got to his office a couple of his staff were waiting for him. They had come in to be there with him and to see if they could help. They put the kettle on and sat around his desk. The phone was positioned in the middle of the desk.

The sound of distant gun fire came from the North but apart from that, it was just the gentle ticking of the clock that disturbed the quiet as they waited for the call that might never come.

Once they had finished their tea Ambrose Sherwill broke the silence. 'Gentlemen, it would be an abuse of our position of trust not to prepare for every eventuality on this momentous day. Let's prepare for our Liberation first and how we will celebrate it, then we must accept that the invasion might fail and decide how we will tell our people that the occupation is not over. But let us be positive, we will start with how we announce the Liberation of the Island and how we will celebrate. We must also remember those who have died and are dying for our freedom.'

With that they began by setting out ideas as to where the announcements would be made. While they planned, all over the Island the people they had looked after for the last four years of occupation were coming out of their houses, smiling and hugging their neighbours.

Those in the North of the Island took every opportunity to welcome any British troops that were in their locale. Hands were shaken and gifts of flowers and cups of tea were offered. The relief was tangible.

On the beaches more munitions and supplies were coming ashore and where possible rations were already being handed out. Trucks travelled to and fro from the beaches and the centre of the common was starting to look like a freight depot.

Newly promoted Brigadier Phillips moved his HQ to the grounds of the Vale Church where the first action took place. The Royal Army Medical Corps set up a large facility next to the Vale Church using the inside of the building as well as their tents to provide as much help to the injured as they could.

Around a thousand captured German troops were now being shipped off the Island using Landing Craft to ferry them to waiting transports or were being treated by the medical teams. More casualties were coming in all the time as medics in the field used the lull in the fighting to retrieve casualties. Both sides were doing the same during the unofficial pause in the battle, the Germans moving their injured to the huge underground hospital in the centre of the Island as well as several field stations they had established just behind their front line.

But not all sectors were quiet. In the cottages around the L'Islet crossroads area, the house to house, cottage to cottage fighting was still intense. In some cases, cottages changed hands more than once as the battle ebbed and flowed. With little open land there was not enough room for heavy guns so machine guns, rifles and at times knives and bare hands were the tools of that terrible trade.

Captain David Morgan of the 6th Division of the Durham Light Infantry was in the thick of the fight. He was in a small cottage just off the crossroads which was at the centre of all the action. Two of his men had died alongside him as they had taken that cottage and now he was on his own. He was convinced the cottage next door was occupied by the Germans and was not sure where the rest of his men were. Morgan was covered in dust from bullets ricocheting off the walls. His uniform was also covered in the blood of his dead comrades.

This was the third house he had taken during the battle.

He reloaded his sten gun and his revolver, using ammunition from his dead colleagues and added a couple of grenades to his belt.

Gun fire from the cottage next door confirmed his suspicions as the unmistakable sound of an MG fired several bursts which were followed by a cry of pain as another member of his regiment was hit.

Sneaking out of the back door of the cottage, he vaulted the low wall between the two buildings and kicked in the old wooden back door.

Bursting through into the kitchen he almost shot the two elderly residents who were sheltering behind a table. He continued through to the front room and saw two Germans firing out of one of the windows.

Without breaking step, he shot them both without warning. No quarter and no pity.

'That's for my pals!'

His mouth was full of dust and automatically he spat on the carpet. Immediately he regretted it, remembering he was in someone's house. He went back into the kitchen and spoke to the couple.

'Sorry about the mess, we'll clean up later.'

With a smile he headed back into the garden and climbed into the next garden to carry on his deadly work.

BREAK OUT

Brigadier Phillips was drawing new lines on one of his maps. His Radio operator had been bringing him reports and he was getting a better picture of progress.

He had a good idea of where his front line was, but he was still worried about his right flank. He knew the 6th Battalion of the Durham regiment were under intense pressure at that moment and the Germans facing them seemed to be constantly reinforced.

Thank goodness we have the Imps over there, he thought to himself.

The Brigadiers radio operator had just reported that they had received a coded signal from a German radio saying 'Glenn Miller had landed' which he took to be from Colonel Willcocks to confirm he had taken the airport.

He had heard from Colonel Krimp that Delancy Park had been secured but nothing had been received since. Worried about heavy casualties he had decided to pin the Germans in their garrisons at Fort Doyle and the Vale Castle and not to waste any lives unnecessarily in taking those positions. Phillips hoped that the German Commander would see sense and surrender the Island before too long.

That meant he could use the 5th Battalion, East Yorkshire Regiment who had been with the 69th Infantry Brigade on his left flank to help with the breakout from their current position.

He called back Brigadier Heaume from his role in the Devonshires and ordered him to join the East Yorkshires and help them enact his plan for the breakout. Phillips explained how he saw this happening and then sent Heaume on his way together with some trucks to help move the men as fast as possible to their jump off point.

The East Yorkshires were stationed in some open land behind masses of greenhouses just South of La Moye. They had been positioned there to provide support if needed for the troops around Fort Doyle and those surrounding the Vale Castle. Their CO was Colonel Kevin Clarke, a veteran of Dunkirk and Africa who was considered one of the finest leaders of men in the regiment. He welcomed Mark Heaume to his HQ tent like a long-lost friend.

'What's the plan Brigadier?'

'Brigadier Phillips sends his compliments Colonel and asks if you would advance to the Saltpans to lead the breakout from our current position.'

Heaume pulled out a map showing the front line and indicated where Phillips wanted the East Yorkshires to position themselves.

'The Brigadier has also supplied some transport as he wants to start the push by 11am.'

'Thank you, Brigadier, we'll get cracking straight away. Will we have any support?'

'We are going to create a feint using some armour here.' Heaume pointed to the land to the West of the Military Road opposite the Saltpans. 'You'll be backed by elements of the 231st and across to the right, the Durham lads of the 8th and 9th will cover our flank. They have to stay close to the 6th who are still heavily engaged.'

'Good, are you staying with us or going back to your unit?'

'I'll stay with you if you don't mind. I used to live here so can help if you need a local guide.'

'Perfect, let's get going then, between us we can position the men safely so that the jump off comes as a surprise to jerry.'

Clarke busied himself getting his HQ tent packed up and before long they were heading off in the lead truck towards the Saltpans.

Phillips plan was simple. He had succeeded in securing the North of the Island and saw the best route forward was to bite off another chunk of territory to the South of St Sampson's Harbour. From there he could then push into St Peter Port to take the town and the German HQ. Phillips hoped when they saw the position was hopeless the Germans would surrender.

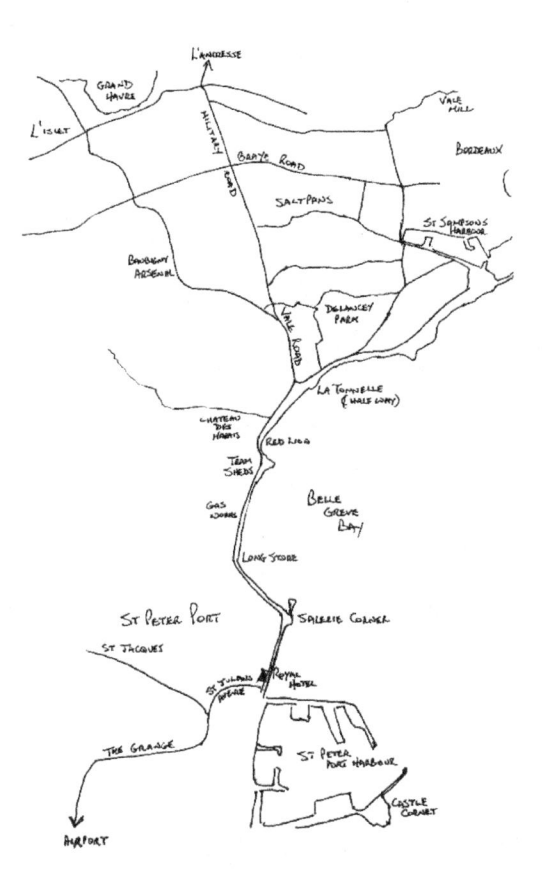

From L'Ancresse to St Peter Port

For the plan to work they needed to push out from the Saltpans through to the coast. By doing that they would cut off St Sampsons harbour and the land to the East of their line of attack.

That would give him control of a significant portion of the Island and a port. Phillips knew that should the battle go on to become a war of attrition, something he desperately did not want to happen, a harbour would be a useful asset.

General Hood came to see Phillips while he was planning his next move and expressed his concern about the situation in the L'Islet area. 'That fight has been going on too long Roy. We need a solution.'

'The problem is General, that the 6th is having to take those houses one by one. More enemy troops keep coming from along the coast and as soon as our lads make a few yards of ground they get pushed back.'

'Let's see if we can arrange a few air strikes. That might curb jerries enthusiasm for the fight.'

'I'd be happy with that General, but I am worried about civilian casualties. Warn the RAF to avoid striking buildings wherever possible. Too many people have died already.'

'Will do Roy, but the clock is ticking, we need to secure this Island so the RAF can use that airfield and the Navy can use St Peter Port Harbour. This Island has a vital job to do until we secure Cherbourg. Only then will these people be able to start rebuilding their lives.'

'Let's finish what we've started then.'

The men shook hands and Hood left Phillips to his work and walked up to the church to visit the injured men.

Phillips looked at his plans for the final time. He called in the air strikes and puffed at his pipe. They were committed.

******

'Message from HQ Sir, we're good to go in five minutes.'

Clarke looked at Mark Heaume then turned to his Company commanders. 'Gentlemen, you know our targets. Let's push these bastards back. I fancy getting my boots off and enjoying a paddle in Belle Greve Bay. Let's get to it. Up the Yorks!'

'Up the Yorks,' came the echoed reply and the Company commanders rushed off to join their men.

Unseen from their position, away to their right, a dozen Churchill tanks pushed towards the German lines supported by the Hampshires and elements of the Dorsetshires. The German defenders rushed to reinforce the positions under threat, drawing men from both flanks.

Five minutes after that attack began the East Yorks rose from their positions and, leapfrogging the Devonshires, rushed the German lines that were centred around the Saltpans. The area was full of greenhouses interspersed with cottages and the fighting was messy. Bullets smashed through glass causing the worst kind of shrapnel and the German defenders used cottages and houses as defensive positions.

Many of the locals had taken the opportunity during the lull in the fighting to evacuate their premises and many were now on Delancey Park hoping to avoid the fighting. Some though had stayed at home and were now in the firing line as the East Yorks stormed through the German lines, pushing towards Belle Greve Bay on Guernsey's East coast.

*****

After his success on Delancey Park, Colonel Krimp had moved down to the coast and had engaged and put out of action a large bunker which overlooked the bay. The Paras had then established a defensive position at La Tonnelle around the T Junction where the Vale Road met the coast.

Krimp had his men occupy several houses on the junction and had moved the residents to safer locations.

His men were positioned on rooftops and in upper floor windows. Troops were spread along the top of the beach line and behind the tram stop ready to intercept any German movements from either direction.

Krimp did not have to wait long. A column of around 200 German troops was soon spotted, moving towards the North to support the defenders trying to halt the British advance.

He waited until they were in the killing zone he had created and then signaled his men to open fire.

Completely taken by surprise the German column was devastated by Bren and sten gun fire. Trapped between the houses, the beach and the tram stop, under fire from all sides, it was a massacre.

A few troops managed to escape down the odd pathway or alley between the houses, but the vast majority fell where they stood until the last few surrendered to the overwhelming fire power directed at them.

The roadway ran with blood.

Apart from a few cuts from flying glass, Krimps men took no casualties. The few prisoners they had taken were placed in one of the houses as Krimp reset the trap, dragging bodies from the road, and hiding them either on the beach, down alleys or behind walls.

They appropriated some of the German guns and ammunition and waited.

*****

As the big push continued, the tanks in front of the 231st caused more than just a diversion. With the support of the Hampshires, the Germans were pushed back in the centre towards the open land to the West of the coast road. There the German troops regrouped and used the open terrain to slow the British advance.

Meanwhile the East Yorkshires, moving up hill, faced difficult terrain amongst narrow lanes and stone walls but managed to gain ground. The Germans used every greenhouse and cottage in the area as an opportunity to set up defences and create ambushes. As the German troops were forced to retreat, many fell back towards Delancey Park.

Captain Flatterly, aware the fighting was getting nearer, anticipated the move and had positioned his men around the Northern perimeter of the park. He had relocated the civilians behind some of the big houses which faced the park to keep them out of the firing line.

When the first Germans fell back, intent on making a stand on Delancey Park, they were completely surprised to come under the guns of Flatterly's men. With just 60 men facing hundreds of panicked German troops, Captain Flatterly knew he was in trouble.

He soon started to take casualties as the weight of numbers started to tell. The Germans were using grenades whenever they could and kept trying to climb over the park wall. It looked as if Flatterly was about to be overwhelmed when from behind the Germans the East Yorkshires came into sight.

This effectively pinned the Germans on both sides. Some tried to break to the right and left of the park but others, seeing the hopelessness of their position, threw down their weapons and surrendered to the British troops. Many got away but most surrendered.

Colonel Kevin Clarke had been in the thick of the action and once the firing had died out, he walked up towards the park where he met Captain Flatterly.

'Well done, Captain, inspired piece of leadership.' He shook John's hand and looked around at his men. 'Is this your total force?'

'Yes Colonel, we took the hill earlier with Colonel Krimp. He left us here in case any Germans popped out of those bunkers.' He pointed across the park.

'Well, I am quite sure the Colonel will get his own fair share of the action. The Germans seem to be falling back on all fronts.'

He paused for a moment and took a deep breath.

'Right let's get this lot tidied up.'

With that he arranged for all the prisoners to be held in a small chapel just to the North of Delancey park and after talking to some of the householders set up field hospitals in three of the bigger houses which looked over the park.

Many of the householders, sensing the end of the action had come out of their houses and rushed to help the medics tend the wounded.

Two companies were sent to follow the Germans that had broken to the left and right of the park while Clarke with the rest of his men and Captain Flatterly's survivors followed the path Colonel Krimp had taken down to the coast.

Krimp meanwhile was fighting again as troops retreating from the advance of the tanks and the Hampshires headed down the Vale Road to the coast. Many had fallen into his trap and had died or surrendered in equal numbers. The troops following those caught in Krimp's trap realised they were cornered and most surrendered to the advancing troops.

In just a few minutes, hundreds of Germans were lined up in the Vale Road with their hands on their heads, having had enough of the battle.

The first Churchill tank rolled on to the coast road just before 11am and effectively the breakout from the beach head was complete.

Ahead the road led straight to St Peter Port. To their right behind some houses and greenhouses the main body of German troops were fighting to hold the open land and stop the advance on St Peter Port, but they quickly realised they had been flanked and began to fall back to a rough line around the Chateau de Marais fortifications.

They had bunkers with MG posts in an area on the coast, known locally as the tram sheds, and were using that to anchor their right flank.

In truth they had been devastated by the British advance and the tremendous force that had been brought to bear against them and were struggling. Communications and leadership had broken down under the intense pressure.

******

Captain David Morgan of the 6th Battalion of the Durham Regiment was not on his own anymore. After relieving the Germans of two more cottages he had met up with several men of his regiment who had taken cottages from the other end of the row. They had achieved a sort of front line but there were so many cottages in the area the fight had literally ranged from garden to garden and house to house.

Morgan was preparing to move against an old barn that he was convinced was occupied by Germans when the sound of aircraft drew his attention. A flight of three typhoons appeared above where he was holed up and arrowed down towards the coast road about 200 yards from his position.

He could not see the action from his position, but he could hear the scream of rockets, swiftly followed by explosions. The planes pulled away but were soon attacking again, this time machine guns adding to the chaos they must have caused on the ground.

Three more typhoons appeared and once again rockets screamed away, and explosions followed.

What Morgan could not see was that a large column of troops had been heading in his direction and the sudden appearance and attack by the Typhoons had caused absolute carnage and confusion amongst the enemy.

The aircraft were largely unopposed, apart from sporadic rifle and machine gun fire from the ground.

After one last pass with machine guns firing, the aircraft swung away and headed north. Morgan felt hope for the first time in a while, which was heightened when a column of Churchill tanks appeared from the direction of the landing beaches. They rolled past his position, heading towards the area where the planes had attacked.

Behind them came more troops to support the 6th and suddenly the situation changed as German troops came out of several buildings waving white flags or with their hands on their heads. They had decided further resistance against the overwhelming force around them was futile.

As he walked out into the road to wave to the relief column of tanks and troops more planes flew overhead. This time they were Dakotas, supported by several fighters and just like the typhoons they all sported distinctive black and white stripes on their wings.

*****

At the Airport, Captain Willcocks and several of his Commandos who had been enjoying a rest were disturbed by the sound of aircraft. For a couple of minutes, they thought they were facing a German attack and the 88mm was readied for action as the Commandos took up positions around the terminal building.

To their relief a Hurricane came out of the summer haze and buzzed the airfield in a low fly past. The pilot must have seen the Union Jack flying from the flagstaff as he wiggled his wings and flew up into the blue performing a lazy victory roll. Confident the airport was in safe hands a stream of Dakotas descended on the airport to be welcomed by Willcocks and his men.

Colonel Brian Hunter walked down the steps of the lead Dakota and shook Willcock's hand.

'Well done, Captain, excellent performance in securing the Airport. We are from the Essex Regiment part of 6th Airborne. General Morgan thought you might appreciate some support.'

'Thank you, Colonel, we have everything pretty much tied up here.'

'Well, we understand Jerry is putting up a bit of a fight down in St Peter Port so we thought we might head down there and join the party.'

'Well Colonel, the Commandos don't like to miss a party. Mind if we tag along.'

'It would be an honour to have you by my side Captain. I'll leave a platoon here to guard the shop and we'll crack on and maybe give them a bit of a surprise.'

'A surprise and a party, I'll see if we can rustle up a bottle or two. I'd hate to turn up empty handed.'

Colonel Hunter shook Willcocks by the hand. With a big smile he put his arm around Willcock's huge shoulders.

'Come on Captain, no time to lose. We don't want to get there and find the party is all over.'

Together they organised their troops and set off along the Forest Road towards St Peter Port.

As they were leaving the Airport the vicar of Forest Church walked across the road and stopped in front of the column. Colonel Hunter halted the column.

'How can I help you, Father?'

The vicar did not know the Colonel's rank. 'Commander, I am guessing you are marching to St Peter Port. I want to come with you, and I think others will too.'

'I'm not sure that would be a good idea, Father. We may come under fire.'

'That's why I am suggesting it. We have lived with the Germans for nearly four years now and I don't believe the Germans will fire on civilians.'

Colonel Hunter had been joined by Captain Willcocks which caused the vicar to take a step back as the huge Commando towered over the preacher. The officers looked around and sure enough outside all the houses people were standing, eager to join the column.

'You know we can't guarantee your safety Vicar.'

'I know my son, but I think we can guarantee yours.'

Hunter turned to Willcocks who returned a subtle nod. 'Well let's get going then, the more the merrier.'

'And the Colonel has promised a party when we reach St Peter Port.' Willcocks added with a smile.

'Good, wait there a minute,' the Vicar added, then ran off to the Church, returning quickly with a brass cross on a staff. He turned to the assembled people.

'People of Guernsey, we have God on our side. Let us march with these brave men and keep them safe from evil. Are you with me?'

A big cheer went up and dozens of men, women and children joined the column as the vicar took the lead.

As they walked along the Forest Road more and more people joined the column and before long hundreds of men, women and children walked alongside the troops.

Some carried flags and ribbons; everyone was smiling and laughing. At times they burst into song. Sarnia Cherie was the most popular with Onward Christian Soldiers and Land of Hope and Glory as well as a bunch of songs from the First World War being sung by the mass of people. Even the battle-hardened troops joined in and smiled as they walked towards St Peter Port.

'Looks like the party's started.' Willcocks said to the Colonel.

'You could be right.' Hunter replied patting the captain on the back.

*****

General Hood and newly promoted Brigadier Phillips had followed the advance of the Hampshires and together they walked past the lines of German prisoners and out on to the coast road, setting their binoculars across the bay towards Salarie Corner. Beyond that bend in the coast road lay St Peter Port Harbour and their target, the German HQ in the Royal Hotel.

In front of them six Churchill tanks sat on the road engines purring. Their guns were pointing towards the Tram sheds. Hood turned to Phillips.

'There used to be a Loophole tower where that bunker is now. It was always an important location on the East Coast back to Napoleonic times.'

Roy Phillips puffed at his pipe and looked at his pocket watch, a present from his father.

'Are you happy if we blast that bunker with our tanks?'

Hood looked through his binoculars again. 'There's little chance of collateral damage Roy, let's press our advantage. Have we a flame thrower tank?'

Phillips looked behind him as more tanks rolled up the Vale Road.

'London buses General, here come three of the bastards now.'

'Why do you call them that?'

'Just don't feel its cricket General. I like a good honest fight; these things seem bloody cruel.'

'Well, I wouldn't like to be on the receiving end of one of those that's for sure, but as long as we have an ace up our sleeve I think we should use it.'

Hood thought for a moment. 'What about we give them a chance to surrender?'

'Sounds good to me General, if we can save a few lives, I am all for it.'

While they had been talking Colonel Clarke and Brigadier Heaume had joined them along with a rather bedraggled and bloodied Captain Best.

Hood turned to the young Captain. 'Been having fun Ian?'

'Yes General, had a few narrow squeaks but I'm still here.' Ian was smiling despite a bandage around the top of his left arm and another around the top of his head.

Hood shook his head smiling. 'How's your German Ian?'

'Not great General, but I can get by.'

'Would you be happy to offer those Germans the chance to surrender?'

'Yes sir, if we can save some lives, I am happy to give it a try.'

'Good.' He turned to Colonel Clarke. 'Kevin, can you ask your men to find me the most senior German officer we have amongst our prisoners and bring him here.'

'Yes General.'

While Kevin arranged for a German officer to be brought to General Hood, he explained his idea to Phillips and Ian.

After ten minutes, which seemed like an hour, a very scared looking young Hauptmann was brought to where Hood and Phillips were discussing their move on St Peter Port. Clarke introduced him as Hauptmann Lautner.

'Ah, Herr Hauptmann, thank you for agreeing to see me.'

'I didn't think I had a choice, Herr General.' Hauptmann Lautner replied with a nervous smile and in excellent English.

'Well, I guess you didn't.' Hood smiled back.

Hood took stock of the young man and made his decision. 'Hauptmann, I want you to help me save some lives, both those of your men and those of ours.'

'How, Herr General. You have invaded our land and my countrymen are determined to protect it from you.'

Hood smiled. 'I think you'll find this is our land Herr Hauptmann and has been since 1066 so I think we have a prior claim.'

'Maybe you should have defended it in 1940 when you gave it to us without a fight.'

'Maybe we should, Herr Hauptmann, but I haven't called you here to discuss semantics. We need to save the lives of our comrades.'

'What would you have me do Herr General.'

'We want you to go to that bunker under a flag of truce with Captain Best here and ask your men to lay down their arms. British and American forces are now in France and soon the war will be over. You and your fellow soldiers will spend the rest of the war in captivity in England and before long you will be able to go home to your families and live the rest of your lives in peace. There is no dishonour in saving lives. In fact, I believe it would be the honourable thing to do.'

Hauptmann Lautner took in the news about the invasion of France and thought for a moment. 'I will do as you ask General, but I cannot guarantee the success of your offer.'

'I know Hauptmann Lautner, but if I can save your men from those flame throwing tanks, then I have to try. Brigadier Phillips here thinks they are awful inventions.'

'On that we agree.' Hauptmann Lautner replied.

General Hood shook Lautner's hand. 'You have my word on safe passage for your men, Herr Hauptmann. Good Luck. Ian, good luck to you too.'

With that Captain Best took the hastily put together white flag, left his gun with General Hood, and walked past the tanks with Lautner towards the German defensive position. When they got within shouting distance one of the German defenders shouted at them. 'Halt!'

Hautner shouted back asking to speak to their senior officer. In less than a minute an Oberleutnant appeared from behind the bunker.

'What do you want Herr Hauptmann?'

'Oberleutnant, the British are offering you the chance to surrender. They have flame throwing tanks and more artillery and they will destroy your position. They have invaded France and say the war will be over soon. There is nothing left to fight for. If you drop your weapons, their General has offered you safe passage to England where we will be safe until the end of the war.'

'Do you believe them Hauptmann?'

The hairs on the back of Lautner's neck stood on end. The Oberleutnant had dropped the term of respect and seemed to be sneering as he spoke.

'If I didn't believe them, I wouldn't be here.'

'Wait!'

The Oberleutnant walked back behind the bunker and Ian looked at Lautner. 'I don't like this, Captain. Let's step back a few paces.'

They started to edge back when the Oberleutnant appeared again next to the MG on top of the bunker.

He pushed the German behind the gun out of the way.

'You are a traitor Hauptmann, this is our Island, and we will save it for the Reich, just as the Fuhrer ordered. There will be no surrender.'

With that he opened fire with the MG and mercilessly gunned both men down where they stood.

Back at La Tonnelle, Hood witnessed the whole thing through his binoculars.

'Jesus Christ, they've killed Ian.'

'Roy, send those bastard tanks of yours in. Let them burn!'

The tank commanders, stunned by what they had just witnessed, were waiting for the signal. Roy waved them forward and soon they were bathing the bunker and the surrounding defences in flame. Troops followed them in and any Germans that ran or crawled out of that bunker were killed without mercy.

Once the firing was over General Hood, despite protests from Phillips, followed the tanks in and bent over Ian's body. Four bullets had ended his young life. Hood bent down and cradled the man's head in his arms.

'I am so sorry Ian, forgive me.'

Hood looked across at the burning bunker and the pall of black smoke. 'What a bloody waste.'

He remembered the first time he had met the young Captain who could have stayed with General Morgan. Morgan had doted on the lad, but Ian had wanted to be involved in the action. Hood had promised General Morgan he would look after his friend, and he knew he had let Morgan down.

Hood had been so convinced the Germans would surrender he hadn't considered the fanaticism of some of their troops. *What a fool I am*, he thought to himself. By now Medics were surrounding the General.

'We'll take care of him General. He was a brave man.' A young Corporal bent down next to the General. At that moment they were just two men, mourning a dead comrade.

'Do that Corporal, he was my friend.'

Hood stood up and watched the tanks rolling by as they carried on along the road to St Peter Port. He looked at his watch.

It was 11.30am.

I've had enough of this. He walked over to Phillips.

'I want this done by noon Roy. Let's go.'

Colonel Clarke and Colonel Heaume were standing a few yards away from the two commanders. Roy took a big puff of his pipe and then tapped it on the granite kerb alongside the road.

'Gentlemen, I'll not light this pipe again until we are in the German HQ enjoying a whiskey. I get twitchy if I don't have a puff for half an hour and you wouldn't like to see me twitchy. Take your men and follow those tanks into St Peter Port. Whatever it takes gentlemen, whatever it takes.'

Both Clarke and Heaume saluted and went over to their men and within minutes they were all heading South on the last leg of their journey.

THE COUP DE GRACE

The British tanks slowly rumbled along the coast road towards St Peter Port in groups of three. The first with its main gun pointing straight ahead, the second focused on the land and buildings on their right and the third aiming to the immediate right of the first tank.

Troops followed the advance in close order. The men kept the tanks to their right, walking between the massive vehicles and the sea wall. They were worried about potential attacks from the Gas works and assorted buildings they were passing.

It was approaching high tide now and it was a disciplined man that didn't glance to his left at the beautiful sight of the sun glittering off the sea and the distant Islands of Herm, Brecqhou, and further away Sark.

They could see the Destroyer in the distance and its flashing message and the sharp eyed could see the movement of German helmets as troops on Salarie Corner reinforced that key defensive position. It was the final defensive position on the approach to the heart of St Peter Port.

The lead tank reached the left turn in the road at the Long Store. Just as it reached the junction it was attacked by German troops using a Panzerfaust. The men had been behind the last building on the right that made the corner. The third tank in the column reacted quickly and fired at the position while the machine gun on the second tank engaged the small group of German troops next to the man with the panzerfaust who were firing at the column using an MG.

Another German soldier that had been hiding in the building fired his Panzerfaust through the window and the first tank in the column was forced to stop. Men supporting the tanks quickly rushed across the road and grenades were thrown through the window. That stopped further attacks from that direction.

At the same moment, a hastily positioned mobile 88mm on Salerie Corner opened up from across the bay, firing at the column of tanks. Tanks in the rest of the column immediately traversed their guns towards the danger and started to pound the area above the small harbour at La Salerie. One of the flame throwing Churchill tanks was hit by the 88mm and erupted in flames.

German units that had been shadowing the column took the firing as a signal to engage the British column all along the road by the Gas works. These were troops that had been filtering back towards St Peter Port from the Bouet area near the Chateau de Marais. They had been working their way through the vineries and buildings, inland from where the engagement had taken place at the tram sheds.

The British troops supporting the tanks immediately engaged this new threat and several platoons entered the gas works and surrounding spaces to root out the enemy.

The 88mm at La Salerie was well positioned and was causing severe damage to the column despite the return fire. Three tanks were now out of commission and two more were damaged. Phillips, recognising the danger, immediately ordered Colonel Clarke to push his men forward to try and engage the German position. As soon as they were in range the East Yorks brought their mortars to bear on the German position as more tanks pushed forward. As the infantry worked their way closer, machine gun fire was added to the pressure being brought to bear on Salerie Corner.

*****

GeneralMajor Von Graf was getting frantic.

He had walked out of the front of the Royal Hotel and could see the pressure being brought on his position at La Salerie. It was the first action he had seen during the invasion, and he was surprised by the ferocity of the attack. The Kommandant had managed to get a mobile 88mm there from the Harbour area, but he could see it was only a matter of time before one of the shells exploding around it found their target.

Now he was arranging for a defence work to be created across the road in front of his HQ. Sandbags and barbed wire barriers had been dragged from the entrance to the harbour to build a barricade across the road. MGs had been put in place on the barricade as well as two smaller PAK 75mm field guns.

More troops lined the harbour wall, aiming their guns and MGs towards Salarie Corner, waiting for the moment the British rounded the bend in the road. German troops were also on roof tops and in the upper floors of many of the buildings that lined the road armed with Grenades and rifles.

Von Graf was determined to make the British pay for every yard of that last stretch of road between La Salerie and his HQ. All the soldiers he could muster were being concentrated around his position. He still held a glimmer of hope that the harbour might provide an opportunity for him to get support or at the very least provide him and his men with a means of escape. With that in mind he wanted to protect it at all costs.

The chances of any forces coming to his aid were remote and he knew that. The reports he had received from France were confused. Paratroopers had landed on the Cotentin, troops had landed on the beaches, but some of the senior officers still believed this was a feint and that the Pas de Calais would be the main target.

Nothing had been heard from Hitler himself and many of the senior Generals were still in Rennes, refusing to accept what was happening around Cherbourg. As a result, it had been down to senior officers on the ground to do the best they could with what troops they had available.

The Commander in Cherbourg had called for help but so far there had been little response to that request or to the British and American landings. German units, in particular the panzer reserves, were yet to push towards Cherbourg to try and ensure the port was not cut off from the rest of the German army in France.

Von Graf had also seen in the reports that there had been widespread disruption to communications, rail, and road links in France due to action by French Maquis resistance groups. The Kommandant was grateful that he wasn't facing such a backlash from the locals here in Guernsey.

Suddenly a huge explosion from Salerie corner caused everyone to look in that direction. The 88mm disappeared in a cloud of smoke and flame as stockpiled ammunition was hit by a well-aimed mortar shell. A few disorientated survivors from the explosion began staggering back towards the last line of defence outside the Royal Hotel. Everything went quiet.

*****

Colonel Hunter and Captain Willcocks had now reached the top of the Grange, the main route into town. They had passed several German troops on their march, but all had either turned away or had laid down their weapons. One young Guernsey girl had latched on to a young Lance Corporal from the Essex regiment and they had been chatting and walking arm in arm for well over a mile. Betty liked the look of this handsome young man and Dennis was enjoying the moment. It was a moment that would lead to a lifetime together, not that they knew that at the time.

As they turned to walk down the Grange, the column, still led by the Vicar, was faced by a small group of German officers that were stationed in the Grange Hotel.

An Oberleutnant walked forward to confront the column. He spoke to the Vicar. 'Father what are you doing, the fighting is still going on, this isn't over.'

The Vicar looked the young man straight in the eye.

'Son, it is all over. You must know they are not going to stop now they are here. You can choose to try and kill us, or you can let us pass and put down your weapons. If you kill us, you will have to remember what you have done for the rest of your life, which will not be long. Then you will rot in hell. Is that what you want?'

The Oberleutnant looked at the large column of people and troops. He turned to his colleagues and shrugged his shoulders then turned back.

'No Father, I do not want that. We will let you pass and await orders but be aware you are walking into a battle.'

'Thank you,' the Vicar said, placing a hand on the young man's shoulder and with a wave of his hand the column walked on.

Captain Willcocks caught the eye of the young officer and shrugged his shoulders with a smile. The young officer smiled back and turned away as the huge parade of dancing and singing people walked by.

Ahead they could hear explosions and gun fire but there was no stopping the column as they walked towards the huge edifice which is Elizabeth College.

There waiting for them was Ambrose Sherwill, the Bailiff of Guernsey. He stood in the road and held his hand up to stop the march. Colonel Hunter walked past the Vicar of Forest Church.

'Commander, my name is Ambrose Sherwill and I am the head of the Guernsey Civil Government.'

'Nice to meet you Sir, my name is Colonel Brian Hunter,' the Colonel replied offering his hand. The men shook hands to a huge roar from the crowd.

'I think I need to warn you Colonel that I offered the Kommandant of the German forces the chance to surrender earlier. He told me he was determined to fight to the last man.'

'He may think that, but a lot of his men don't feel the same way.'

Sherwill looked back at the crowd. 'I don't want to endanger my people, Colonel. They have put up with a lot over the last four years.'

'I have had no say in this Sir, this has been a spontaneous reaction from your people. I have had some time to think about this on the way here and it may just work. When the Germans ahead of us see this crowd, they may realise this is all over and put down their weapons.'

Sherwill thought for a moment.

'Well, if that is the case, I will walk with you.'

'Proud to have you with us Mr Sherwill.'

'Call me Ambrose, please.'

With a wave from Colonel Hunter, and a huge cheer, the column started its journey again, past St James Church and down St Julian's Avenue. This was the last stretch of road before the seafront and the Royal Hotel.

*****

The German troops manning the last barricade braced themselves for what was coming next. Von Graf stood in the doorway of the Royal Hotel and knew the situation was hopeless. He looked around the defences, smiled at the troops that were looking at him to try and encourage them, and then like them watched for the first sign of the British troops.

Two things happened next, first a low rumble from Salerie Corner heralded the arrival of the first British tank accompanied by supporting troops who were hugging the walls, looking for whatever cover they could get. Then came the sound of singing, this time from behind where he was standing. Von Graf noticed several of the troops manning the harbour walls, were looking, and pointing up St Julian's Avenue.

He ran over to the corner and looked up the avenue. Coming down the hill were around a thousand people led by a Vicar with a cross and Ambrose Sherwill, flanked by two officers of the British army.

At that moment Von Graf knew it was over. He could not order his men to fire on innocent civilians. The Kommandant ran back to the front of the Hotel and shouted across to all the troops. 'Hold your fire! Officers, stand your men down.'

Rushing into the hotel he called for his aides to hang out bedsheets as white flags. He got his radio operator to send a message to the head of the Kriegsmarine in Guernsey to come down to the Royal Hotel to meet the British commander. Once he had done that, he told the radio operator to transmit their surrender to the British vessel. Finally, he sent out an order to all the troops on the Island to lay down their arms and surrender to the British troops.

The most senior Kriegsmarine officer in Guernsey, Konteradmiral Manfred Jarmann read the message and knew this was the end of their resistance. He called all his staff together in his HQ bunker in St Jacques.

'Gentlemen, the war is over for us. We must accept defeat, in the same way we have fought, with pride and honour. Can one of you radio operators send one last message, signing off and then destroy all the code machines and associated equipment. Do we have a staff car here?'

'Yes, Herr Konteradmiral.'

'Good, can I have one volunteer to drive me down to the Kommandants HQ and please take off the swastikas and replace them with white flags.'

'It will be my honour to drive you,' a Leutnant zur See volunteered.

'Thank you, son. Let us get this over with and please leave your weapons here.'

With that Jarmann headed out followed by his driver and once the flags were replaced, they started the short journey down to the Royal Hotel through the massed crowds in St Julian's Avenue.

Von Graf retired to his room and got dressed in his finest dress uniform. He looked out of the window and could see his troops laying down their guns and could hear the approaching tanks of the British invaders. Out in the Little Russell the British Destroyer sailed in closer.

'At least that infernal flashing has stopped.'

There was no-one there to hear him. He picked up the book he had been reading, Volk ohne Raum, and flicked through the pages. *I wonder how it finishes*, he thought to himself with a smile.

He looked at the picture of Hitler on the wall and poured himself a stiff glass of whiskey. He raised his glass. 'Herr Hitler. Enjoy it while it lasts. It will your turn soon.'

Draining the glass, he went back and laid down on his bed. He took the book in his left hand and pulled his Luger out with his right. Without a moment's hesitation he put the gun in his mouth and pulled the trigger.

His aide rushed into the room at the sound of the gunshot and realised instantly what had happened.

*****

Konteradmiral Jarmann's car pulled up outside the hotel after driving through the crowd and he stepped out to a chorus of boos from the mass of people. He took off his cap and walked up the steps just as Von Graf's aide was rushing down to the front door of the hotel. The aide whispered the news into Jarmann's ear and the Konteradmiral bowed his head in a moment of respect for his friend. He took a deep breath.

'Well, I guess it is down to me now.'

He looked at the assembled crowd and saw Colonel Hunter and waved him over. Hunter pushed through the crowd followed by Ambrose Sherwill and the three men went into the Hotel foyer.

Jarmann held out a hand and Colonel Hunter took it with a firm grip. 'The Island is yours Herr Colonel.'

'Not sure of Jarmann's rank but noting the Kreigsmarine uniform he simply replied. 'Thank you, Admiral. Let me find our Commander, General Hood and he will attend to the formalities.'

Hunter walked back outside of the Hotel and waved Captain Willcocks over.

'Captain, will you do me the favour of finding General Hood. The German Admiral has offered his surrender.'

'Yes Colonel, it will be my pleasure,' and with a smart salute he pushed his way back through the crowd to find General Hood.

Hood and Phillips had been following the advance and when the firing stopped had been making their way forward to see what was happening. They were accompanied by Captain Larch of the US contingent.

Willcocks spotted them and ran over to give them a situation report. Buoyed by the good news the three of them, led by Willcocks who cleared the way, walked up the steps of the Royal Hotel to meet Jarmann who was waiting in the foyer.

They all shook hands and Jarmann in perfect English informed the men present that all the remaining German forces in the Island had been ordered to lay down their arms. He explained that he couldn't be sure that all of them would have received the news, but he was happy to send out messengers to all the positions around the Island if necessary.

'Thank you, Admiral. Your cooperation is much appreciated.' Hood turned to Ambrose Sherwill.

'Mr Sherwill I presume. Would you be happy to oversee the surrender paperwork?'

'General, I have the papers already prepared. Everything is waiting up at Elizabeth College.'

'It seems a shame to waste a balcony, Ambrose. Can we make an interim announcement and then arrange for everyone to attend Elizabeth College at say,' he looked at his watch, '1pm, British time!' He emphasised the time with a smile.

'Of course, General.'

Admiral if you would join us.

Together the four of them went up the staircase in the hotel and out on to the balcony of the Royal Hotel. The crowd roared their approval and Hood lifted his cap and waved it in the air. Cheers resounded around the town and the harbour.

Phillips held up his hands to call for quiet.

Hood cleared his throat.

'Ladies and Gentlemen of Guernsey, British and German troops. I am pleased to announce that all hostilities in Guernsey have ended with the surrender of the German forces. Men of the German army and navy, you have my word that you will be given passage to England where you will be safe until the end of the war. We may need your help to clear some of the damage we have all caused to this beautiful Island but if you cooperate, I guarantee your safety.' He took a deep breath.

'Today is a day of celebration but first we must complete the formalities. I would ask that you join us outside Elizabeth College at 1pm, British time, for the formal announcements.'

Another huge cheer came from the crowd and a chorus of Sarnia Cherie broke out. The men all waved, apart from Jarmann who had kept to the back of the balcony. He led them back into the Hotel.

'Mr Sherwill, can I leave you to make the arrangements. I need to talk to my men and Admiral Jarmann here.'

'Of course, General. I will see you in 45 minutes and on behalf of everyone in Guernsey, thank you.'

After Sherwill left, Hood turned to Jarmann. 'Where's the bar. I made Roy here a promise and the sun is over the yard arm as they say.'

Jarmann smiled. 'This way Gentlemen.'

A civilian bar tender poured each man a drink as they stood at the bar.

'I just wanted to say thank you Admiral, for surrendering as you did. You have saved a lot of lives.'

'In truth General, the decision was made by GeneralMajor Von Graf. He couldn't live with his order and took his life not 15 minutes ago upstairs in his quarters.'

There was a moment of reflection then Hood spoke.

'In that case Gentlemen, let us toast GeneralMajor Von Graf.'

'And to peace,' Phillips added. 'Peace!' They all echoed.'

With that Brigadier Roy Phillips began to fill his pipe. 'Just in time, you wouldn't like me when I'm twitchy!'

Hood laughed, for probably the first time since the whole invasion build up had begun, and the two friends called for another drink.

*****

In the Naval HQ in St Jacques the last radio operator on duty typed out a message to all German stations that might be listening. 'This is German command in Guernsey, signing out, forever.'

He then took a sledgehammer and smashed the radio and coding equipment before walking out of the bunker into the sunshine. He joined his friends sitting on a bench and enjoyed a cigarette.

*****

On a table set out on the top of the steps outside the main entrance to Elizabeth College General Hood and Konteradmiral Jarmann sat ready to sign the official surrender document. The school was bathed in sunlight and a Union Jack flew proudly from the mast at the top of the huge building. It flapped gently in the light breeze.

Ambrose Sherwill placed the surrender agreement in front of them and they took turns to sign it. He then witnessed the document with his own signature and added the date, 6th June 1944. A Major commanding the Wehrmacht troops and Brigadier Phillips added their signatures to the document.

Ambrose Sherwill lifted the paper for the assembled crowds to see. The throng went mad.

A microphone and speakers had been set up on the steps and General Hood walked over to say a few words. The men of the Guernsey Team were also present. Colonel Harry Vaudin, Brigadier Mark Heaume, Colonel Bruce Mahy, Colonel Ronnie Krimp.

Others were present too, Captain Larch, Colonel Hunter, Captain Willcocks and many more, several were showing signs of battle, with temporary bandages covering wounds. Others just sported the filth and grime of warfare.

'Ladies and Gentlemen. This is an historic day. Today British Forces under the leadership of Brigadier Roy Phillips and myself have liberated Guernsey from occupation. Sadly, many good men and women have lost their lives today and we should always remember their sacrifice. I would ask now that we are silent for a minute in their memory.'

The crowd went silent, so silent you could hear a pin drop. In the background birds sang in the trees but little else intruded on the silence until General Hood spoke again.

'I would ask now that you fly every flag you can find; that you ring every church bell and that you enjoy today, your Liberation Day, and look to a future full of peace and serenity once this dreadful war is over.'

The crowd cheered and clapped in celebration as Ambrose Sherwill took over the microphone.

'People of Guernsey. We have undergone almost four years of occupation. The true indomitable spirit of the Sarnian people has shone through and thanks to these gentlemen and their brave soldiers we are free once again. All of us will have lost friends and family in this terrible war, many on this day. That is why we will forever more remember the 6th June as our Liberation Day. Tomorrow, we start to rebuild, tomorrow we have much work to do but today we celebrate and say a prayer of gratitude to everyone that made this day possible. People of Guernsey three cheers for the heroes who gave us back our freedom. Hip Hip, Hooray, Hip Hip, Hooray, Hip Hip, HOORAY!'

The crowd joined in with each Hooray, getting louder and louder. As if they could hear the announcement, the bells of the town church began to ring out and others around the island echoed the sound. The hooter of the Destroyer Bulldog, which was now just outside the pier heads, added to the sounds of triumph. At that moment a flight of Tornadoes flew over followed by three spitfires, all turning to land at Guernsey Airport.

The sight was magnificent and no-one who was present that day would ever forget the sights and sounds of Guernsey's Liberation Day.

Half an hour later, General Hood's hand was aching from all the handshakes he had given after the formalities were ended.

Eventually he managed to break away from the crowds and walked back down to the Royal Hotel. The German flags and bedsheets were all gone, and a Union Jack was flying from the flagpole outside the front of the building. Hood went inside and walked up to the German Operations room.

Von Graf's staff had gone but all their maps and equipment were still lying around. He found the room Von Graf had used and entered. Someone had placed a sheet over his body.

Hood gently pulled the sheet back and saw his opponent for the first time. It wasn't a pretty sight, but he could measure the strength of the man. The person who had covered him had placed the gun back in his holster and put his right arm back by his side. The book still lay next to his open left hand. Hood picked it up and opened it. There was a handwritten inscription inside the front cover. It read *He who would live must fight*. He thought he had read or been told of that quote before but could not place it.

Flicking through the rest of the pages he noted a corner of a page near the back of the book had been turned over and realised with some sadness that the General had never finished the book.

He looked again at the man lying on the bed.

'Thank you General Von Graf, for all the lives you have saved. I'll finish this book for you if I may.' He saluted the General, put the book in his pocket and gently placed the sheet back over the Kommandant's body.

The General walked slowly back down to the bar and poured himself a stiff whiskey. Roy Phillips walked in as Hood stood behind the bar. 'Join me Roy?'

'Don't mind if I do.' Roy replied. He tapped his pipe out in an ashtray on the bar and refilled it with fresh tobacco. Hood saw an ornate lighter behind the bar and offered it to Phillips who used it to light his pipe. After a few puffs Phillips gave a sigh of contentment and lifted his glass.

'Can I offer a toast?'

'Yes, you can.' He knew what Roy was about to say.

'To Ian, one of the bravest of the brave. We will always remember him.'

'Ian.' Hood replied and they both took a large sip.

'What do we do now?' Roy asked.

'Well, I suggest we have a couple more of these and then we have work to do. We need to get the prisoners organised, get our men fed and watered, find somewhere for them to sleep, treat the injured, get more supplies in for the locals, help clear up the mess we've made and then get ready to be shipped out to France.'

'Is that all?' Roy laughed. He looked at his pocket watch. I think we can spare an hour before we get started.

The two men clinked glasses and finished their drinks. It would be a long day.

FRANCE

In France the battle raged on. By mid-afternoon firm beachheads had been established on all four landing beaches and US troops were moving out towards Cherbourg from both East and West beaches.

The Cotentin Peninsula was now completely cut off from the rest of France by a combination of paratroop regiments and troops from the landings so reinforcements could no longer get to Cherbourg. Not that reinforcements were coming. While Hitler slept and his staff were too frightened to wake him, the Panzer regiments held in readiness for just this moment, drank coffee, read magazines, and enjoyed the sun in their reserve positions.

In Cherbourg, the defenders knew they were in trouble but resolved to hold out until relief came. To the south a battle had taken place around the strategic town of Periers which was now in the hands of the 6th Airborne Paratroop regiment. They were now in touch with the British divisions which had landed on Blackpool beach and units had pushed across to East beach to create a front line.

The Americans on West Beach had moved off the beaches swiftly and were on the outskirts of Cherbourg. Naval forces were shelling coastal defences around the harbour and more commandos and troops were being held offshore ready to assault the harbour itself. When the opportunity presented itself.

However, it would be a week before resistance was finally crushed. In a final act of defiance, the Germans wrecked the harbour with explosives. That meant the allies would still be without that harbour for at least three weeks. The small fishing port of Dielette fell to the allies on the first day and until Cherbourg was secured it became the main supply port for the allied troops in France. Floating jetties were created off the small fishing quay to allow vehicles and tanks to come ashore.

Guernsey's harbours were used as staging and storage areas for materials and a steady stream of vessels ferried back and forth between the Island and Dielette. A large depot was established near the Gas works.

Guernsey's airport also became a frontline base for air raids on targets around the Cotentin. When the German tanks did roll towards the British front line they were attacked and strafed by fighter bombers from Guernsey on a regular basis.

British planes could be over a target within minutes from Guernsey, much quicker than they could arrive from English bases. This was good news for the men on the ground who needed aerial support to help fend off German attacks.

Five weeks after the original landings masses of troops were located within the main country areas south of Cherbourg and the signal was given to push out. The Americans headed West and the British, Free French and Canadians pushed South and Southeast. With Cherbourg Harbour back in working order an undersea pipeline had been rolled out between Weymouth and Cherbourg to provide fuel for the invasion.

Paratroopers were used again and again to drive the push across France towards Germany, but resistance was dogged. It would take until May 1945 before the war in Europe was eventually over.

THE AFTERMATH

In Guernsey, the day after the invasion, the party atmosphere was still in place but for the military there was much work to do.

There was no rest for the Paratroopers who were flown back to the UK that day to train for further drops over France. General Hood was at the airport to see off Colonel Krimp and his men. Krimp watched as the planes carrying his men took off. When it was time for him to go he turned and saluted the General. 'It has been a pleasure sir!'

'Same here Ronnie, it was good to have you on our team. I wish you and your men good fortune. I hope you get your arm back in full working order soon. Happy landings.'

Hood saluted Krimp and Ronnie turned and jogged over to his waiting plane. The Dakota taxied away then took off into the blue Guernsey sky. Sadly, that would be the last time Hood would see Colonel Krimp.

On the second day the first freighters docked in both St Peter Port and St Sampson's harbours bringing food and supplies for the troops, prisoners, and general population.

They took away many of the German prisoners while others were put to work clearing minefields and beach defences.

Many of the Russian and French prisoners, happy to be freed, volunteered to help with the clear up. Landing craft were also bringing in supplies on the original landing beach, so it was decided to create proper slipways at each end of the beach using the gaps blasted by the bouncing bombs.

Though temporary at first in years to come these would become permanent fixtures.

The last Germans actually surrendered on the 7th June. British and German officers had travelled all over the Island to find pockets of soldiers hidden in defensive positions to pass on the surrender message. The most stubborn were the defenders of the Vale Castle who refused to surrender.

An aerial bombardment and the approach of tanks was enough to change their mind. That was the last military action on Guernsey.

Brigadier Mark Heaume had been with the troops surrounding the Vale Castle. Once the troops started to file out with their hands on their heads, he took the opportunity to walk around to where he had come ashore five months before. He followed the lane to his brother's cottage and this time knocked on the front door. Laura opened the door and seeing Mark flung her arms around his neck.

'You came back.'

'Of course. Are you all OK?'

She did not need to answer, the kids ran to the front door and embraced the Brigadier, closely followed by Rob who had been in the back garden.

'I have something for you.'

Mark emptied his pockets and produced several bars of chocolate and handed them out. 'There are plenty more where these came from. Supplies are flooding ashore as we speak.

'I am so glad you made it,' Rob said hugging his brother. 'I see your hair has grown back.' Rob smiled at his brother. 'We didn't know if you had even made it off the Island.'

'Just about Rob and it has been a long road since. We are not finished yet though. I think we may have a week here and then we will be shipped off to France for the big push to Berlin.'

'Stay with us until you leave?' Laura asked.

'Thank you, I'll have a word with the General and see if he is OK with that. I am sure it won't be a problem.' He looked at his watch. 'I need to get back now but I'll bring some food with me when I return. I'll see you at 5pm, British time,' he added with a smile.

Across the Island the Guernsey team and Guernsey born soldiers met with their families for the first time in at least four years and families across Guernsey ate food, the likes of which they had not seen for many years.

For many it was a party for some it was a time of mourning as the true death toll of the local population was counted. Over 200 local men, women and children had died during the fighting. Planning was already in process to create a memorial to all those that had died.

Ambrose Sherwill had also decreed that in future years the 6th of June would be celebrated as Liberation Day in the Island. One of the major events during that annual celebration became the 'People's March' when a cavalcade of vehicles, individuals and floats reenacted the walk from the Airport to St Peter Port.

The Battle for Guernsey was truly over.

The day after the battle Winston Churchill announced to the nation that Guernsey had been freed from Nazi oppression. It would take another three months before Jersey was liberated. The garrison there had been starved into submission and not a shot was fired. As the end of the year approached the Kommandant of Jersey realised they would not survive the winter and in late October British troops landed in St Helier and the last British soil occupied by Hitler's regime in the second world war was liberated.

Captain Morgan's links to Guernsey went on after the war. He visited the family he had met in that cottage during the battle of the L'islet pocket several times and became firm friends with many of the people living in the area. He was a successful businessman in his civilian life and eventually sponsored the twinning of L'islet with Durham and paid for matching plaques to be erected in the small chapel at L'islet and in Durham Cathedral, commemorating all those who died in the battle.

That was not the only memorial to the invasion.

A memorial to the liberation was built to celebrate the 50th anniversary of Liberation in 1994. It is located near the Royal Hotel and commemorates the exact moment the Germans surrendered. It is in the form of a large sundial which, as the sun rotates each year on the 6th June, marks out the time of the events of that day on a set of stone benches. Another memorial to the airborne elements of the invasion was recently erected outside Guernsey Airport.

Several plaques around the harbour record the names of those that died that day and Captain Willcocks is commemorated at the Airport with that photograph of the moment the Guernsey flag was raised above the old terminal building. It is proudly displayed in the main departures lounge.

BATTLE HONOURS

After the Battle was over several men were recognized for their bravery.

The most notable awards were as follows:

Captain Ian Best was awarded the highest award for bravery, the Victoria Cross, posthumously.

Brigadier Roy Phillips was awarded the George Cross for his outstanding bravery and leadership during the invasion.

Colonel Ronald 'Ronnie' Krimp, for his attack on the Panzers at the Vale Church crossroads was awarded the second Distinguished Service Order of his illustrious career. He did not live to receive his medal.

Captain David Morgan was awarded the Distinguished Service Cross for his bravery in the L'Islet Pocket and Captain Flatterly was also awarded the same medal for his heroic defence of Delancey Park in the face of the retreating German Forces.

In all 28 medals were awarded that day and in time a Guernsey Medal was awarded to all those who took part in the Guernsey campaign.

THE END

ABOUT THE AUTHOR

I started writing The Battle of Guernsey in 2017 while I was working on my second novel, The Ball, which followed Ten Days One Guernsey Summer. The idea for this story had been in my head for a while but a chance conversation with someone who had seen the second world war archives relating to the plans for the invasion of Guernsey inspired me to push on and create this story.

In that respect I owe a debt of gratitude to Chris Oliver and Colin Vaudin who both encouraged me to bring the story to life. I am also indebted to my wife for reminding me to write one book at a time.

As regards my background, I spent a long career in the Civil Service, acquiring a wide knowledge of Guernsey and have a keen interest in the Island's heritage and culture, in a wide range of areas.

For many years I was known as the Island's native guide, within the Civil Service, and have escorted VIPs at the highest level, including a Deputy Prime Minister, when they visited Guernsey. My only experience of being in an escorted cavalcade.

When I left the Civil Service, I established a local tour company called Experience Guernsey Limited and operated that business until 2008. At the end of 2019 my role as a Business Advisor for the Guernsey Enterprise Agency, trading as Startup Guernsey, ended when the Guernsey Government withdrew our funding. At the same time, I retired from my role as Branch Office for the IoD Guernsey Branch.

As well as writing, I build, host, and maintain websites for businesses and private individuals through the domain www.newebsites.co.uk.

At the end of January 2020 I moved with my wife to Sunderland, where she was born. Shortly after we had settled down the Coronavirus struck, and we were forced into lock down. That has given me the time and opportunity to finish this book.

My unique perspective on Guernsey, through a lifetime based on the Island, and from a family who were evacuated, inspired me to write Ten Days one Guernsey Summer and Journey Home. This book seemed the perfect conclusion of my Second World War era trilogy based around the history of Guernsey between 1940 and 1945.

Please remember this is a work of fiction. I think the terminology is Alternative History.

However, this could easily have been a true story. It was the equivalent of the toss of a coin as to where the D-Day landings would take place and of course the decision could have been made to recapture Guernsey.

When I started writing this book, I was going to use the names of people I have known over the years. In the end I decided not to do that and all the names apart from the main historical characters are fictional.

Please remember this is a work of fiction. Names, characters, places and incidents either are products of the author's imagination or are used fictitiously. Any resemblance to actual events or persons, living or dead, is entirely coincidental.

Obviously, the key characters like Winston Churchill, General Morgan, Ambrose Sherwill and others were all real characters and had to be included as befits a novel of this type.

However, all of their actions and dialogues are my creation based around the events that were taking place at that time. These are included for historical reference.

I hope you enjoyed this book.

Tony Brassell
June 2020

ACKNOWLEDGEMENTS

Throughout this book I have drawn on research on the Internet through websites such as Wikipedia.

I have also researched some of the background through books such as the History of the Second World War, which was a weekly publication and The War in Pictures. This specific period was covered in the Fifth-Year edition of the book.

Other regimental websites and reference material from individuals posted on the web helped me paint a picture of what life was like for the invaders in the buildup to the landings and during the battle itself.

I used a 1934 edition Ordnance Survey map as the basis for my Battle plans and the illustration setting out the attack routes is adapted from plans for the Allied Invasions I found on Wikipedia.

Other Books by the Author:

Ten Days One Guernsey Summer
Journey Home, and
The Kangaroo Ace

My science fiction series includes:

Project 75
A New Future, A New Union.

All my novels are available on Amazon in Paperback or Kindle Format

Printed in Great Britain
by Amazon